OXFORD READINGS IN PHILOSOPHY

Series Editor G. J. Warnock

CAUSATION AND CONDITIONALS

Also published in this series

Other volumes are in preparation

CAUSATION AND CONDITIONALS

Edited by
ERNEST SOSA

OXFORD UNIVERSITY PRESS

Oxford University Press, Walton Street, Oxford OX2 6DP

OXFORD LONDON GLASGOW
NEW YORK TORONTO MELBOURNE WELLINGTON
KUALA LUMPUR SINGAPORE JAKARTA HONG KONG TOKYO
DELHI BOMBAY CALCUTTA MADRAS KARACHI
NAIROBI DAR ES SALAAM CAPE TOWN

ISBN 0 19 875030 7

First published 1975
Reprinted 1980

PRINTED AND BOUND IN GREAT BRITAIN
BY RICHARD CLAY (THE CHAUCER PRESS) LTD
BUNGAY, SUFFOLK

CONTENTS

INTRODUCTION

CAUSATION, conditionals, explanation, confirmation, dispositions, and laws form a cluster of closely related issues in metaphysics, philosophy of language, and philosophy of science. There is no weighty justification for my choice of the first two as the topics of this book—only the fact that a choice had to be made, for even having thus delimited our scope, I was able to include only a few of the many excellent papers available.

1

Easily the most favoured line of inquiry into the nature of causation is that which extends back to Mill and on to Hume. Let us begin by discussing two familiar accounts of causation within this tradition.

> I. C is a cause of E if and only if C and E are actual and C is *ceteris paribus* sufficient for E.

(If we put aside temporal considerations, this answer is essentially equivalent to the views of J. S. Mill (*System of Logic*, Book III, ch. V); R. B. Braithwaite (*Scientific Explanation*, pp. 315–18); H. L. A. Hart and A. M. Honoré (*Causation in the Law*, Part I, pp. 106–7); C. G. Hempel (*Aspects of Scientific Explanation*, p. 349); and K. Popper (*Objective Knowledge*, p. 91), to mention only a few. It is perhaps the most popular answer.)

> II. C is a cause of E if and only if C and E are actual and C is *ceteris paribus* necessary for E.

(Putting aside temporal considerations, this answer is essentially equivalent to the view of E. Nagel (*The Structure of Science*, pp. 559–60). It is also considered seriously but rejected by M. Scriven ('Causes, Connections, and Conditions in History', in *Philosophical Analysis and History*, ed. W. H. Dray, particularly section 8, pp. 258–62. Something very similar is defended by Raymond Martin ('The Sufficiency Thesis', *Philosophical Studies*, 23 (1972), 205–11). R. Taylor (*Action and Purpose*, ch 3) considers seriously but ultimately rejects a combination of answers I and II: C is a cause of E

if and only if C is *ceteris paribus* both sufficient and necessary for E. Several of the objections brought against I and II below apply against this combination of the two.)

According to answer I, C is a cause of E if and only if (i) C and E are actual, and (ii) there is an actual condition D such that C necessitates E on condition D. (C necessitates E on condition D if and only if there is a law L such that (C & D & L) logically implies E but neither of (C & D) or (D & L) by itself logically implies E.) A weakness of this account is now demonstrable. For it entails that if E has a cause then everything actual that satisfies some minimal independence requirements also causes E. Proof: Suppose C causes E. There is then a D such that C and D are actual and C necessitates E on condition D. This means that there is a law L such that (C & D & L) logically implies (entails) E but neither of (C & D) or (D & L) by itself entails E. Assume that X is actual and satisfies the following minimal independence requirements: X & $[D$ & $(X \supset C)]$ does not entail E; and $[D$ & $(X \supset C)]$ & L does not entail E. Since C is actual, it follows that $(X \supset C)$ is actual. It now follows, moreover, that X and E are actual, that $[D$ & $(X \supset C)]$ is actual, and that X necessitates E on condition $[D$ & $(X \supset C)]$. Therefore, X causes E by the present account. But no restriction was placed on X save that it be actual and satisfy the minimal independence requirements. (Thus, by the present account, if a fire causes some smoke, then Antarctica's being cold also causes that smoke.)

According to answer II, C is a cause of E if and only if (i) C and E are actual, and (ii) there is an actual condition D such that E necessitates C on condition D. This again has a demonstrable weakness. For it again entails that if something has a cause, then everything actual that satisfies certain minimal independence requirements is its cause. Proof: Suppose that C is a cause of E. There is then an actual D such that E necessitates C on condition D. This means that there is a law L such that (E & D & L) logically implies (entails) C but neither of (E & D) or (D & L) by itself entails C. Assume that X is actual and satisfies the following minimal independence requirements: $\{E$ & $[D$ & $(C \supset X)]\}$ does not entail X; and $\{[D$ & $(C \supset X)]$ & $L\}$ does not entail X. Since X is actual, it follows that $(C \supset X)$ is actual. It now follows, moreover, that E and X are actual, that $[D$ & $(C \supset X)]$ is actual, and that E necessitates X on condition $[D$ & $(C \supset X)]$. Therefore, X causes E by the present account. But no restriction was placed on X save that it be actual and satisfy the minimal independence requirements. (Thus, by the present account, it again turns out that if a fire causes some smoke, then Antarctica's being cold also causes that smoke.)

Ingenuity may remove these obstacles before our first two accounts. But there are other, more weighty obstacles in each case.

With respect to *ceteris paribus* sufficiency (answer I) there is the problem posed by what we may call 'undeterminative sufficiency'.[1] Thus the position of a table top relative to the floor is caused by the length of the legs that support the top. And this seems to be exactly the sort of thing that supports answer I. For the length of the legs is *ceteris paribus* sufficient for the position of the top relative to the floor. Unfortunately, the position of the top is also *ceteris paribus* sufficient for the length of the legs. Ironically, this makes the present example a refutation of answer I, for according to that answer the position of the top relative to the floor must now be said to cause the length of the legs.

With respect to *ceteris paribus* necessity, there is the problem posed by over-determination. If two bullets pierce a man's heart simultaneously, it is reasonable to suppose that each is an essential part of a distinct sufficient condition of the death, and that neither bullet is *ceteris paribus* necessary for the death, since in each case the other bullet is sufficient. Hence neither bullet is a cause of the death (neither is a 'causal factor' of the death, neither 'contributes causally' to the death).[2]

Returning to the earlier example, note that the position of the table top relative to the floor is *ceteris paribus* both necessary and sufficient for the length of the legs. This shows that undeterminative sufficiency is a problem not only for answer I but also for answer II and even for that combination of the two according to which *C* causes *E* if and only if *C* is *ceteris paribus* both necessary and sufficient for *E*.

We may thus conclude that neither of our opening answers is satisfactory.

2

A third idea has recently attracted some attention:

III. If *C* is a cause of *E* (on a certain occasion) then *C* is an INUS condition of *E*, i.e. *C* is an insufficient but necessary part of a condition which is itself unnecessary but exclusively sufficient for *E* (on that occasion).[3]

Thus when experts declare a short-circuit the cause of a fire they '. . . are saying, in effect, that the short-circuit is a condition of this sort, that it

---

[1] On pp. 35–7 of his *Action and Purpose*, included below, Richard Taylor offers several interesting examples of such 'undeterminative sufficiency'.

[2] Cf. the selection from Scriven's 'Causes, Connections, and Conditions in History', in W. Dray (ed.), *Philosophical Analysis and History*.

[3] J. L. Mackie, 'Causes and Conditions', *American Philosophical Quarterly* 2 (1965), 245–64; p. 245. (This is article I below.)

occurred, that the other conditions which conjoined with it form a sufficient condition were also present, and that no other sufficient condition of the house's catching fire was present on this occasion'.[4]

(A little later (on p. 247) Mackie offers a more explicit and slightly modified version of III—call it IIIa. But IIIa is not essentially different from III in any respect that will matter for our discussion. In so far as our discussion locates difficulties with III, it will do so *mutatis mutandis* with respect to IIIa.)

Thesis III gives us Mackie's explanation of an INUS condition. According to this thesis, however, an INUS condition is very little different from a condition that is *ceteris paribus* sufficient. (The only significant difference is that if C is an INUS condition of E then C is an essential part of a condition that is *uniquely* sufficient for E on that occasion, whereas C may be *ceteris paribus* sufficient for E in circumstances where there are several sufficient conditions for E, including some that do not contain C as a part.) Thus we are not yet in a better position to surmount some of the obstacles mentioned earlier.

As Kim shows, moreover, the ontology implicit in Mackie's (and other) discussions of causality needs to be thought through; otherwise there is a risk of an obscurity within which dangers lurk.[5]

3

We have touched on a large number of attempts to explain causation in terms of necessary or sufficient conditions (see references in sections 1 and 2). The difficulties encountered by such attempts have led some to abandon the whole strategy of looking for an account of causation simply in terms of conditionality or lawfulness. Some (e.g. Ducasse) try to offer an account of causation without relying at all on conditionality or lawfulness. Others (e.g. von Wright) supplement conditionality with some other notions (e.g. agency) in attempting to explain causation. Others yet (e.g. Davidson) postpone the problem of the analysis of causation and address themselves to a more 'modest' task: finding the logical form of causal statements. Finally, some (e.g. Anscombe) seem to hold the view that causation is what it is and nothing else—and that there is no analysis of causation that essentially involves conditionality or lawfulness.

[4] Mackie, p. 245. Essentially similar views are attributed by Mackie to Konrad Marc-Wogau ('On Historical Explanation', *Theoria*, 28 (1962), 213–33) and to Michael Scriven (Review of Nagel's *The Structure of Science*, *Review of Metaphysics* (1964)).
[5] See also his 'Causation, Nomic Subsumption and the Concept of Event', *Journal of Philosophy*, 70 (1973).

4

I have nothing to add about Miss Anscombe's contribution. The view that a certain concept (e.g. causation) cannot be analysed is difficult to refute except by producing an analysis. So far as I know no one has published a successful analysis of causation by reference to conditionality or lawfulness, and this is not the place for me to try.

5

Davidson's attempt to give the logical form of causal statements without commitment about the analysis of causation raises questions about his conception of logical form. Suppose we conceive of the logical form of a sentence S of natural language as the form of the correlate of S in canonical notation (in an 'Ideal Language'), all abbreviations or defined terms having been eliminated in favour of primitives. Thus if we suppose that 'is-a-brother-of' and 'falls' are primitives of our canonical notation, then according to Russell the logical form of 'Jill's brother falls' is *not Fa* but the form of 'The brother of Jill falls', which (assuming 'Jill' to be a logically proper name) is the form of this:

$(\exists x)$ [x is-a-brother-of Jill) & (y) (y is-a-brother-of Jill $\supset y = x$) & x falls]. But if 'is-a-brother-of' is not to be taken as primitive but is to be defined by reference to 'is-male' and 'is-a-sibling-of', the logical form of 'The brother of Jill falls' is *not* that given above but is presumably the form of this:

$(\exists x)$ [x is-male & x is-a-sibling-of Jill) & (y) (y is-male & y is-a-sibling-of Jill $\supset y = x$) & x falls].

Here 'is-male', 'is-a-sibling-of', and 'falls' are counted as canonical primitives. Greater complication would be induced, of course, if one or more of these were in turn to be considered an abbreviation or a defined term.

According to Davidson's view the logical form of 'The short circuit caused the fire' is that of '$(\dot{\tau} e)$ *Fe* caused $(\dot{\tau} e)$ *Ge*'. (Perhaps this is to be analysed further *à la* Russell. But this would make no difference to the point that follows.) According to our conception of logical form, if this gives the logical form of 'The short circuit caused the fire', then 'caused must be a *primitive* of canonical notation. But then how can 'caused' possibly have an analysis? Can Davidson hold his intermediate position that offers the logical form of causal statements without commitment about the analysis of causation?

6

Von Wright develops his ideas by reference to a model of the world that satisfies requirements of Logical Atomism.[6] There is a set of n basic states. A state of the world is conjunction with n terms such that each of the basic states or its negation appears as a term. Occasions are basic units of time (and space). On any occasion 2^n different states are logically possible. Over m occasions 2^{mn} different histories are logically possible.

Not everything that is logically possible is physically possible. Systems define what is physically possible. A system is relative to a series of occasions, a set of basic states, and a starting-point or state. It contains all the *physically possible* historical ramifications of the world defined by the n basic states through the m occasions starting with the given starting point or state.

Consider a set of two basic states: p and q, and consider two occasions #1 and #2. Supposing that $p \& q$ is our starting-point or state at #1, there are four logically possible histories:

But suppose only the top one and the bottom one are physically possible. Then our relevant system (for the two basic states, the two occasions, and our starting state) is this:

Note that according to my interpretation of von Wright, systems are defined in part by reference to a kind of physical possibility.

Consider now a system with four occasions.

---

[6] The article in this anthology may be compared with his recent book *Explanation and Understanding* (Ithaca, 1972). Cf. the review by Jaegwon Kim in the *Philosophical Review*, 82 (1973), 380–8.

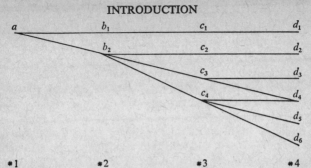

Each node is a state of the system with basic states $p_1 \ldots p_n$. Von Wright defines the top row as the course that nature *would* take unless (active) interference with the course of nature takes place. (See p. 104 below, 'On the Logic and Epistemology of the Causal Relation'.) Thus aTb_1 (a and next b_1) would happen on occasion #1 unless someone acted so that aTb_2. And if we are given that b_2 obtains at #2, then b_2Tc_2 unless someone acted so that b_2Tc_3 or b_2Tc_4. And so on.

An interesting consequence follows: Nature obeys an ironclad determinism but for the interference of agents. (At least nature as modelled in von Wright's 'systems' does so.) What I mean is that on every occasion nature not only does but *would* behave in a certain way but for the interference of agents.

Von Wright then defines causation by reference to the interference of agents: p is a cause relative to q, and q an effect relative to p, if and only if by doing p we could bring about q or by suppressing p we would remove q or prevent it from happening.[7]

It seems clear that the definiens here is *not* to be interpreted so as to mean simply that it is logically (physically) possible that we bring about q by doing p, etc. An equally idiomatic reading seems more plausible: 'by doing p we could bring about q' may be read as 'if we were to do p, we would thus bring about q'. This does not require that we should be able to do p here and now, so the reign of causation can range far beyond the actual reach of agents.

Some difficulties appear discernible. For instance, is not the proper conceptual order reversed? Is not causation essential in understanding what it is for one to *bring about* q *by doing* p? In some cases this involves p causing q, in others p entailing q via conventions, etc.; and so on. (See Goldman on level generation.).[8] In any case, as it stands the definition seems open to the objection that one brings it about that one obeys the traffic laws by stop-

---

[7] *Explanation and Understanding*, p. 70.
[8] Alvin Goldman, *A Theory of Human Action* (Englewood Cliffs, N.J., 1970).

ping at the red light, but one's obedience of the traffic laws is not caused by one's stopping at the red light.[9]

Whatever one may think about von Wright's definition of causation in terms of action, there seem to be other reasons why causation necessarily involves action for von Wright.

Relative to a 'system' it seems clear that what causes what depends not only on what actually follows what, etc. (which may be accidental), but also on what *would* follow what under different conditions. Von Wright's definition of a system permits reference to might-have-beens, reference to conditions other than those that in fact obtain on the various occasions; *but all such reference carries with it reference to a changed pattern of action by the relevant agents.* Given a system and a set pattern of action by the agents involved, the actual course of events is uniquely determined: given such conditions, everything must happen in a certain determined way. Thus any supposition that the actual course of events in a given system had been different will necessarily imply the supposition that the agents involved had acted differently. But surely the idea that generic state *p* is a cause relative to *q* entails not only that *q* is always there when *p* is there or the converse, but at least that either *q would be* there *were p* there or *q would not be* there *were not p* there. But this involves a reference to might-have-beens, to conditions other than those that in fact obtain on the various occasions. And this will necessarily imply a reference to (changed) activity by the agents involved. Thus the very notion of causation essentially involves a reference to (changed) activity.

It should be noted, however, that the foregoing argument for the thesis that causation necessarily involves action rests on the assumption that causation is to be understood within the confines of von Wright's 'systems'. And we have seen reasons to question this assumption.

7

Hume complains about his own first (regularity) definition of causation that it is 'drawn from circumstances foreign to the cause' and 'from something extraneous and foreign to it'.

Ducasse is impressed by this, and concentrates on the actual situation where the cause has its effect. His definition does not look beyond that situation:

Considering two changes, *C* and *K* (which may be either of the same or of different objects), the change *C* is said to have been sufficient to, i.e. to have caused, the change *K* if:

Thanks to Jaegwon Kim.

1. The change C occurred during a time and through a space terminating at the instant I at the surface S.

2. The change K occurred during a time and through a space beginning at the instant I at the surface S.

3. No change other than C occurred during the time and through the space of C, and no change other than K during the time and through the space of K.[10]

But surely not only changes but also unchanges can be causally relevant (as Ducasse elsewhere recognizes). So it is the total complex of changes and unchanges that is the cause. And it won't do to say that the unchanges are irrelevant since the effect did not take place when these unchanges were present without the change that triggered the effect. Why *won't* this do as a reply? For one thing, why *must* there have been a change to trigger the effect? And for another, what Ducasse urges as follows concerning changes is equally applicable to unchanges: 'Step on a man's foot and apologize. Then repeat in precisely the same manner. Then repeat accurately a third time, and so on.' How many times a change has occurred within a certain interval may be causally relevant, and the same applies to how long an unchange has been present.

Furthermore, the definition must surely be broadened to cover causes and effects that are not changes or unchanges at the surfaces of particular objects.

Ducasse's definition thus yields the following picture: take any continuous spatio-temporal volume and slice through it once on a plane perpendicular to the time axis. The total complex of events, states, and processes in the earlier part of the volume causes the corresponding totality in the later part. Furthermore, every concrete cause and its effect form the contents of the earlier and later parts, respectively, of such a sliced volume, and that they do so is all that is meant when, strictly speaking, one says that the first *causes* the second.

As Ducasse explicitly recognizes,[11] the definition just given is not true to '. . . the way in which the word "cause" is actually used'. But his avowed principal aim is to give us an account of a concept of causation commonly accepted, that involved in such ubiquitous ideas as those of breaking, bending, killing, heating, twisting, melting, etc. So he uses his definition of strict causation to provide an analysis of ordinary causation.

With some minor (but, I think, necessary) modifications, Ducasse's analysis of ordinary causation appears to be this:

[10] C. J. Ducasse, 'On the Nature and the Observability of the Causal Relation', *Journal of Philosophy*, 23 (1926), 3–4. (This is article VIII below.)

[11] Ibid., p. 11.

This case of C caused$_o$ (caused in the ordinary sense) this case of E *iff* this case of C caused$_s$ (caused in the strict sense defined above) this case of E, and every case of C causes$_s$ a case of E.[12]

But this seems only terminologically different from a Humean account of causation:

This case of C caused this case of E *iff* this case of C was spatio-temporally immediately followed by this case of E, and every case of C is thus followed by a case of E.

If so, then the present account is subject to all the difficulties that attach to such a Humean account.

8

In 'The Problem of Counterfactual Conditionals', Nelson Goodman raises the following problem. Suppose it is a law that dry matches light when scratched. And suppose that on a certain occasion t a particular dry match m is not scratched and does not light. It would seem true to say (i) that if m had been scratched at t, then it would have lighted at t. But then what are the grounds for this claim? Is it not simply the fact that the match is dry at t and the law that dry matches light when scratched? But if so, then it would seem equally true to say (ii) that if m had been scratched at t then it would not (could not) have been dry at t. For it is a fact that the match does *not* light at t and it is a law that matches that are scratched without lighting cannot be dry. (Temporal considerations alone will not solve the problem, or so it seems to me. If need be, we can replace the match conditionals with the following (in the situation of a table with a one-piece table top that rests directly on upright legs that rest directly on the floor): (iii) if the table legs had been longer, the table top would have been farther from the floor (since the top rests directly on the upright legs which stand directly on the floor); (iv) if the table legs had been longer, the legs would have been buried into the floor or would have protruded through the top (since the top is just so far from the floor).[13]

9

According to Wilfrid Sellars, it is relevant to note that dry matches *begin* to burn when scratched, whereas it is not generally true that matches that are scratched without lighting begin to be wet. But this cannot be a complete solution (or so it seems to me) inasmuch as it *is* generally true that

[12] pp. 11–13.
[13] Nor will it do to require in addition that there be no set of conditions and laws which in conjunction with the antecedent of the conditional will entail the negate of the consequent. This still will not distinguish between (i) and (ii).

matches that are non-burning and dry, etc., up to time t and are scratched without lighting at t, do begin to be not-(dry, etc.) at t. And there is a further reason why Sellars's suggestion does not give us a complete solution: namely, that the same (analogous?) problems arise when 'starting to Φ' does not play a role. Thus consider a wood house that is wet and thus burns long only because gasoline is poured on the fire. And compare the following conditionals: (v) if the gasoline had not been poured on the fire, the house would not have burned long (since it was wet); (vi) if the gasoline had not been poured on the fire, the house would not (could not) have been wet (since it burned long). It seems clear that (v) is true and (vi) false. But nothing of the form 'starts to Φ' plays a significant role here.

Sellars's more general solution relies on a distinction between kinds, conditions, actions, and results, and highlights laws of the form 'Φ'ing K's in condition C yields result Ψ': $(x)[(Kx \, \& \, Cx) \rightarrow (\Phi x \supset \Psi x)]$. It can then be argued that $(x)[(x$ is a match & x is dry, etc.) $\rightarrow (x$ is scratched $\supset x$ lights)] fits this pattern, whereas $(x)[(x$ is a match & x does not light) $\rightarrow (x$ is scratched $\supset x$ is not-(dry, etc.))] does not. And it may be concluded that this is what accounts for the distinction we make between conditionals (i) and (ii) above, holding (i) to be true and (ii) to be false. But this apparently relies on an equally obscure distinction: that between 'conditions' and 'non-conditions'. On what basis can we hold that dryness is a 'condition', whereas not-lighting is not? It may be replied, however, that we can appeal to a further distinction, that between 'results' and 'non-results'. Whatever may be thought of 'conditions', at least it is clear that its lighting is normally a 'result' of scratching a dry match, whereas its being wet is *not* normally a 'result' of a match's being scratched without lighting. Thus it is true that scratching dry matches causes them to light but it is *not* true that a match's being scratched without lighting causes it to be wet. And this may be what lies behind the fact that conditional (i) is true whereas conditional (ii) is false. But we are left with a difficult question: *What is the distinction between results and non-results?* If a dry, etc. match is scratched, it lights, and its lighting is normally a *result* of its having been scratched. However, if a match is scratched without lighting, it is not dry, but its not being dry is not normally a result of its having been scratched. What is the difference between the two cases? In each case we have a set of actualities that yield a certain further actuality by law of nature, where the law of nature is essential to the deduction. What is it that makes the first case one where what is yielded is a consequence (a result), whereas in the second case it is merely a consequent (and not a result)? Does Sellars's complete paper contain an answer for this question?

10

One of the central positive themes of both the Chisholm and the Rescher contributions is the thesis that strong (i.e. counterfactual, subjunctive, etc.) conditionals are *semantically indeterminate* and depend for their determinate content when asserted on the pragmatic vagaries of the occasion. These papers contain not only a critique of opposing views but also a wealth of examples and a lucid exposition of the indeterminacy view.

11

Stalnaker agrees with the indeterminacy view, but thinks that there is enough determinate content in strong conditionals to induce an interesting logical theory with its corresponding (alternative worlds) semantics. Stalnaker's semantics includes a selection function f which takes a proposition and a possible world as arguments and a world as its value. (The symbol for the strong conditional is '$>$', named 'the corner'.)

$A > B$ is true in α if B is true in $f(A, \alpha)$;
$A > B$ is false in α if B is false in $f(A, \alpha)$.

The world selected by $f(A, \alpha)$ must 'differ minimally' from the world α. This means that there can be no differences between $f(A, \alpha)$ and α except those required implicitly or explicitly by the (assumed) truth of A in $f(A, \alpha)$. Moreover, among the alternative ways of making the required changes one must choose the one that does the 'least violence' to the correct description and explanation of the actual world (α).

The following conditions are imposed on the selection functions:

  (i) For all A and α, A must be true in $f(A, \alpha)$.
 (ii) For all A and α, $f(A, \alpha) = \lambda$ only if there is no world possible with respect to α in which A is true (λ is the absurd world, where everything is true).
(iii) For all A and α, if A is true in α, then $f(A, \alpha) = \alpha$.
(iv) For all A and A' and all α, if A is true in $f(A', \alpha)$ and A' is true in $f(A, \alpha)$, then $f(A', \alpha) = f(A, \alpha)$.

Stalnaker's paper is an attempt to expound and formalize a version of the indeterminacy thesis. However, it leads to the following two questions.

First, the semantics validates the principle that whenever A and B are both true, then $A > B$ and $B > A$ are true, and the principle that for every A and B either ($A > B$) or ($A >$ not-B) is true. But does this not jar intuitions, particularly when one reflects on concrete examples?

Secondly, in my opinion it is not quite clear how Goodman's problem is to be solved. In the case described by Goodman, indeterminacy does not figure significantly. Consider an ordinary situation where there is (and has been) a well-made match that is dry, in oxygen, etc., and that has not been scratched and has not lighted. In such a situation practically everyone would agree that one of the following conditionals is true and the other false.

(a) If the match had been scratched, it would have lighted.
(b) If the match had been scratched, it would not (could not) have been dry.

The question is: Why is it that practically everyone holds constant the dryness and concludes that the match would have lighted on the assumption that it had been scratched? And why is it that practically no one holds constant the non-lighting and concludes that the match could not have been dry on the assumption that it had been scratched? Is there some principle at work here or is it just a huge random coincidence? Does Stalnaker provide an answer—or can we derive an answer from his theory? Apparently we cannot—at least, not until we are told more about what it is for a possible world α to differ minimally from a possible world β relative to a proposition A. Is it enough to be told that choosing α over other alternative worlds does the 'least violence' to the correct description and explanation of β? But what more precisely is it to do 'least violence' or 'less violence'? Actually, these are questions raised in Rescher's paper, which should be compared.

Returning to the Goodman problem, it seems plausible to argue thus: In choosing conditional (a) over conditional (b) we are reasoning as follows. *Given the assumption that the match had been scratched*, an assumption made when the match is known not to be scratched, not to light, and to be dry, etc., we have two choices: either (i) we can conclude that since it is dry, etc., it would have lighted, or (ii) we can conclude that since it does not light, it would not (could not) have been dry, etc. But the second conclusion requires that the past would have been different in many other ways, for the conclusion that the match would have been wet (not-(dry, etc.)) leaves us with the question: How would it have got wet? (And presumably one would not want to assume that the past in our hypothetical situation would have been just the same in every way as the actual past whereas in the hypothetical present the match is wet (not-(dry, etc.)) and in the actual present the match is dry, etc.) This seems in sharp contrast to what is required by the *first* conclusion ((i) above): that since the match is dry, it would have lighted. Here there is no such requirement that the past would have been different as that which we noted with respect to the second conclusion. For although the conclusion that the match would have lighted may raise the question 'How would it have come to light?' this time the question can be answered easily by saying that it would have come to light *because* it would have been scratched when dry, etc. And this would not require the postulation of further differences in the past.

The reasoning in the last paragraph suggests that even if the 'similarity' or 'least violence' that pertains to possible worlds is not quite clear and distinct, Stalnaker's idea is nevertheless pregnant and promising.

Similar ideas have been worked out in detail by David Lewis in his book on *Counterfactuals* and in his paper on 'Causation' (both fresh off the press as I write). In the paper, Lewis sketches the theory of counterfactual conditionals developed in the book, and he then uses that theory to construct an analysis of causation. In his discussion of 'Causes and Counterfactuals', Kim focuses attention on some of the more salient obstacles that Lewis's analysis must surmount and also puts the issue in a broader context. These two papers about the relation between causation and conditionals seem a fitting close for a collection on *Causation and Conditionals*.

Concerning both causation and conditionals it seems fair to say that there is no established paradigm—or at least nothing that deserves that status. Another view of the matter is that there is no fossilized orthodoxy, but a diversity of opinion that generates lively ongoing discussions. We may thus hope for deeper insight and broader understanding, not only about causation and conditionals, but also about explanation, laws, dispositions, and confirmation. In my opinion, the papers collected here are among those most responsible for what depth of insight and breadth of understanding we now enjoy, and among those that will be most helpful to those who want more.[14]

[14] Thanks to Jaegwon Kim, Philip Quinn, James Van Cleve, and the students in my seminar at Brown for helpful comments.

I

CAUSES AND CONDITIONS

J. L. MACKIE

ASKED what a cause is, we may be tempted to say that it is an event which precedes the event of which it is the cause, and is both necessary and sufficient for the latter's occurrence; briefly that a cause is a necessary and sufficient preceding condition. There are, however, many difficulties in this account. I shall try to show that what we often speak of as a cause is a condition not of this sort, but of a sort related to this. That is to say, this account needs modification, and can be modified, and when it is modified we can explain much more satisfactorily how we can arrive at much of what we ordinarily take to be causal knowledge; the claims implicit within our causal assertions can be related to the forms of the evidence on which we are often relying when we assert a causal connection.

1. SINGULAR CAUSAL STATEMENTS

Suppose that a fire has broken out in a certain house, but has been extinguished before the house has been completely destroyed. Experts investigate the cause of the fire, and they conclude that it was caused by an electrical short-circuit at a certain place. What is the exact force of their statement that this short-circuit caused this fire? Clearly the experts are not saying that the short-circuit was a necessary condition for this house's catching fire at this time; they know perfectly well that a short-circuit somewhere else, or the overturning of a lighted oil stove, or any one of a number of other things might, if it had occurred, have set the house on fire. Equally, they are not saying that the short-circuit was a sufficient condition for this house's catching fire; for if the short-circuit had occurred, but there had been no inflammable material near by, the fire would not have broken out, and even given both the short-circuit and the inflammable material, the fire would not have occurred if, say, there had been an efficient automatic sprinkler at just the right spot. Far from being a condition both necessary and sufficient for the fire, the short-circuit was, and is known to

From *American Philosophical Quarterly*, 2.4 (October 1965), 245–55 and 261–4. Reprinted by permission of the editor of *American Philosophical Quarterly*.

the experts to have been, neither necessary nor sufficient for it. In what sense, then, is it said to have caused the fire?

At least part of the answer is that there is a set of conditions (of which some are positive and some are negative), including the presence of inflammable material, the absence of a suitably placed sprinkler, and no doubt quite a number of others, which combined with the short-circuit constituted a complex condition that was sufficient for the house's catching fire—sufficient, but not necessary, for the fire could have started in other ways. Also, of *this* complex condition, the short-circuit was an indispensable part: the other parts of this condition, conjoined with one another in the absence of the short-circuit, would not have produced the fire. The short-circuit which is said to have caused the fire is thus an indispensable part of a complex sufficient (but not necessary) condition of the fire. In this case, then, the so-called cause is, and is known to be, an *insufficient* but *necessary* part of a condition which is itself *unnecessary* but *sufficient* for the result. The experts are saying, in effect, that the short-circuit is a condition of this sort, that it occurred, that the other conditions which conjoined with it form a sufficient condition were also present, and that no other sufficient condition of the house's catching fire was present on this occasion. I suggest that when we speak of the cause of some particular event, it is often a condition of this sort that we have in mind. In view of the importance of conditions of this sort in our knowledge of and talk about causation, it will be convenient to have a short name for them: let us call such a condition (from the initial letters of the words italicized above), an INUS condition.[1]

This account of the force of the experts' statement about the cause of the fire may be confirmed by reflecting on the way in which they will have reached this conclusion, and the way in which anyone who disagreed with it would have to challenge it. An important part of the investigation will have consisted in tracing the actual course of the fire; the experts will have ascertained that no other condition sufficient for a fire's breaking out and taking this course was present, but that the short-circuit did occur and that conditions were present which in conjunction with it were sufficient for the fire's breaking out and taking the course that it did. Provided that there is some necessary and sufficient condition of the fire—and this is an assumption that we commonly make in such contexts—anyone who wanted to deny the experts' conclusion would have to challenge one or another of these points.

We can give a more formal analysis of the statement that something is an INUS condition. Let '*A*' stand for the INUS condition—in our example,

---

[1] This term was suggested by D. C. Stove who has also given me a great deal of help by criticizing earlier versions of this article.

the occurrence of a short-circuit at that place—and let 'B' and '$\bar{C}$' (that is, 'not-C', or the absence of C) stand for the other conditions, positive and negative, which were needed along with A to form a sufficient condition of the fire—in our example, B might be the presence of inflammable material, $\bar{C}$ the absence of a suitably placed sprinkler. Then the conjunction '$AB\bar{C}$' represents a sufficient condition of the fire, and one that contains no redundant factors; that is, $AB\bar{C}$ is a minimal sufficient condition for the fire.[2] Similarly, let $D\bar{E}F$, $\bar{G}\bar{H}I$, etc., be all the other minimal sufficient conditions of this result. Now provided that there is some necessary and sufficient condition for this result, the disjunction of all the minimal sufficient conditions for it constitutes a necessary and sufficient condition.[3] That is, the formula '$AB\bar{C}$ or $D\bar{E}F$ or $\bar{G}\bar{H}I$ or . . .' represents a necessary and sufficient condition for the fire, each of its disjuncts, such as '$AB\bar{C}$', represents a minimal sufficient condition, and each conjunct in each minimal sufficient condition, such as 'A', represents an INUS condition. To simplify and generalize this, we can replace the conjunction of terms conjoined with 'A' (here '$B\bar{C}$') by the single term 'X', and the formula representing the disjunction of all the other minimal sufficient conditions—here '$D\bar{E}F$ or $\bar{G}\bar{H}I$ or . . .'— by the single term 'Y'. Then an INUS condition is defined as follows:

A is an INUS condition of a result P if and only if, for some X and for some Y, (AX or Y) is a necessary and sufficient condition of P, but A is not a sufficient condition of P and X is not a sufficient condition of P.

We can indicate this type of relation more briefly if we take the provisos for granted and replace the existentially quantified variables 'X' and 'Y'

[2] The phrase 'minimal sufficient condition' is borrowed from Konrad Marc-Wogau, 'On Historical Explanation', *Theoria*, 28 (1962), 213–33. This article gives an analysis of singular causal statements, with special reference to their use by historians, which is substantially equivalent to the account I am suggesting. Many further references are made to this article, especially in n. 9 below.

[3] Cf. n. 8 on p. 227 of Marc-Wogau's article, where it is pointed out that in order to infer that the disjunction of all the minimal sufficient conditions will be a necessary condition, 'it is necessary to presuppose that an arbitrary event C, if it occurs, must have sufficient reason to occur'. This presupposition is equivalent to the presupposition that there is some (possibly complex) condition that is both necessary and sufficient for C.

It is of some interest that some common turns of speech embody this presupposition. To say 'Nothing but X will do,' or 'Either X or Y will do, but nothing else will,' is a natural way of saying that X, or the disjunction (X or Y), is a *necessary* condition for whatever result we have in mind. But taken literally these remarks say only that there is no sufficient condition for this result other than X, or other than (X or Y). That is, we use to mean 'a necessary condition' phrases whose literal meanings would be 'the only sufficient condition', or 'the disjunction of all sufficient conditions'. Similarly, to say that Z is 'all that's needed' is a natural way of saying that Z is a sufficient condition, but taken literally this remark says that Z is the only necessary condition. But, once again, that the only necessary condition will also be a sufficient one follows only if we presuppose that some condition is both necessary and sufficient.

by dots. That is, we can say that A is an INUS condition of P when $(A \ldots$ or $\ldots)$ is a necessary and sufficient condition of P.

(To forestall possible misunderstandings, I would fill out this definition as follows.[4] First, there could be a set of minimal sufficient conditions of P, but no necessary conditions, not even a complex one; in such a case, A might be what Marc-Wogau calls a moment in a minimal sufficient condition, but I shall not call it an INUS condition. I shall speak of an INUS condition only where the disjunction of all the minimal sufficient conditions is also a necessary condition. Secondly, the definition leaves it open that the INUS condition A might be a conjunct in each of the minimal sufficient conditions. If so, A would be itself a necessary condition of the result. I shall still call A an INUS condition in these circumstances: it is not part of the definition of an INUS condition that it should *not* be necessary, although in the standard cases, such as that sketched above, it is not in fact necessary.[5] Thirdly, the requirement that X by itself should not be sufficient for P insures that A is a non-redundant part of the sufficient condition AX; but there is a sense in which it may not be strictly necessary or indispensable even as a part of *this* condition, for it may be replaceable: for example KX might be another minimal sufficient condition of P.[6] Fourthly, it *is* part of the definition that the minimal sufficient condition, AX, of which A is a non-redundant part, is not also a necessary condition, that there is another sufficient condition Y (which may itself be a disjunction of sufficient conditions). Fifthly, and similarly, it *is* part of the definition that A is not by itself sufficient for P. The fourth and fifth of these points amount to this: I shall call A an INUS condition only if there are terms which actually occupy the places occupied by 'X' and 'Y' in the formula for the necessary and sufficient condition. However, there may be cases where there is only one minimal sufficient condition, say AX. Again, there may be cases where A is itself a minimal sufficient condition, the disjunction of all minimal sufficient conditions being $(A$ or $Y)$; again, there may be cases where A itself is the only minimal sufficient condition, and is itself both necessary and sufficient for P. In any of these cases, as well as in cases where A is an INUS condition, I shall say that A is *at least an* INUS *condition*. As we shall see, we often have evidence which supports the conclusion that something is *at least* an INUS condition; we may or may not have other evidence which shows that it is *no more than* an INUS condition.)

---

[4] I am indebted to the referees for the suggestion that these points should be clarified.

[5] Special cases where an INUS condition is also a necessary one are mentioned at the end of § 3.

[6] This point, and the term 'non-redundant', are taken from Michael Scriven's review of Nagel's *The Structure of Science*, in *Review of Metaphysics*, 1964. See especially the passage on p. 408 quoted below.

I suggest that a statement which asserts a singular causal sequence, of such a form as 'A caused P,' often makes, implicitly, the following claims:

(i) A is at least an INUS condition of P—that is, there is a necessary and sufficient condition of P which has one of these forms: (AX or Y), (A or Y), AX, A.

(ii) A was present on the occasion in question.

(iii) The factors represented by the 'X', if any, in the formula for the necessary and sufficient condition were present on the occasion in question.

(iv) Every disjunct in 'Y' which does not contain 'A' as a conjunct was absent on the occasion in question. (As a rule, this means that whatever 'Y' represents was absent on this occasion. If 'Y' represents a single conjunction of factors, then it was absent if at least one of its conjuncts was absent; if it represents a disjunction, then it was absent if each of its disjuncts was absent. But we do not wish to exclude the possibility that 'Y' should be, or contain as a disjunct, a conjunction one of whose conjuncts is A, or to require that *this* conjunction should have been absent.) [7]

I do not suggest that this is the whole of what is meant by 'A caused P' on any occasion, or even that it is a part of what is meant on every occasion: some additional and alternative parts of the meaning of such statements are indicated below.[8] But I am suggesting that this is an important part of the concept of causation; the proof of this suggestion would be that in many cases the falsifying of any one of the above-mentioned claims would rebut the assertion that A caused P.

This account is in fairly close agreement, in substance if not in terminology, with at least two accounts recently offered of the cause of a single event.

Konrad Marc-Wogau sums up his account thus: 'when historians in singular causal statements speak of a cause or the cause of a certain individual event β, then what they are referring to is another individual event α which is a moment in a minimal sufficient and at the same time necessary condition *post factum* β.[9]

---

[7] See example of the wicket-keeper discussed below.

[8] See §§ 7, 8.

[9] See pp. 226–7 of the article referred to in n. 2 above. Marc-Wogau's full formulation is as follows:

'Let "msc" stand for minimal sufficient condition and "nc" for necessary condition. Then suppose we have a class K of individual events $a_1, a_2, \ldots a_n$. (It seems reasonable to assume that K is finite; however even if K were infinite the reasoning below would not be affected.) My analysis of the singular causal statement: α is the cause of β, where α and β stand for individual events, can be summarily expressed in the following statements:

(1) $(EK) (K = \{a_1, a_2, \ldots, a_n\})$;
(2) $(x) (x \in K \equiv x \text{ msc } β)$;

He explained his phrase 'necessary condition *post factum*' by saying that he will call an event a_1 a necessary condition *post factum* for x if the disjunction 'a_1 or a_2 or a_3 . . . or a_n' represents a necessary condition for x, and of these disjuncts only a_1 was present on the particular occasion when x occurred.

Similarly Michael Scriven has said:

> Causes are *not* necessary, even contingently so, they are not sufficient—but they are, to talk that language, *contingently sufficient*. . . . They are part of *a* set of conditions that does guarantee the outcome, and they are non-redundant in that the rest of *this* set (which does not include all the other conditions present) is not alone sufficient for the outcome. It is not even true that they are relatively necessary, i.e., necessary with regard to that set of conditions rather than the total circumstances of their occurrence, for there may be several possible replacements for them which happen not to be present. There remains a ghost of necessity; a cause is a factor from a set of possible factors the presence of one of which (*any* one) is necessary in order that a set of conditions actually present be sufficient for the effect.[10]

There are only slight differences between these two accounts, or between each of them and that offered above. Scriven seems to speak too strongly when he says that causes are not necessary: it is, indeed, not part of the definition of a cause of this sort that it should be necessary, but, as noted above, a cause, or an INUS condition, may be necessary, either because there is only one minimal sufficient condition or because the cause is a moment in each of the minimal sufficient conditions. On the other hand, Marc-Wogau's account of a minimal sufficient condition seems too strong. He says that a minimal sufficient condition contains 'only those moments relevant to the effect' and that a moment is relevant to an effect if 'it is a necessary condition for β: β would not have occurred if this moment had not been present.' This is less accurate than Scriven's statement that the cause only needs to be non-redundant.[11] Also, Marc-Wogau's requirement, in

----

(3) $(a_1 \lor a_2 \lor \ldots a_n)$ nc β;

(4) $(x) (x \in K\, x \neq a_1) \supset x$ is not fulfilled when α occurs);

(5) α is a moment in a_1.

(3) and (4) say that a_1 is a necessary condition *post factum* for β. If a_1 is a necessary condition *post factum* for β, then every moment in a_1 is a necessary condition *post factum* for β, and therefore also α. As has been mentioned before (note 6) there is assumed to be a temporal sequence between α and β; β is not itself an element in K.'

[10] Op. cit., p. 408.

[11] However, in n. 7 on pp. 222–33, Marc-Wogau draws attention to the difficulty of giving an accurate definition of 'a moment in a sufficient condition'. Further complications are involved in the account given in § 5 below of 'clusters' of factors and the progressive localization of a cause. A condition which is minimally sufficient in relation to one degree of analysis of factors may not be so in relation to another degree of analysis.

his account of a necessary condition *post factum*, that only one minimal sufficient condition (the one containing α) should be present on the particular occasion, seems a little too strong. If two or more minimal sufficient conditions (say a_1 and a_2) were present, but α was a moment in each of them, then though neither a_1 nor a_2 was necessary *post factum*, α would be so. I shall use this phrase 'necessary *post factum*' to include cases of this sort: that is, α is a necessary condition *post factum* if it is a moment in every minimal sufficient condition that was present. For example, in a cricket team the wicket-keeper is also a good batsman. He is injured during a match, and does not bat in the second inning, and the substitute wicket-keeper drops a vital catch that the original wicket-keeper would have taken. The team loses the match, but it would have won if the wicket-keeper had *both* batted *and* taken that catch. His injury was a moment in two minimal sufficient conditions for the loss of the match; either his not batting, or the catch's not being taken, would on its own have ensured the loss of the match. But we can certainly say that his injury caused the loss of the match, and that it was a necessary condition *post factum*.

This account may be summed up, briefly and approximately, by saying that the statement '*A* caused *P*' often claims that *A* was necessary and sufficient for *P* in the circumstances. This description applies in the standard cases, but we have already noted that a cause is non-redundant rather than necessary even in the circumstances, and we shall see that there are special cases in which it may be neither necessary or non-redundant.

2. DIFFICULTIES AND REFINEMENTS[12]

Both Scriven and Marc-Wogau are concerned not only with this basic account, but with certain difficulties and with the refinements and complications that are needed to overcome them. Before dealing with these I shall introduce, as a refinement of my own account, the notion of a causal field.[13]

This notion is most easily explained if we leave, for a time, singular causal statements and consider general ones. The question 'What causes

---

[12] This section is something of an aside: the main argument is resumed in § 3.

[13] This notion of a causal field was introduced by John Anderson. He used it, e.g., in 'The Problem of Causality', first published in the *Australasian Journal of Psychology and Philosophy*, 16 (1938), and reprinted in *Studies in Empirical Philosophy* (Sydney, 1962), pp. 126–36, to overcome certain difficulties and paradoxes in Mill's account of causation. I have also used this notion to deal with problems of legal and moral responsibility, in 'Responsibility and Language', *Australasian Journal of Philosophy*, 33 (1955), 143–59.

influenza?' is incomplete and partially indeterminate. It may mean 'What causes influenza in human beings in general?' If so, the (full) cause that is being sought is a difference that will mark off cases in which human beings contract influenza from cases in which they do not; the causal field is then the region that is to be thus divided, *human beings in general*. But the question may mean, 'Given that influenza viruses are present, what makes some people contract the disease whereas others do not?' Here the causal field is *human beings in conditions where influenza viruses are present*. In all such cases, the cause is required to differentiate, within a wider region in which the effect sometimes occurs and sometimes does not, the sub-region in which it occurs: this wider region is the causal field. This notion can now be applied to singular causal questions and statements. 'What caused this man's skin cancer?'[14] may mean 'Why did this man develop skin cancer now when he did not develop it before?' Here the causal field is the career of this man: it is within this that we are seeking a difference between the time when skin cancer developed and times when it did not. But the same question may mean 'Why did this man develop skin cancer, whereas other men who were also exposed to radiation did not?' Here the causal field is the class of men thus exposed to radiation. And what is the cause in relation to one field may not be the cause in relation to another. Exposure to a certain dose of radiation may be the cause in relation to the former field: it cannot be the cause in relation to the latter field since it is part of the description of that field, and being present throughout that field it cannot differentiate one sub-region of it from another. In relation to the latter field, the cause may be, in Scriven's terms, 'some as-yet-unidentified constitutional factor'.

In our first example of the house which caught fire, the history of this house is the field in relation to which the experts were looking for the cause of the fire: their question was 'Why did this house catch fire on this occasion, and not on others?' However, there may still be some indeterminacy in this choice of a causal field. Does this house, considered as the causal field, include all its features, or all its relatively permanent features, or only some of these? If we take all its features, or even all of its relatively permanent ones, as constituting the field, then some of the things that we have treated as conditions—for example the presence of inflammable material near the place where the short-circuit occurred—would have to be re-

---

[14] These examples are borrowed from Scriven, op. cit., pp. 409–10. Scriven discusses them with reference to what he calls a 'contrast class', the class of cases where the effect did not occur with which the case where it did occur is being contrasted. What I call the causal field is the logical sum of the case (or cases) in which the effect is being said to be caused with what Scriven calls the contrast class.

garded as parts of the field, and we could not then take them also as conditions which in relation to this field, as additions to it or intrusions into it, are necessary or sufficient for something else. We must therefore take the house, in so far as it constitutes the causal field, as determined only in a fairly general way, by only some of its relatively permanent features, and we shall then be free to treat its other features as conditions which do not constitute the field, and are not parts of it, but which may occur within it or be added to it. It is in general an arbitrary matter whether a particular feature is regarded as a condition (that is, as a possible causal factor) or as part of the field, but it cannot be treated in both ways at once. If we are to say that something happened to this house because of, or partly because of, a certain feature, we are implying that it would still have been *this* house, the house in relation to which we are seeking the cause of this happening, even if it had not had this particular feature.

I now propose to modify the account given above of the claims often made by singular causal statements. A statement of such a form as 'A caused P' is usually elliptical, and is to be expanded into 'A caused P in relation to the field F.' And then in place of the claim stated in (i) above, we require this:

(ia) A is at least an INUS condition of P in the field F—that is, there is a condition which, given the presence of whatever features characterize F throughout, is necessary and sufficient for P, and which is of one of these forms: (AX or Y), (A or Y), AX, A.

In analysing our ordinary causal statements, we must admit that the field is often taken for granted or only roughly indicated, rather than specified precisely. Nevertheless, the field in relation to which we are looking for a cause of this effect, or saying that such-and-such is a cause, may be definite enough for us to be able to say that certain facts or possibilities are irrelevant to the particular causal problem under consideration, because they would constitute a shift from the intended field to a different one. Thus if we are looking for the cause, or causes, of influenza, meaning its cause(s) in relation to the field *human beings*, we may dismiss, as not directly relevant, evidence which shows that some proposed cause fails to produce influenza in rats. If we are looking for the cause of the fire in *this house*, we may similarly dismiss as irrelevant the fact that a proposed cause would not have produced a fire if the house had been radically different, or had been set in a radically different environment.

This modification enables us to deal with the well-known difficulty that it is impossible, without including in the cause the whole environment, the whole prior state of the universe (and so excluding any likelihood of repetition), to find a genuinely sufficient condition, one which is 'by itself, adequate to secure the effect'.[15] It may be hard to find even a complex condition which was absolutely sufficient for this fire because we should have to include, as one of the negative conjuncts, such an item as the earth's not being destroyed by a nuclear explosion just after the occurrence of the suggested INUS condition; but it is easy and reasonable to say simply that such an explosion would, in more senses than one, take us outside the field in which we are considering this effect. That is to say, it may be not so difficult to find a condition which is sufficient in relation to the intended field. No doubt this means that causal statements may be vague, in so far as the specification of the field is vague, but this is not a serious obstacle to establishing or using them, either in science or in everyday contexts.[16]

It is a vital feature of the account I am suggesting that we can say that A caused P, in the sense described, without being able to specify exactly the terms represented by 'X' and 'Y' in our formula. In saying that A is at least an INUS condition for P in F, one is *not* saying what other factors, along with A, were both present and non-redundant, and one is *not* saying what other minimal sufficient conditions there may be for P in F. One is not even claiming to be able to say what they are. This is in no way a difficulty: it is a readily recognizable fact about our ordinary causal statements, and one which this account explicitly and correctly reflects.[17] It will be shown (in § 5 below) that this elliptical or indeterminate character of our causal statements is closely connected with some of our characteristic ways of discovering and confirming causal relationships: it is precisely for state-

[15] Cf. Bertrand Russell, 'On the Notion of Cause', *Mysticism and Logic* (London, 1917), p. 187. Cf. also Scriven's first difficulty, op. cit., p. 409: 'First, there are virtually no known sufficient conditions, literally speaking, since human or accidental interference is almost inexhaustibly possible, and hard to exclude by specific qualification without tautology.' The introduction of the causal field also automatically covers Scriven's third difficulty and third refinement, that of the contrast class and the relativity of causal statements to contexts.

[16] J. R. Lucas, 'Causation', *Analytical Philosophy*, ed. R. J. Butler (Oxford, 1962), pp. 57–9, resolves this kind of difficulty by an informal appeal to what amounts to this notion of a causal field: '. . . these circumstances [cosmic cataclysms, etc.] . . . destroy the whole causal situation in which we had been looking for Z to appear . . . predictions are not expected to come true when quite unforeseen emergencies arise'.

[17] This is related to Scriven's second difficulty, op. cit., p. 409: 'there still remains the problem of saying what the other factors are which, with the cause, make up the sufficient condition. If they can be stated, causal explanation is then simply a special case of subsumption under a law. If they cannot, the analysis is surely mythological.' Scriven correctly replies that 'a combination of the thesis of macro-determinism . . . and observation-plus-theory frequently gives us the very best of reasons for saying that a certain factor combines with an unknown sub-set of the conditions present into a sufficient condition for a particular effect'. He gives a statistical example of such evidence, but the whole of my account of typical sorts of evidence for causal relationships in §§ 5 and 7 below [omitted from this volume] is an expanded defence of a reply of this sort.

ments that are thus 'gappy' or indeterminate that we can obtain fairly direct evidence from quite modest ranges of observation. On this analysis, causal statements implicitly contain existential quantifications; one can assert an existentially quantified statement without asserting any instantiation of it, and one can also have good reason for asserting an existentially quantified statement without having the information needed to support any precise instantiation of it. I can know that there is someone at the door even if the question 'Who is he?' would floor me.

Marc-Wogau is concerned especially with cases where 'there are two events, each of which independently of the other is a sufficient condition for another event'. There are, that is to say, two minimal sufficient conditions, both of which actually occurred. For example, lightning strikes a barn in which straw is stored, and a tramp throws a burning cigarette butt into the straw at the same place and at the same time. Likewise for a historical event there may be more than one 'cause', and each of them may, on its own, be sufficient.[18] Similarly Scriven considers a case where '. . . conditions (perhaps unusual excitement plus constitutional inadequacies) [are] present at 4.0 p.m. that guarantee a stroke at 4.55 p.m. and consequent death at 5.0 p.m.; but an entirely unrelated heart attack at 4.50 p.m. is still correctly called the cause of death, which, as it happens, does occur at 5.0 p.m.[19]

Before we try to resolve these difficulties let us consider another of Marc-Wogau's problems: Smith and Jones commit a crime, but if they had not done so the head of the criminal organization would have sent other members to perform it in their stead, and so it would have been committed anyway.[20] Now in this case, if 'A' stands for the actions of Smith and Jones, what we have is that AX is one minimal sufficient condition of the result (the crime), but $\bar{A}Z$ is another, and both X and Z are present. A combines with one set of the standing conditions to produce the result by one route; but the absence of A would have combined with another set of the standing conditions to produce the same result by another route. In this case we *can* say that A was a necessary condition *post factum*. This sample satisfies the requirements of Marc-Wogau's analysis, and of mine, of the statement that A caused this result; and this agrees with what we would ordinarily say in such a case. (We might indeed add that there was *also* a deeper cause—the existence of the criminal organization, perhaps—but this does not matter; our formal analyses do not insure that a particular result will have

---

[18] Op. cit., pp. 228–33.
[19] Op. cit., pp. 410–11: this is Scriven's fourth difficulty and refinement.
[20] Op. cit., p. 232: the example is taken from P. Gardiner, *The Nature of Historical Explanation* (Oxford, 1952), p. 101.

a unique cause, nor does our ordinary causal talk require this.) It is true that in this case we cannot say what will usually serve as an informal substitute for the formal account, that the cause, here A, was necessary (as well as sufficient) in the circumstances; for $\bar{A}$ would have done just as well. We cannot even say that A was non-redundant. But this shows merely that a formal analysis may be superior to its less formal counterparts.

Now in Scriven's example, we might take it that the heart attack prevented the stroke from occurring. If so, then the heart attack *is* a necessary condition *post factum*: it is a moment in the only minimal sufficient condition that was present in full, for the heart attack itself removed some factor that was a necessary part of the minimal sufficient condition which has the excitement as one of its moments. This is strictly parallel to the Smith and Jones case. Again it is odd to say that the heart attack was in any way necessary, since the absence of the heart attack would have done just as well: this absence would have been a moment in that other minimal sufficient condition, one of those other moments was the excitement. Nevertheless, the heart attack was necessary *post factum*, and the excitement was not. Scriven draws the distinction, quite correctly, in terms of continuity and discontinuity of causal chains: 'the heart attack was, and the excitement was not the cause of death because the "causal chain" between the latter and death was interrupted, while the former's "went to completion".' But it is worth noting that a break in the causal chain corresponds to a failure to satisfy the logical requirements of a moment in a minimal sufficient condition that is also necessary *post factum*.

Alternatively, if the heart attack did not prevent the stroke, then we have a case parallel to that of the straw in the barn, or of the man who is shot by a firing squad, and two bullets go through his heart simultaneously. In such cases the requirements of my analysis, or Marc-Wogau's, or of Scriven's, are not met: each proposed cause *is* redundant and not even necessary *post factum*, though the disjunction of them is necessary *post factum* and non-redundant. But this agrees very well with the fact that we *would* ordinarily hesitate to say, of either bullet, that it caused the man's death, or of either the lightning or the cigarette butt that it caused the fire, or of either the excitement or the heart attack that it was the cause of death. As Marc-Wogau says, 'in such a situation as this we are unsure also how to use the word 'cause'.' Our ordinary concept of cause does not deal clearly with cases of this sort, and we are free to decide whether or not to add to our ordinary use, and to the various more or less formal descriptions of it, rules which allow us to say that where more than one at-least-INUS-condition, and its conjunct conditions, are present, each of them caused the result.[21]

The account thus far developed of singular causal statements has been expressed in terms of statements about necessity and sufficiency: it is therefore incomplete until we have added an account of necessity and sufficiency themselves. This question is considered in § 4 below. But the present account is independent of any particular analysis of necessity and sufficiency. Whatever analysis of these we finally adopt, we shall use it to complete the account of what it is to be an INUS condition, or to be at least an INUS condition. But in whatever way this account is completed, we can retain the general principle that at least part of what is often done by a singular causal statement is to pick out, as the cause, something that is claimed to be at least an INUS condition.

3. GENERAL CAUSAL STATEMENTS

Many general causal statements are to be understood in a corresponding way. Suppose, for example, that an economist says that the restriction of credit causes (or produces) unemployment. Again, he will no doubt be speaking with reference to some causal field; this is now not an individual object, but a class, presumably economies of a certain general kind; perhaps their specification will include the feature that each economy of the kind in question contains a large private enterprise sector with free wage-earning employees. The result, unemployment, is something which sometimes occurs and sometimes does not occur within this field, and the same is true of the alleged cause, the restriction of credit. But the economist is not saying that (even in relation to this field) credit restriction is either necessary or sufficient for unemployment, let alone both necessary and sufficient. There may well be other circumstances which must be present along with credit restriction, in an economy of the kind referred to, if unemployment is to result; these other circumstances will no doubt include various negative ones, the absence of various counteracting causal factors which, if they were present, would prevent this result. Also, the economist will probably be quite prepared to admit that in an economy of this kind unemployment would be brought about by other combinations of circumstances in which the restriction of credit plays no part. So once again the claim that he is making is merely that the restriction of credit is, in economies of this kind, a non-redundant part of one sufficient condition for unemployment: that is, an INUS condition. The economist is probably assuming that there

---

[21] Scriven's fifth difficulty and refinement are concerned with the direction of causation. This is considered briefly in § 8 below.

is some condition, no doubt a complex one, which is both necessary and sufficient for unemployment in this field. This being assumed, what he is asserting is that, for some X and for some Y (AX or Y) is a necessary and sufficient condition for P in F, but neither A nor X is sufficient on its own, where 'A' stands for the restriction of credit, 'P' for unemployment, and 'F' for the field, economies of such-and-such a sort. In a developed economic theory the field F may be specified quite exactly, and so may the relevant combinations of factors represented here by 'X' and 'Y'. (Indeed, the theory may go beyond statements in terms of necessity and sufficiency to ones of functional dependence, but this is a complication which I am leaving aside for the present.) In a preliminary or popular statement, on the other hand, the combinations of factors may either be only roughly indicated or be left quite undetermined. At one extreme we have the statement that (AX or Y) is a necessary and sufficient condition, where 'X' and 'Y' are given definite meanings; at the other extreme we have the merely existentially quantified statement that this holds for *some* pair X and Y. Our knowledge in such cases ordinarily falls somewhere between these two extremes. We can use the same convention as before, deliberately allowing it to be ambiguous between these different interpretations, and say that in any of these cases, where A is an INUS condition of P in F (A . . . or . . .) is a necessary and sufficient condition of P in F.

A great deal of our ordinary causal knowledge is of this form. We know that the eating of sweets causes dental decay. Here the field is human beings who have some of their own teeth. We do not know, indeed it is not true, that the eating of sweets by any such person is a sufficient condition for dental decay: some people have peculiarly resistant teeth, and there are probably measures which, if taken along with the eating of sweets, would protect the eater's teeth from decay. All we know is that sweet-eating combined with a set of positive and negative factors which we can specify, if at all, only roughly and incompletely, constitutes a minimal sufficient condition for dental decay—but not a necessary one, for there are other combinations of factors, which do not include sweet-eating, which would also make teeth decay, but which we can specify, if at all, only roughly and incompletely. That is, if 'A' now represents sweet-eating, 'P' dental decay, and 'F' the class of human beings with some of their own teeth, we can say that, for some X and Y (AX or Y) is necessary and sufficient for P in F, and we *may* be able to go beyond this merely existentially quantified statement to at least a partial specification of the X and Y in question. That is, we can say that (A . . . or . . .) is a necessary and sufficient condition, but that A itself is only an INUS condition. And the same holds for many general causal statements of the form 'A causes (or produces) P'. It is in this sense that the application of a potential difference to the ends of a copper wire produces an electric current in the wire; that a rise in the temperature of a piece of metal makes it expand; that moisture rusts steel; that exposure to various kinds of radiation causes cancer, and so on.

However, it is true that not all ordinary general causal statements are of this sort. Some of them are implicit statements of functional dependence. Functional dependence is a more complicated relationship of which necessity and sufficiency can be regarded as special cases. Here too what we commonly single out as causing some result is only one of a number of factors which jointly affect the result. Again, some causal statements pick out something that is not only an INUS condition, but also a necessary condition. Thus we may say that the yellow fever virus is the cause of yellow fever. (This statement is not, as it might appear to be, tautologous, for the yellow fever virus and the disease itself can be independently specified.) In the field in question—human beings—the injection of this virus is not by itself a sufficient condition for this disease, for persons who have once recovered from yellow fever are thereafter immune to it, and other persons can be immunized against it. The injection of the virus, combined with the absence of immunity (natural or artificial), and perhaps combined with some other factors, constitutes a sufficient condition for the disease. Beside this, the injection of the virus is a necessary condition of the disease. If there is more than one complex sufficient condition for yellow fever, the injection of the virus into the patient's bloodstream (either by a mosquito or in some other way) is a factor included in every such sufficient condition. If 'A' stands for this factor, the necessary and sufficient condition has the form (A ... or A ... etc.), where A occurs in every disjunct. We sometimes note the difference between this and the standard case by using the phrase 'the cause'. We may say not merely that this virus *causes* yellow fever, but that it is *the cause* of yellow fever; but we would say only that sweet-eating *causes* dental decay, not that it is *the cause* of dental decay. But about an individual case we could say that sweet-eating was *the cause* of the decay of this person's teeth, meaning (as in § 1 above) that the only sufficient condition present here was the one of which sweet-eating is a non-redundant part. Nevertheless, there will not in general be any one item which has a unique claim to be regarded as *the cause* even of an individual event, and even after the causal field has been determined. Each of the moments in the minimal sufficient condition, or in each minimal sufficient condition, that was present can equally be regarded as the cause. They may be distinguished as predisposing causes, triggering causes, and so on, but it is quite arbitrary to pick out as 'main' and 'secondary', different moments which are equally non-redundant items in a minimal sufficient condition, or which are moments in two minimal sufficient conditions each of which makes the other redundant.[22]

4. NECESSITY AND SUFFICIENCY

One possible account of general statements of the forms 'S is a necessary condition of T' and 'S is a sufficient condition of T'—where 'S' and 'T' are general terms—is that they are equivalent to simple universal propositions. That is, the former is equivalent to 'All T are S' and the latter to 'All S are T.' Similarly, 'S is necessary for T in the field F' would be equivalent to 'All FT are S,' and 'S is sufficient for T in the field F' to 'All FS are T.' Whether an account of this sort is adequate is, of course, a matter of dispute; but it is not disputed that these statements about necessary and sufficient conditions at least *entail* the corresponding universals. I shall work on the assumption that this account is adequate, that general statements of necessity and sufficiency are equivalent to universals: it will be worth while to see how far this account will take us, how far we are able, in terms of it, to understand how we use, support, and criticize these statements of necessity and sufficiency.

A directly analogous account of the corresponding singular statements is not satisfactory. Thus it will not do to say that 'A short-circuit here was a necessary condition of a fire in this house' is equivalent to 'All cases of this house's catching fire are cases of a short-circuit occurring here,' because the latter is automatically true if this house has caught fire only once and a short-circuit has occurred on that occasion, but this is not enough to establish the statement that the short-circuit was a necessary condition of the fire; and there would be an exactly parallel objection to a similar statement about a sufficient condition.

It is much more plausible to relate singular statements about necessity and sufficiency to certain kinds of non-material conditionals. Thus 'A short-circuit here was a necessary condition of a fire in this house' is closely related to the counterfactual conditional 'If a short-circuit had not occurred here this house would not have caught fire,' and 'A short-circuit here was a sufficient condition of a fire in this house' is closely related to what Goodman has called the factual conditional, 'Since a short-circuit occurred here, this house caught fire.'

However, a further account would still have to be given of these non-material conditionals themselves. I have argued elsewhere[23] that they are

---

[22] Cf. Marc-Wogau's concluding remarks, op. cit., pp. 232–3.
[23] 'Counterfactuals and Causal Laws', *Analytical Philosophy*, ed. R. J. Butler (Oxford, 1962), pp. 66–80.

best considered as condensed or telescoped *arguments*, but that the statements used as premisses in these arguments are no more than simple factual universals. To use the above-quoted counterfactual conditional is, in effect, to run through an incomplete argument: 'Suppose that a short-circuit did not occur here, then the house did not catch fire.' To use the factual conditional is, in effect, to run through a similar incomplete argument, 'A short-circuit occurred here; therefore the house caught fire.' In each case the argument might in principle be completed by the insertion of other premisses which, together with the stated premiss, would entail the stated conclusion. Such additional premisses may be said to *sustain* the non-material conditional. It is an important point that someone can use a non-material conditional without completing or being able to complete the argument, without being prepared explicitly to assert premisses that would sustain it, and similarly that we can understand such a conditional without knowing exactly how the argument would or could be completed. But to say that a short-circuit here was a necessary condition of a fire in this house is to say that there is some set of true propositions which would sustain the above-stated counterfactual, and to say that it was a sufficient condition is to say that there is some set of true propositions which would sustain the above-stated factual conditional. If this is conceded, then the relating of singular statements about necessity and sufficiency to non-material conditionals leads back to the view that they refer indirectly to certain simple universal propositions. Thus, if we said that a short-circuit here was a necessary condition for a fire in this house, we should be saying that there are true universal propositions from which, together with true statements about the characteristics of this house, and together with the supposition that a short-circuit did not occur here, it would follow that the house did not catch fire. From this we could infer the universal proposition which is the more obvious, but unsatisfactory, candidate for the analysis of this statement of necessity, 'All cases of this house's catching fire are cases of a short-circuit occurring here,' or, in our symbols, 'All *FP* are *A*.' We can use this to represent approximately the statement of necessity, on the under-standing that it is to be a consequence of some set of wider universal propositions, and is not to be automatically true merely because there is only this one case of an *FP*, of this house's catching fire.[24] A statement that

[24] This restriction may be compared with one which Nagel imposes on laws of nature: 'the vacuous truth of an unrestricted universal is not sufficient for counting it a law; it counts as a law only if there is a set of other assumed laws from which the universal is logically derivable' (*The Structure of Science* (New York, 1961), p. 60). It might have been better if he had added 'or if there is some other way in which it is supported (ultimately) by empirical evidence'. Cf. my remarks in 'Counterfactuals and Causal Laws', pp. 72–4, 78–80.

A was a sufficient condition may be similarly represented by 'All FA are P.' Correspondingly, if all that we want to say is that $(A \ldots \text{or} \ldots)$ was necessary and sufficient for P in F, this will be represented approximately by the pair of universals 'All FP are $(A \ldots \text{or} \ldots)$ and all $F(A \ldots \text{or} \ldots)$ are P,' and more accurately by the statement that there is some set of wider universal propositions from which, together with true statements about the features of F, this pair of universals follows. This, therefore, is the fuller analysis of the claim that in a particular case A is an INUS condition of P in F, and hence of the singular statement that A caused P. (The statement that A is *at least* an INUS condition includes other alternatives, corresponding to cases where the necessary and sufficient condition is $(A \text{ or} \ldots)$, $A \ldots$, or A).

Let us go back now to general statements of necessity and sufficiency and take F as a class, not as an individual. On the view that I am adopting, at least provisionally, the statement that Z is a necessary and sufficient condition for P in F is equivalent to 'All FP are Z and all FZ are P.' Similarly, if we cannot completely specify a necessary and sufficient condition for P in F, but can only say that the formula '$(A \ldots \text{or} \ldots)$' represents such a condition, this is equivalent to the pair of incomplete universals, 'All FP are $(A \ldots \text{or} \ldots)$ and all $F(A \ldots \text{or} \ldots)$ are P.' In saying that our general causal statements often do no more than specify an INUS condition, I am therefore saying that much of our ordinary causal knowledge is knowledge of such pairs of incomplete universals, of what we may call elliptical or *gappy* causal laws.

. . . .

8. THE DIRECTION OF CAUSATION

This account of causation is still incomplete, in that nothing has yet been said about the direction of causation, about what distinguishes A causing P from P causing A. This is a difficult question, and it is linked with the equally difficult question of the direction of time. I cannot hope to resolve it completely here, but I shall state some of the relevant considerations.[25]

First, it seems that there is a relation which may be called *causal priority*, and that part of what is meant by 'A caused P' is that this relation holds in one direction between A and P, not the other. Secondly, this relation is not identical with temporal priority; it is conceivable that there should be evidence for a case of backward causation, for A being causally prior to

---

[25] As was mentioned in n. 21, Scriven's fifth difficulty and refinement are concerned with this point (op. cit., pp. 411–12), but his answer seems to me inadequate. Lucas touches on it (op. cit., pp. 51–3). The problem of temporal asymmetry is discussed, e.g. by J. J. C. Smart, *Philosophy and Scientific Realism* (London, 1963), pp. 142–8, and by A. Grünbaum in the article cited on p. 35 n. 28 below.

P whereas *P* was temporally prior to *A*. Most of us believe, and I think with good reason, that backward causation does not occur, so that we can and do normally use temporal order to limit the possibilities about causal order; but the connection between the two is synthetic. Thirdly, it could be objected to the analysis of 'necessary' and 'sufficient' offered in § 4 above that it omits any reference to causal order, whereas our most common use of 'necessary' and 'sufficient' in causal contexts includes such a reference. Thus '*A* is (causally) sufficient for *B*' says 'If *A*, then *B*, and *A* is causally prior to *B*,' but '*B* is (causally) necessary for *A*' is not equivalent to this: it says 'If *A*, then *B*, and *B* is causally prior to *A*.' However, it is simpler to use 'necessary' and 'sufficient' in senses which exclude this causal priority, and to introduce the assertion of priority separately into our accounts of '*A* caused *P*' and '*A* causes *P*.' Fourthly, although '*A* is (at least) an INUS condition of *P*' is not synonymous with '*P* is (at least) an INUS condition of *A*,' this difference of meaning cannot exhaust the relation of causal priority. If it did exhaust it, the direction of causation would be a trivial matter, for, given that there is some necessary and sufficient condition of *A* in the field, it can be proved that if *A* is (at least) an INUS condition of *P*, then *P* is also (at least) an INUS condition of *A*: we can construct a minimal sufficient condition of *A* in which *P* is a moment.[26]

Fifthly, it is often suggested that the direction of causation is linked with controllability. If there is a causal relation between *A* and *B*, and we can control *A* without making use of *B* to do so, and the relation between *A* and *B* still holds, then we decide that *B* is not causally prior to *A* and, in general, that *A* is causally prior to *B*. But this means only that if one case of causal priority is known, we can use it to determine others: our rejection of the possibility that *B* is causally prior to *A* rests on our knowledge that our action is causally prior to *A*, and the question how we know the latter, and even the question of what causal priority is, have still to be answered. Similarly, if one of the causally related kinds of event, say *A*, can be randomized, so that occurrences of *A* are either not caused at all, or are caused by something which enters this causal field *only* in this way, by causing *A*, we can reject both the possibility that *B* is causally prior to *A* and the possibility that some common cause is prior both to *A* and separately to *B*, and we can again conclude that *A* is causally prior to *B*. But this still means only that we can infer causal priority in one place if we first know that it is absent from another place. It is true that our knowledge of the direction of causation in ordinary cases is thus based on what we find to be controllable, and on what we either find to be random or find that we can randomize;

---

[26] I am indebted to one of the referees for correcting an inaccurate statement on this point in an earlier version.

but this cannot without circularity be taken as providing a full account either of what we mean by causal priority or of how we know about it.

A suggestion put forward by Popper about the direction of time seems to be relevant here.[27] If a stone is dropped into a pool, the entry of the stone will explain the expanding circular waves. But the reverse process, with contracting circular waves, 'would demand a vast number of distant coherent generators of waves the coherence of which, to be explicable, would have to be shown . . . as originating from one centre'. That is, if *B* is an occurrence which involves a certain sort of 'coherence' between a large number of separated items, whereas *A* is a single event, and *A* and *B* are causally connected, *A* will explain *B* in a way in which *B* will not explain *A* unless some other single event, say *C*, first explains the coherence in *B*. Such examples give us a *direction of explanation*, and it may be that this is the basis, or part of the basis, of the relation I have called causal priority.

9. CONCLUSIONS

Even if Mill was wrong in thinking that science consists mainly of causal knowledge, it can hardly be denied that such knowledge is an indispensable element in science, and that it is worth while to investigate the meaning of causal statements and the ways in which we can arrive at causal knowledge. General causal relationships are among the items which a more advanced kind of scientific theory explains, and is confirmed by its success in explaining. Singular causal assertions are involved in almost every report of an experiment: doing such and such *produced* such and such an effect. Materials are commonly identified by their causal properties: to recognize something as a piece of a certain material, therefore, we must establish singular causal assertions about it, that this object affected that other one, or was affected by it, in such and such a way. Causal assertions are embedded in both the results and the procedures of scientific investigation.

The account that I have offered of the force of various kinds of causal statements agrees both with our informal understanding of them and with accounts put forward by other writers: at the same time it is formal enough to show how such statements can be supported by observations and experiments, and thus to throw a new light on philosophical questions about the nature of causation and causal explanation and the status of causal knowledge.

One important point is that, leaving aside the question of the direction

[27] 'The Arrow of Time', *Nature*, 177 (1956), 538; also ibid., 178, p. 382 and 179, p. 1297.

of causation, the analysis has been given entirely within the limits of what can still be called a regularity theory of causation, in that the causal laws involved in it are no more than straightforward universal propositions, although their terms may be complex and perhaps incompletely specified. Despite this limitation, I have been able to give an account of the meaning of statements about singular causal sequences, regardless of whether such a sequence is or is not of a kind that frequently recurs: repetition is not essential for causal relation, and regularity does not here disappear into the mere fact that this single sequence has occurred. It has, indeed, often been recognized that the regularity theory could cope with single sequences if, say, a unique sequence could be explained as the resultant of a number of laws each of which was exemplified in many other sequences; but my account shows how a singular causal statement can be interpreted, and how the corresponding sequence can be shown to be causal, even if the corresponding complete laws are not known. It shows how even a unique sequence can be directly recognized as causal.

One consequence of this is that it now becomes possible to reconcile what have appeared to be conflicting views about the nature of historical explanation. We are accustomed to contrast the 'covering-law' theory adopted by Hempel, Popper, and others with the views of such critics as Dray and Scriven who have argued that explanations and causal statements in history cannot be thus assimilated to the patterns accepted in the physical sciences.[28] But while my basic analysis of singular causal statements in

[28] See, for example, C. G. Hempel, 'The Function of General Laws in History', *Journal of Philosophy*, 39 (1942), reprinted in *Readings in Philosophical Analysis*, ed. H. Feigl and W. Sellars (New York, 1949), pp. 459–71; C. G. Hempel and P. Oppenheim, 'Studies in the Logic of Explanation', *Philosophy of Science*, 15 (1948), reprinted in *Readings in the Philosophy of Science*, ed. H. Feigl and M. Brodbeck (New York, 1953), pp. 319–52; K. R. Popper, *Logik der Forschung* (Vienna, 1934), translation *The Logic of Scientific Discovery* (London, 1959), pp. 59–60, also *The Open Society and its Enemies* (London, 1952), ii, 262; W. Dray, *Laws and Explanation in History* (Oxford, 1957); N. Rescher, 'On Prediction and Explanation', *British Journal for the Philosophy of Science*, 9 (1958), 281–90; various papers in *Minnesota Studies in the Philosophy of Science*, vol. 3, ed. H. Feigl and G. Maxwell (Minneapolis, 1962); A. Grünbaum, 'Temporally-asymmetric Principles, Parity between Explanation and Prediction, and Mechanism versus Teleology', *Philosophy of Science*, 29 (1962), 146–70.

Dray's criticisms of the covering-law theory include the following: we cannot state the law used in a historical explanation without making it so vague as to be vacuous (op. cit., especially pp. 24–37) or so complex that it covers only a single case and is trivial on that account (p. 39); the historian does not come to the task of explaining an event with a sufficient stock of laws already formulated and empirically validated (pp. 42–3); historians do not need to replace judgement about particular cases with deduction from empirically validated laws (pp. 51–2). It will be clear that my account resolves each of these difficulties. Grünbaum draws an important distinction between (1) an asymmetry between explanation and prediction with regard to the grounds on which we claim to know that the explanandum is true, and (2) an asymmetry with

§§ 1 and 2 agrees closely with Scriven's, I have argued in § 4 that this analysis can be developed in terms of complex and elliptical universal propositions, and this means that wherever we have a singular causal statement we shall still have a covering law, albeit a complex and perhaps elliptical one. Also, I have shown in § 5, and indicated briefly, for the functional dependence variants, in § 7 [both omitted from this volume], that the evidence which supports singular causal statements also supports general causal statements or covering laws, though again only complex and elliptical ones. Hempel recognized long ago that historical accounts can be interpreted as giving incomplete 'explanation sketches', rather than what he would regard as full explanations, which would require fully stated covering laws, and that such sketches are also common outside history. But in these terms what I am saying is that explanation sketches and the related elliptical laws are often all that we can discover, that they play a part in all sciences, that they can be supported and even established without being complete, and so not serve merely as preliminaries to or summaries of complete deductive explanations. If we modify the notion of a covering law to admit laws which not only are complex but also are known only in an elliptical form, the covering-law theory can accommodate many of the points that have been made in criticism of it, while preserving the structural similarity of explanation in history, and in the physical sciences. In this controversy, one point at issue has been the symmetry of explanation and prediction, and my account may help to resolve this dispute. It shows, in agreement with what Scriven has argued, how the actual occurrence of an event in the observed circumstances—the I_1 of my formal account in § 5—may be a vital part of the evidence which supports an explanation of

---

respect to the logical relation between the explanans and the explanandum; he thinks that only the former sort of asymmetry obtains. I suggest that my account of the use of gappy laws will clarify both the sense in which Grünbaum is right (since an explanation and a tentative prediction can use similarly gappy laws which are similarly related to the known initial conditions and the result) and the sense in which, in such a case, we may contrast an entirely satisfactory explanation with a merely tentative prediction. Scriven (in his most recent statement, the review cited in n. 10 above) says that 'we often pin down a factor as a cause by excluding other possible causes. Simple—but disastrous for the covering-law theory of explanation, because we can eliminate causes only for something *we know has occurred*. And if the grounds for our explanation of an event *have* to include knowledge of that event's occurrence, they cannot be used (without circularity) to predict the occurrence of that event' (p. 414). That is, the observation of this event in these circumstances may be a vital part of the evidence that justifies the particular causal explanation that we give of this event: it may itself go a long way toward establishing the elliptical law in relation to which we explain it (as I have shown in § 5), whereas a law used for prediction cannot thus rest on the observation of the event predicted. But as my account also shows, this does not introduce an asymmetry of Grünbaum's second sort, and is therefore not disastrous for the covering-law theory.

that event, which shows that it was A that caused P on this occasion. A prediction on the other hand cannot rest on observation of the event predicted. Also, the gappy law which is sufficient for an explanation will not suffice for a prediction (or for a retrodiction): a statement of initial conditions together with a gappy law will not entail the assertion that a specific result will occur, though of course such a law may be, and often is, used to make tentative predictions the failure of which will not necessarily tell against the law. But the recognition of these differences between prediction and explanation does not affect the covering-law theory as modified by the recognition of elliptical laws.

Although what I have given is primarily an account of physical causation, it may be indirectly relevant to the understanding of human action and mental causation. It is sometimes suggested that our ability to recognize a single occurrence as an instance of mental causation is a feature which distinguishes mental causation from physical or 'Humean' causation.[29] But this suggestion arises from the use of too simple a regularity account of physical causation. If we first see clearly what we mean by singular causal statements in general, and how we can support such a statement by observation of the single sequence itself, even in a physical case, we shall be better able to contrast with this our awareness of mental causes, and to see whether the latter has any really distinctive features.

This account also throws light on both the form and the status of the 'causal principle', the deterministic assumption which is used in any application of the methods of eliminative induction. These methods need not presuppose determinism in general, but only that each specific phenomenon investigated by such a method is deterministic. Moreover, they require not only that the phenomenon should have some cause, but that there should be some restriction of the range of possibly relevant factors (at least to spatio-temporally neighbouring ones, as explained in § 5). Now the general causal principle, that every event has some cause, is so general that it is peculiarly difficult either to confirm or to disconfirm, and we might be tempted either to claim for it some *a priori* status, to turn it into a metaphysical absolute presupposition, or to dismiss it as vacuous. But the specific

---

[29] See, for example, G. E. M. Anscombe, *Intention* (Oxford, 1957), especially p. 16; J. Teichmann, 'Mental Cause and Effect', *Mind*, 70 (1961), 36–52. Teichmann speaks (p. 36) of 'the difference between them and ordinary (or "Humean") sequences of cause and effect' and says (p. 37) 'it is sometimes in order for the person who blinks to say absolutely dogmatically that the cause is such-and-such, and to say this independently of his knowledge of any previously established correlations', and again 'if the noise is a cause it seems to be one which is known to be such in a special way. It seems that while it is necessary for an observer to have knowledge of a previously established correlation between noises and Smith's jumpings, before he can assert that one causes the other, it is not necessary for Smith himself to have such knowledge.'

assumption that this phenomenon has some cause based somehow on factors drawn from this range, or even that this phenomenon has some neighbouring cause, is much more open to empirical confirmation and disconfirmation: indeed the former can be conclusively falsified by the observation of a positive instance I_1 of P, and a negative case N_1 in which P does not occur, but where each of the factors in the given range is either present in both I_1 and N_1 or absent from both. This account, then, encourages us to regard the assumption as something to be empirically confirmed or disconfirmed. At the same time it shows that there must be some principle of the confirmation of hypotheses other than the eliminative methods themselves, since each such method rests on an empirical assumption.

II

THE METAPHYSICS OF CAUSATION

RICHARD TAYLOR

IF we can now cite clear examples of causal connections wherein those conditions that constitute the cause and those that constitute the effect are entirely contemporaneous, neither occurring before the other, then it will have been proved that the difference between a cause and its effect cannot be a temporal one, but must consist of something else.

In fact such examples are not at all hard to find. Consider, for instance, a locomotive that is pulling a caboose, and to make it simple, suppose this is all it is pulling. Now here the motion of the locomotive is sufficient for the motion of the caboose, the two being connected in such a way that the former cannot move without the latter moving with it. But so also, the motion of the caboose is sufficient for the motion of the locomotive, for given that the two are connected as they are, it would be impossible for the caboose to be moving without the locomotive moving with it. From this it logically follows that, conditions being such as they are—both objects are in motion, there are no other moves present, no obstructions to motion, and so on—the motion of each object is also necessary for the motion of the other. But is there any temporal gap between the motion of one and the motion of the other? Clearly there is not. They move together, and in no sense is the motion of one temporally followed by the motion of the other.

Here it is tempting to say that the locomotive must *start* moving before the caboose can start moving, but this is both irrelevant and false. It is irrelevant, because the effect we are considering is not the caboose's *beginning* to move, but its moving. And it is false because we can suppose the two to be securely connected, such that as soon as either begins to move the other must move too. Even if we do not make this supposition, and suppose, instead, that the locomotive does begin moving first, and moves some short distance before overcoming the looseness and elasticity of its connection with the caboose, still it is no cause of the motion of the caboose until that looseness is overcome. When that happens, and not until then, the

From *Action and Purpose* (Englewood Cliffs, N.J.: Prentice-Hall, 1966; reptd.: New York: Humanities Press, 1974), pp. 35–9. Reprinted by permission of the author.

locomotive imparts its motion to the caboose. Cause and effect are, then, perfectly contemporaneous.

Again, consider the relationships between one's hand and a pencil he is holding while writing. We can ignore here the difficult question of what causes the *hand* to move. It is surely true, in any case, that the motion of the pencil is caused by the motion of the hand. This means, first, that conditions are such that the motion of the hand is sufficient for the motion of the pencil. Given precisely *those* conditions, however, the motion of the pencil is sufficient for the motion of the hand; neither can move, under the conditions assumed—that the fingers are grasping the pencil—without the other moving with it. It follows, then, that under these conditions the motion of either is also necessary for the motion of the other. And, manifestly, both motions are contemporaneous; the motion of neither is *followed* by the motion of the other.

Or again, consider a leaf that is being fluttered by the wind. Here it would be quite clearly erroneous to say that the wind currents impinge upon the leaf and then, some time later, the leaf flutters in response. There is no gap in time at all. One might want to say that the leaf, however light, does offer some resistance to the wind, and that the wind must overcome this slight resistance before any fluttering occurs. But then we need only add that the wind is no cause of the leaf's motion until that resistance is overcome. Cause and effect are again, then, contemporaneous.

What, then, distinguishes cause and effect in the foregoing examples? It is not the time of occurrence, for both occur together. It is not any difference in the relations of necessity and sufficiency, for these are identical both ways. But there is one thing which, in all these cases, appears to distinguish the cause from the effect; namely, that the cause acts upon something else to produce some change. The locomotive *pulls* the caboose, but the caboose does not *push* the locomotive; it just follows passively along. The hand pushes the pencil and imparts motion to it, while the pencil is just passively moved. The wind acts upon the leaf to move it; but it is no explanation of the wind's blowing to say that the leaf is moving. In all these cases, to be sure, what has been distinguished as the cause is itself moved by something else—the locomotive by steam in its cylinders, the hand by a man, the wind by things more complex and obscure; but that only calls attention to the fact that causes can themselves be the effects of other causes. Whether all causes must be such or whether, on the contrary, something—such as a man, for example—can be a 'first cause' is something we shall consider later on.

ARE ALL CAUSES CONTEMPORANEOUS WITH THEIR EFFECTS?

In order to show that it can be no part of the analysis of a causal connection that causes precede their effects in time, all that is needed is a *single* clear example of a cause or set of causal conditions which is entirely contemporaneous with its effect, and examples of this, we have just seen, are easy enough to point out. It should, in any case, be obvious just from philosophical considerations, for it is not difficult to imagine beginningless processes producing effects throughout all time past, even though it is doubtful whether any such processes exist. If it were discovered, for example, that the sun had always shone upon the moon, that this state of affairs had always existed, no one would be led by that alone to doubt that moonlight is caused by the sun, or to suppose that it would be arbitrary, in such a state of affairs, what one called the cause and what the effect.

It has, however, sometimes been argued most acutely that *all* causes are contemporaneous with their effects, that just in the nature of things neither a cause nor its effect *can* occur before or after the other. Thus it is sometimes maintained that a ball, for example, which is moved by the impact of another ball, is not caused to move by anything happening *prior* to such impact, but by the impact itself, and that this is simultaneous with the initial motion of the ball that is thus moved. Again, it can be argued that water is not caused to boil by *first* being heated to a certain point. Rather, it boils as soon as it is heated to that point, and not sometime later, such that cause and effect are again contemporaneous. And we get the same result, it is sometimes claimed, in the case of any causal connection described with sufficient exactness.

Now it is in no way essential, for the point of this chapter, either to affirm or to deny this. In order to show that a cause *need* not precede its effect in time, which has already been done, it is by no means necessary to show that *no* cause ever precedes its effect. Nor need we address ourselves to the arguments upon which this latter claim rests. They are, in my opinion, impossible to meet, for they involve enormous unresolved problems concerning the continuity of processes and the continuity of time itself. The reason we nevertheless need not address ourselves to them is that, however difficult they may be of refutation, their conclusion—that *all* causes are contemporaneous with their effects—is provably false. For if this were true, then there would be no such thing as a causal chain. Indeed, it would be impossible for any two events whatever to have any causal connection with each other if there were any lapse of time at all between their occurrences. If some event *A*, for example, causes *B*, which in turn causes C, which in turn causes D, then if every cause is simultaneous with its effect, it follows that when A occurs, then the others, and indeed every event in the universe that is in any way causally connected with A, must occur *at the same time*. This, however, is false. There *are* causal chains, and sometimes temporally separated events are causally related in one way or another. When a stone is dropped into the middle of a pond, for instance, this has at least *some* causal connection with the ripples that appear at the shore some moments later. There are, to be sure, many intervening causal connections, but this common state of affairs would be logically impossible if every cause were simultaneous with its effect—for all the intervening causal connections would then have to occur simultaneously with both the initial disturbance of the water and the subsequent appearance of ripples at the shore, which is absurd.

My conclusions, then, are compatible with the supposition that causes sometimes precede their effects in time. I only deny that they *must* precede them, and hence that this supposition plays any part in the nature or analysis of a causal connection. My conclusions are also compatible with saying that a given set of conditions, which is *antecedently* necessary for, or sufficient for, or both necessary and sufficient for another state of affairs, is the *cause* of that state of affairs. I only deny that its causal relationship to that state of affairs *consists* in that relationship, for a cause, as I have maintained, must *also* be something having the power to produce that state of affairs. My conclusions are *not* compatible with saying that a given set of conditions, which is subsequently necessary for, or sufficient for, or both necessary and sufficient for another state of affairs, is the cause of that state of affairs. This, however, is no consequence of 'the way we use words'. On the contrary, the reason we use words as we do here, and refuse to call such a set of conditions the cause of something happening earlier on, is that it would be absurd to do so. And the only basis for this, as far as I can see, is that causes have no power over the past—even though they may have precisely the same relationships of necessity and sufficiency with respect to things past as they have with respect to things future.

WHAT IS A CAUSE?

A true interpreted statement of the form 'A was the cause of B' means, in light of the foregoing, that both A and B are conditions or sets of conditions that occurred; that each was, given all the other conditions that occurred, but only those, both necessary and sufficient for the occurrence of the other; that B did not precede A in time; *and* that A made B happen by virtue of its power to do so. But this final qualification, *alas!* renders the whole analysis empty. For to say that A made B happen obviously only means that *A caused B*, and to say that it did this by virtue of its power to do so obviously means nothing more than that *A* produced *B* by virtue of its efficacy as a *cause*—or, in short, that *A* caused *B*. To say of anything, then, that it was the cause of something else, means simply and solely that it *was* the cause of the thing in question, and there is absolutely no other conceptually clearer way of putting the matter except by the introduction of mere synonyms for causation. Positively, what this means is that causation is a philosophical category, that while the concept of causation can perhaps be used to shed light upon other problems or used in the analysis of other relationships, no other concepts can be used to analyse it.

III

DEFECTS OF THE NECESSARY
CONDITION ANALYSIS OF CAUSATION

MICHAEL SCRIVEN

THE foregoing analysis has represented causes as selected on pragmatic grounds from conditions which are (a) known to be possible causes, (b) known to be present in the case under consideration, and (c) not known to operate in a way contra-indicated by known data about the case.

But this only defines 'cause' in terms of 'possible cause'. Can we not proceed further and define 'possible cause' in terms of some combination of necessary and sufficient conditions, these being interpreted as simple regularity notions? The answer appears to be that we cannot. The concept of cause is fundamental to our conception of the world in much the same way as the concept of number: we cannot define it in terms of other notions without conceptual or ostensive [1] circularity.

It is probably best to see the notion of cause, like number, as systematically developed from a simple case which we can exhibit, though not define in non-causal terms. The existence of this developmental sequence does not establish the common idea that later members are simply complex combinations of the earlier ones. (Finding the sum of an infinite series is not done by a complex combination of counting procedures even though the calculus is a development from arithmetic.)

8.1. *Basic Experimental Case.* Suppose that whenever and however we produce C, E occurs, and that E never occurs unless C is produced (so that C is in a sense the only handle by means of which we can manipulate E), then C is the cause of E. (We assume a normal experimental context throughout. E may also turn out to be a cause of C, e.g. where C and E are alterations in pressure and temperature of a cylinder of gas.)

From *Philosophical Analysis and History*, ed. W. Dray (New York: Harper and Row, 1966), pp. 258–62. Copyright © 1966 by William H. Dray. Reprinted by permission of Harper and Row, Publishers Inc.

[1] Ostensive circularity afflicts the Russellian definition of a number, which can only be applied by someone with the capacity to count that number of quantifiers, and hence in an important sense presupposes possession of the concept. (Cf. Tarski's definition of truth.) Neither ostensive nor conceptual circularity are fatal to *all* the purposes of definitions, but generally make their use as eliminative or reductive devices unsatisfactory.

8.2. *Basic Observation Case*. Suppose that C just occurs on various occasions and is accompanied by (perhaps followed by) E, and E never occurs on any other occasions. C is the cause of E if (but not only if) we can conclude that C *would* always be accompanied by E, no matter how or when it was produced (i.e. if we can reduce it to Case 8.1). Since we assume that something is responsible for the occurrence of E (determinism) and C is at least always present, the great problem is to eliminate the possibility that some *other* antecedent of C and E, say X, is bringing them both about *independently*.[2] Thus, the correlation between the early and late symptoms of a disease has often been mistakenly identified as a causal connection until it is discovered both are due to a third factor, the infection itself.

Case 8.1 is immune to this difficulty, since when we experimentally control C we produce it at random moments, i.e. moments not determined by[3] any preceding environmental factor that could possibly determine E (we may use a table of random numbers, dice, a roulette wheel, a decimal clock, or an electronic randomizer).

8.3. *Compound Causes*. Suppose that we need to bring about not only C but also D in order to get E (and that D alone is not sufficient). We may call C and D *causal factors* or *co-causes* of E. Neither can be called *the* cause, except when the context changes so that one or the other can be regarded as a standing condition or an irrelevant factor.

8.4. *Multiple Causes*. If C and D are *each* sufficient to bring about E, and nothing else is, then whichever occurs is the cause. If both occur, one of them may not have had any effect on this occasion, a possibility which we check by examining the situation for the presence of known intermediate links which characterize the *modus operandi* of C and D, i.e. any sets of conditions 'C_1 or C_2 or . . .' (or 'D_1 or D_2 or . . .') which are necessary for C (or D) to act as the cause of E. This test does not apply where no such links are known, and since it is not logically necessary that there be any (C and E may be adjacent links in the chain, or differ only from a certain descriptive standpoint, or represent 'action at a distance'), the test is not part of the meaning, of course. But it is the historian's and the coroner's key test.

---

[2] Of course, even if C is the cause of E, many antecedents of C bring it about and *hence* bring about E. To say X brings about C and E independently means *roughly* that prevention of C's occurrence will not prevent E's occurrence.

[3] Notice that this definition of 'random' itself involves the causal notion of 'determined by', just as the Case 8.1 description involves the notion of 'producing' C. Both are dispensable only in terms of other causal notions, e.g. those of 'independent and dependent variable', 'free act' (in a technical sense).

If one has brought about E before the other could, although it would have in time, we have a case of *independent overdetermination* (Case 8.5), but only one cause.

If both occur, both may have been effective, bringing about E simultaneously, or essentially simultaneously for the purpose at hand, which gives the case of *simultaneous overdetermination* (Case 8.6)—for example, a firing squad—and neither factor can be identified as *the* cause (but cf. the compound cause, Case 8.3).

In any case of an effect for which there are multiple causes we are no longer able to infer to C from E, i.e. C is not a necessary condition for E. However, we can infer from C plus the absence of the other possible causes to E, and since the absence of the other causes is part of the surrounding circumstances, we might still regard the cause as 'necessary in the circumstances' or what Nagel calls 'contingently necessary'. But this situation is complicated by the possibility of overdetermination, i.e. any cases of multiple causation where the causes are not mutually exclusive. If a revolution is overdetermined, as such events frequently are, there are several factors present which will ensure its occurrence, one of which we may assume gets in first. It will be quite incorrect to say that this factor is contingently necessary for the effect if, *ex hypothesi*, the remaining circumstances are quite adequate to bring about the effect by themselves.

We might try to save the situation for the contingently necessary analysis by invoking the fact that the other factors would not bring about the effect at the same time, and we might argue that the effect we are trying to explain is a revolution at the particular time it took place (i.e. the contrast state is peace at that moment). Unfortunately, this possibility is undermined by a species of overdetermination which we may call *linked overdetermination* (Case 8.7). There the factors are not independent; the circumstances are such that the very act of preventing C from occurring will bring about D which will itself cause E ('Damned if he does and damned if he doesn't'). Suppose a radical group attempts a *coup d'état*; the effort is watched attentively by the army, which will take action if the coup is unsuccessful, but not otherwise. In such a case, where the political coup may be slower moving than the military, we cannot argue that the government's downfall would occur at a different time.

Suppose we argue that the cause is necessary to explain the way in which the collapse occurred, if not the time. But *many* facts about the way the collapse occurred are, in a particular case, such that the cause is not a necessary condition for *their* occurrence, e.g. whether communication of the crisis details between members of the tottering cabinet was telephonic or telegraphic. The necessary condition analyst replies that these facts are not historically significant, not relevant to the contrast in which he is interested. He *is* explaining the *exact* historical occurrence, but only historically, i.e. not with an equal interest in all aspects of it. How do we determine which details are historically relevant—since, after all, the delay involved in telegraphing could well be crucial in some such cases? The answer must be, it seems, that it depends on its consequences for the occurrence of the item of principal interest. Alas, this is a *causal* consideration and so we have not analysed cause in terms of necessary condition but in terms of necessary condition and cause. The attempt is not without value, but it is not a reductive analysis. It reflects the good methodological principle of building up a case by finding clues which in their totality can *only* be explained by the hypothesis that C caused E.[4]

In general, then, the search for an acausal definition of 'cause' turns out to be ultimately as unsuccessful as the search for an amoral definition of 'moral'. It is, however, no less illuminating, and in the present discussion we have uncovered two useful approximations to the notion of cause, formulated in terms of considerations which will at least avoid the common failure to allow for overdetermination. It may also be seen from the discussion how historical and psychological analysis proceeds by the development of knowledge of possible causes and their *modus operandi*—a knowledge very unlike explicit knowledge of scientific laws—which is applied to the explanation of particular cases by the process of evidential, formal, and contextual elimination described above.

[4] *Technical footnote:* 'C is the only possible cause of E in circumstances C'' is not the same as 'C is a necessary condition for E in C'' not only for the reasons given (which show the first to include cases the second excludes unless made equivalent by circularity) but because, embarrassingly enough, the second description would identify many an *effect* of E as E's cause. For, with a suitable choice of C', there are many effects of E (call them $G_1, G_2, \ldots$) whose occurrence it is possible to infer from the occurrence of E i.e. the G's must occur if E does—in other words, their occurrence is necessary, given E's occurrence in C'—which makes the G's causes of E on the above proposed definition.

It is possible to salvage the necessary condition analysis here by using a slightly different and possibly more natural definition of necessary condition—unfortunately, it involves a causal notion. An analogous series of difficulties attends the notion of a cause as a non-redundant member of *some* set of conditions which are jointly sufficient for the effect. This handles linked overdetermination nicely but does less well on independent overdetermination, where *it* requires an accessory stipulation about the presence of intervening links, 'links' being a causal notion. Nor can causes be distinguished from effects on this definition. It is possible to give a proof of the equivalence of these two notions under certain plausible assumptions, e.g. the assumption of the thesis of detectivism—the converse of determinism—which asserts that different causes have different effects. It seems clear that the distinction between cause and effect is linked to the *range* of warranted counterfactual claims; we can't say flatly that if C hadn't occurred then E wouldn't have, but the weaknesses in this are less than and different from those in the claim that if G (one of E's effects) hadn't occurred, E couldn't (wouldn't?) have occurred.

IV

CAUSES AND EVENTS:
MACKIE ON CAUSATION

JAEGWON KIM

ANY discussion of causation must presuppose an ontological framework of entities among which causal relations are to hold, and also an accompanying logical and semantical framework in which these entities can be talked about. We often take *events* as causes and also as effects; but entities of other sorts (if indeed they are 'other sorts'), such as *conditions, states, phenomena, processes,* and sometimes even *facts,* are also pressed into service when we engage in causal talk, although with these there is some controversy as to their suitability as terms of causal relations. Coherent causal talk is possible only within a coherent ontological and logical framework of events and perhaps also other entities of appropriate categories; and the adequacy of an analysis of causal relations may very much depend on the sort of ontological and logical scheme underlying it. What I propose to do in this paper is to examine, from an ontological and logical point of view, a recent notable contribution by J. L. Mackie[1] to the analysis of causation. Although what we will say is relevant to an evaluation of the substantive contents of Mackie's analysis, our primary concern is with the ontology of events implicit in Mackie's discussion. We begin with a brief exposition of the central points of Mackie's analysis of singular causal statements.

I

The central idea in Mackie's conception of causation is that a cause of an event is neither a necessary nor a sufficient condition of that event, although it is a condition of a sort closely related to it. Briefly, a cause is often 'an *insufficient* but *necessary* part of a condition which is itself *unnecessary* but *sufficient* for the result' (16); Mackie calls a condition of this kind an 'INUS condition'. As an example: A short-circuit is said to be

From *Journal of Philosophy*, 68 (1971), 426–41. Reprinted by permission of the author and the editor of the journal.

[1] 'Causes and Conditions', *American Philosophical Quarterly*, 2, no. 4 (1965), 245–64. Reprinted in part above, pp. 15–38. With some exceptions, parenthetical references are to pages of this volume.

the cause of a fire in a house. But it is neither necessary nor sufficient for that fire, since the fire might have been caused by a short-circuit elsewhere or the overturning of a lighted oil stove; and also, in the absence of inflammable material near the short-circuit, the fire would not have occurred. So in what sense is the short-circuit said to be the cause of the fire?

At least part of the answer is that there is a set of conditions (of which some are positive and some are negative), including the presence of inflammable material, the absence of a suitably placed sprinkler, and no doubt quite a number of others, which combined with the short-circuit constituted a complex condition that was sufficient for the house's catching fire—sufficient, but not necessary, for the fire could have started in other ways. Also, of *this* complex condition, the short-circuit was an indispensable part: the other parts of this condition, conjoined with one another in the absence of the short-circuit, would not have caused the fire. The short-circuit which is said to have caused the fire is thus an indispensable part of a complex sufficient (but not necessary) condition of the fire (16).

A more general definition of 'INUS condition' is needed. Since the exact wording of Mackie's formulation is important, I quote again:

Let 'A' stand for the INUS condition—in our example, the occurrence of a short-circuit at that place—and let 'B' and '$\bar{C}$' (that is, 'not-C', or the absence of C) stand for the other conditions, positive and negative, which were needed along with A to form a sufficient condition of the fire—in our example, B might be the presence of inflammable material, C the absence of a suitably placed sprinkler. Then the conjunction '$AB\bar{C}$' represents a sufficient condition of the fire, and one that contains no redundant factors; that is, $AB\bar{C}$ is a minimal sufficient condition for the fire (16–17).

Now the disjunction of all the minimal sufficient conditions of a given event, assuming that there is only a finite number of them, constitutes a necessary and sufficient condition of it. Mackie defines 'INUS condition' thus:

A is an INUS condition of a result P if and only if for some X and for some Y, (AX or Y) is a necessary and sufficient condition of P, but A is not a sufficient condition of P and X is not a sufficient condition of P (17).

Here, 'X' represents the conjunction of terms (possibly just one) that together with A constitute a minimal sufficient condition of P; 'Y' stands for the disjunction of other minimal sufficient conditions; both X and Y must be non-null.

Before the singular causal judgement 'A caused P' can be analysed, one more notion is needed. A condition A is said to be *at least an INUS condition* of P provided there is a necessary and sufficient condition of P that has one of these forms: (AX or Y), (A or Y), AX, A. That is, A is at least an INUS condition of P if and only if either A is an INUS condition or A itself is a minimal sufficient condition or a component in the only minimal sufficient condition of P or A is by itself a necessary and sufficient condition of P.

Mackie's analysis of 'A caused P' is this:

   (i) A is at least an INUS condition of P.
  (ii) A was present on the occasion in question.
 (iii) The factors represented by the 'X', if any, in the formula for the necessary and sufficient condition were present on the occasion in question.
  (iv) Every disjunct in 'Y' that does not contain 'A' as a conjunct was absent on the occasion in question.

Mackie does not claim that the conjunction of these four clauses is a complete analysis of 'A caused P'; his only explicit claim is that this is 'an important part of the concept of causation'; Mackie suggests certain refinements, chiefly by the use of the notion of 'causal field', but these do not concern us here. What is of greater importance to us is Mackie's explanation of 'necessary condition' and 'sufficient condition'.

Thus if we said that a short-circuit here was a necessary condition for a fire in this house, we should be saying that there are true universal propositions from which, together with true statements about the characteristics of this house, and together with the supposition that a short-circuit did not occur here, it would follow that the house did not catch fire (31).

This explains 'necessary condition'; 'sufficient condition' is to be explained on the same model, which is to say: 'A is a sufficient condition of P' amounts to 'there are true universal propositions from which, together with additional singular premises and the statement that A was present, it follows that P occurred'. As Mackie points out, his approach is to construe statements of necessity and sufficiency on the model of the counterfactual 'If A had not occurred, P would not have occurred' and the factual conditional 'Since A occurred, P occurred'. Mackie has given elsewhere[2] what may be called a 'nomic-inferential model' of counterfactual conditionals; the essence of this analysis is that a counterfactual of the form 'If P, then Q' is a covert assertion of the existence of an argument whose premises include universal laws, the indicative form of P, and other singular statements of 'relevant conditions' and whose conclusion is the indicative form of Q.

[2] 'Counterfactuals and Causal Laws', in *Analytical Philosophy*, ed. R. J. Butler, (Oxford, 1962). See also Nicholas Rescher, 'Belief-contravening Suppositions', *Philosophical Review*, 70, no. 2 (1961), 176–96 (reprinted below on pages 156–65); Ernest Nagel, *The Structure of Science* (New York, 1961), pp. 68–73.

To recapitulate: singular causal assertions are explained in terms of the notion of 'at least an INUS condition'; a cause of an event is at least an INUS condition of it. The notion of INUS condition in turn is explained on the basis of 'necessary condition' and 'sufficient condition', and these are analysed in terms of counterfactual conditionals. Finally, counterfactuals are explained on the nomic-inferential model. It is at this point that laws and regularities enter into singular causal judgements; according to Mackie, his analysis can be characterized as a form of the regularity theory of causation.

II

Mackie's chief concern is to analyse singular causal statements, e.g. 'This short-circuit caused this fire.' And the letters he uses, 'A', 'B', 'C', ..., are presumably variables taking as values concrete individual events occurring at specific times and places or, at least, dummy variables standing in place of singular terms (names and descriptions) for individual events. Mackie refers to causes and effects as 'events' and also as 'conditions'; 'event' presumably is being used as a wider term which comprehends 'condition', and moreover it must be understood in the broad sense in which it refers to 'states' and 'standing conditions' as well as events narrowly conceived as involving changes.

What sorts of expression can replace these variables over events? That is to say, what sorts of expression can be used to refer to, describe, or name concrete individual events? The following are some of the expressions Mackie uses to specify individual events:

'A fire broke out in a certain house'
'the cause of the fire'
'this house's catching fire at this time'
'the overturning of a lighted oil stove'
'the presence of inflammable material'
'the absence of a suitably placed sprinkler'

The first is a full sentence, and the rest, with the possible exception of the second, are all nominalized sentences. And with the possible exception of the first, they are to be be taken as singular terms referring uniquely or purporting to refer uniquely to individual events; they can flank the identity sign ('the overturning of a lighted oil stove = the cause of the fire') and give way to bound variables. Presumably there would be no theoretical objection to using other kinds of names for individual events; for example, 'the most unforgettable event in Herbert's life', 'Larry', 'event #300', etc.

Now, what is interesting is that Mackie uses such connectives as 'and', 'not', and 'or' to compound event names; for example, a minimal sufficient condition is represented by the 'conjunction' '$AB\bar{C}$', and the bar on 'C' is akin to or is identical with the negation sign. And Mackie represents the necessary and sufficient condition of a given event in 'disjunctive normal form', and this concept presupposes that such truth-functional operations as conjunction, negation, and disjunction are meaningfully defined for event names. Further, Mackie often refers to events represented by such compound expressions as 'ABC' as 'complex events'. Thus, if A, B, and C are 'simple events', then ABC is a complex event; so presumably are $AB\bar{C}$, $\bar{A}BC$, and so on. But precisely how are we to understand these compound event names and the 'complex events' they are supposed to refer to?

Take the simple events A, B, and the complex event AB. What is the nature of the conjunction in 'AB'? One thing certain is that this cannot be understood in the sense of the usual logical conjunction 'and' as in 'Oscar *and* Edith like Mexican food', which is straightforwardly equivalent to 'Oscar likes Mexican food *and* Edith likes Mexican food'. For 'AB is a sufficient condition of P' is not to be taken in the sense of 'A is a sufficient condition of P and B is a sufficient condition of P'. It is perhaps more akin to 'Oscar *and* Edith *together* weigh two hundred and sixty pounds,' where 'Oscar and Edith' denotes a single composite entity (i.e. the 'sum' of Oscar and Edith in the sense of the calculus of individuals). This means that we cannot just depend on the familiar meaning of the sentential connective 'and' to understand what 'AB' means; what seems to be a new mode of linguistic construction is involved here which requires explanation. When we consider disjunction and negation, the situation at first blush is even more puzzling. In the case of ordinary singular terms, e.g. 'Socrates', '$2 + 5$', and 'the husband of Calpurnia', negation makes no sense; consider 'not-Socrates', 'not-$(2 + 5)$', etc. Nor do their disjunctions make sense; there is no object corresponding to such expressions as 'Socrates or Cicero', '7 or the colour blue', etc. The reason disjunction and negation appear to be meaningful for event names may be that event names are often nominalized sentences, although even here we would be hard pressed to attach a meaning to 'the cause of the fire or Socrates' death' or to 'not-the cause of the fire' as a singular term naming a single event.

But perhaps a coherent explanation of these operations is possible. What needs explaining is precisely how the complex events AB, $A \vee B$, and $\bar{A}$ are functionally related to the simple events A and B. And Mackie provides a hint:

If 'Y' represents a single conjunction of factors, then it was absent if at least one of its conjuncts was absent; if it represents a disjunction, then it was absent if each of its disjuncts was absent (19).

'$\bar{C}$' (that is, 'not-C,' or the absence of C . . .) (17).

This suggests a systematic procedure of compounding event names parallel to the truth-functional compounding of sentences. But what precisely is the relationship between the 'complex' events designated by compound event names '$\bar{A}$', 'AB', and '$A \vee B$' on the one hand and the simple events designated by 'A' and 'B'? Following Mackie's hint, we might first try something like this:

$\bar{A} = (Ie)$ [e occurs if and only if A does not occur]; [3]
$AB = (Ie)$ (e occurs if and only if both A and B occur];
$A \vee B = (Ie)$ [e occurs if and only if A occurs or B occurs].

One trouble with this way of explaining event composition is that there is no reason to believe that for event A there exists a unique event $\bar{A}$ as defined; given the usual truth-functional meaning of 'if and only if' as a biconditional, there would be too many events satisfying the description; similar comments apply to 'AB' and '$A \vee B$'.

Thus one may wish to strengthen these definitions by introducing some sort of modality in the definiens; an obvious choice would be to insert the qualifier 'necessarily true' or 'logically true' just after the description operator:

$\bar{A} = (Ie)N$ [e occurs if and only if A does not occur];
$AB = (Ie)N$ [e occurs if and only if both A and B occur];
$A \vee B = (Ie)N$ [e occurs if and only if either A occurs or B occurs].

when we use 'N' to abbreviate 'necessarily'. We shall ignore here the familiar difficulties involving the use of modal terms like this to govern open sentences. Assuming provisional adequacy of these definitions, we can go on to define 'disjunctive normal form', 'truth-functional implication', 'truth-functional equivalence', and other notions for event descriptions along the obvious lines. The following would then be a direct consequence of these definitions:

Equivalence condition: Truth-functionally equivalent event names and descriptions designate the same event.[4]

[3] We use 'I' as the description operator, and 'e' as a variable taking individual events as values. We say 'e occurs' where Mackie would say 'e is present'.

[4] Although Mackie does not explicitly recognize this condition, he seems tacitly to accept it; see, for example, p. 255 [of the complete article], where he talks about

All that needs to be assumed here is that truth-functionally equivalent sentences are interchangeable *salva veritate* in contexts prefixed by the necessity operator 'N'. On this interpretation of event composition it is clear that the complexity of 'complex events' pertains not to events *per se* but to event descriptions. For the equivalence condition tells us that there is no strict correspondence between the complexity of a given compound event name and the event designated by it; to take a simple example, A is the same event as $A\bar{B} \vee AB$. In general, the orthographic features of an event description are not a reliable guide to the ontological structure of the event it describes; and there is no more reason to expect this than to expect the complexity of the description of an object to be an indication of the complexity of the object described.

III

Does the foregoing provide a workable logical and ontological framework for a theory work for a theory of causation, and more specifically for Mackie's analysis of causal relations? I believe there is ample reason for thinking that the answer is in the negative; moreover, it is not at all clear that there is any coherent ontological framework underlying Mackie's analysis. In this section we shall bring out some of the problems and difficulties; in the next section we shall propose an alternative scheme in which Mackie's analysis could be restated.

Let us first consider the notion of 'minimal sufficient condition', which plays a crucial role in Mackie's definition of causation. The only explanation we get from Mackie is this: 'Then the conjunction '$AB\bar{C}$' represents a sufficient condition of the fire, and one that contains no redundant factors; that is, $AB\bar{C}$ is a minimal sufficient condition for the fire' (17). This suggests the following definition:

The event $A_1A_2 \ldots A_n$ is a minimal sufficient condition for an event P if and only if it is a sufficient condition for P, and, for each i ($1 \leqslant i \leqslant n$), $A_1 \ldots A_{i-1}. A_{i+1} \ldots A_n$ is not a sufficient condition for P.

Assume AB is a minimal sufficient condition for P; we can then show, for almost any event C, that C is an INUS condition for P and, hence, a candidate as a cause of P. For, given that AB is minimal-sufficient for P, it follows that $C(\bar{C} \vee A)B$ is also minimal-sufficient (unless $\bar{C} \vee A$ amounts

representing the necessary and sufficient condition of an event in disjunctive normal form. We leave aside the interesting and important question whether the stronger form of the equivalence condition to the effect that all and *only* truth-functionally equivalent event descriptions designate the same event is a consequence of these definitions, and if not, what further assumptions are needed to make it one.

just to A, or else C alone or together with B is sufficient for P). Now, Mackie might say that, when we consider a conjunction of 'factors' for minimal sufficiency, each conjunct must be a single letter; and, more generally, that the necessary and sufficient condition, if it exists, of an event must be represented by a disjunctive normal form each disjunct of which could then be considered as a minimal sufficient condition for that event.[5]

If we follow this line, the troublesome $C(\bar{C} \vee A)B$ reduces to CAB and the difficulty vanishes. Taking this course, however, does have disadvantages; for one thing, it prevents us from taking 'disjunctive events' as INUS conditions and hence as causes; for another, it requires us to identify certain events as 'simple events' for which we shall have non-compound event descriptions. The real difficulty with this approach is seen, however, when we reflect that sentences do not generally have unique disjunctive normal forms (unique up to the order of disjuncts and the order of conjuncts within each disjunct); for the following two disjunctive normal expressions are logically equivalent: $A \vee \bar{A}B$ and $B \vee \bar{B}A$. By the equivalence condition, these two represent the same event, and it is natural to assume that if one of them is a necessary and sufficient condition for an event P, then so must be the other. But, according to the expression '$A \vee \bar{A}B$', the event $\bar{A}$ is an INUS condition for P; according to '$B \vee \bar{B}A$', $\bar{B}$ is an INUS condition for P; further, these expressions are equivalent to '$A \vee B$' which sanctions neither $\bar{A}$ nor $\bar{B}$ as an INUS condition of P. Which one of these—or perhaps the complete disjunctive normal form, in this case '$AB \vee \bar{A}B \vee A\bar{B}$—should be picked, or indeed whether it makes any difference which is picked, is a matter requiring further examination.

For this particular case, however, one might say that '$A \vee B$' is the disjunctive normal form that must be used in determining minimal sufficient conditions; one might say that from '$A \vee B$' we know A and B to be each a minimal sufficient condition for a certain event, from which it follows that neither $\bar{A}B$ nor $\bar{B}A$ is minimal-sufficient. But then are we to require in general that the *shortest* disjunctive normal form be the basis for determining minimal sufficient conditions? Although it is true that any truth-functional formula has a shortest normal equivalent,[6] it is not true that there is a *unique* shortest normal equivalent (up to, of course, the order of disjuncts and the order of conjuncts within each disjunct): e.g. $A\bar{B} \vee \bar{A}B \vee$

[5] Mackie writes: 'For some Z, Z is a necessary and sufficient condition for the phenomenon P in the field F, that is, all FP are Z and all FZ are P, and Z is a condition represented by some formula in disjunctive normal form all of whose constituents are taken from the range of possibly relevant factors, A, B, C, D, E, etc.' (255).

[6] See W. V. Quine, 'Cores and Prime Implicants', reprinted in Quine, *Selected Logical Papers* (New York, 1966).

$A\bar{C}$ and $A\bar{B} \vee \bar{A}B \vee B\bar{C}$. According to the first of these equivalent normal formulas, $A\bar{C}$ is minimal sufficient; according to the second, $B\bar{C}$ is minimal sufficient. Shall we then say that the disjunction of *all* the minimal sufficient conditions, which in this case might be $A\bar{B} \vee \bar{A}B \vee A\bar{C} \vee B\bar{C}$, must be considered the correct representation? Here, the situation seems too fluid for a definite answer. Much deeper analysis of event discourse would be required before one could state and defend a definite stand on this problem.

Let us briefly return to the original definition of 'minimal sufficient condition'. Qua definition it is defective; it does not permit the elimination of the defined predicate 'is a minimal sufficient condition' from all contexts; it permits such elimination only when the event in question is represented in a certain logical form, i.e. conjunction of single-event names with no redundancies; by the use of the definition we cannot eliminate the defined term from, say, 'My most unforgettable event was a minimal sufficient condition for my most embarrassing event.' As stated, whether or not an event is a minimal sufficient condition for another would depend on the logical form of the particular description chosen for it; but the equivalence condition shows that no reliable inference can be made from the logical form of an event name to the ontological structure of the event named by it. A better definition of 'minimal sufficiency' would be something like this:

> An event E is a minimal sufficient condition for P if and only if it is representable (i.e. is named) by an expression of the form '$A_1 \ldots A_n$' containing no redundancies such that $A_1 \ldots A_n$ is sufficient for P and the deletion of any of the A's results in a condition not sufficient for P.

This makes the concept of minimal sufficiency very much dependent on the particular language used, and it is likely to make it easy for any sufficient condition of an event to be a minimal sufficient condition of it as well.

It seems to me that the difficulties under discussion are symptomatic of an underlying confusion of events with their descriptions, a confusion which, I believe, stems from our common use of full sentences and nominalized sentences to pick out events. This confusion manifests itself in the uncritical assumption that truth-functional compositions of event names are intelligible without much further ado; it also leads to the talk of 'disjunctive events', 'conjunctive events', and 'complex events'. A comprehensive theory of events would have to have room for the concept of complex event; intuitively, an earthquake or the pitching of a baseball is a *complex* event that has other events as *parts*; but it would be an illusion to count on the sentential connectives applied to event descriptions to yield a clear explanation of these notions.

The sort of ambivalence with respect to events and their descriptions becomes apparent also when we examine Mackie's explanations of 'necessary condition' and 'sufficient condition'. Mackie's analysis of 'necessary condition' comes to this:[7]

> A is a necessary condition of P if and only if there are true universal propositions L and true singular statements S such that L and S together with the statement that A did not occur logically imply the statement that P did not occur.

This involves the unintelligible assumption that for a given event A there is *the* statement that A occurred. Take as A the death of Socrates. What is *the* statement that asserts the occurrence of this event? Is it 'Socrates died' or 'Xantippe's husband died' or perhaps some other statement? Which of these statements is chosen makes a great deal of difference to the question what other statements are implied by it. The source of this difficulty lies in the fact that the definition involves a cross-reference into the context of quotation, since the expressions 'A did not occur' and 'P did not occur' in the definiens are in effect as though sealed with quotation marks.[8]

One final point concerning Mackie's framework of events: three of the four classes in Mackie's analysis of 'A caused P' have to do with the existence or non-existence ('presence' or 'absence' in his terminology) of certain events. The first of these clauses (which we may call 'existence conditions') requires that the cause event, A, must be 'present on the occasion in question'. What could this mean? The qualification 'on the occasion in question' suggests that A perhaps is not an individual event but rather a generic event or a property, and that the clause in effect says that the generic event must be exemplified on the occasion in question, that is, an individual event falling under this generic event must exist on that occasion. If 'A' is a bona fide singular term denoting a particular individual event, the further requirement that A must exist 'on the occasion in question' over and beyond the existence of A would seem to be completely otiose. This becomes especially clear when the last clause is considered, to the effect that every

---

[7] See the quotation at the end of section 1, p. 50 above.

[8] Let me briefly mention here what seems to be an incongruity between Mackie's analysis of causation and his analysis of 'necessary condition' and 'sufficient condition'. The point of introducing the notion of INUS condition is just that what is said to be the cause of an event is often not a necessary or a sufficient condition, *when taken alone*, for that event. This implies that a sufficient condition for an event, as Mackie understands it here, is a *fully* sufficient condition even if taken alone by itself; and similarly, for a necessary condition. If this is so, it is difficult to understand why, in his explanation of necessity and sufficiency, Mackie allows the use of auxiliary singular statements of 'relevant conditions' (i.e. S in the reconstructed definition in the text above).

minimal sufficient condition other than that in which the cause event figures must *not* exist 'on the occasion in question'. Now, this cannot be construed as meaning that these events must not exist at all, for then it would be hard to see how they could figure as sufficient conditions for any event. But it is also hard to make sense of the requirement that these events must exist *but not on the occasion in question*. If so, where and when? Far enough away from P not to have caused it? In that case, why should they figure at all as sufficient conditions of P?

It is unclear that the existence conditions make any sense at all if 'A', 'B', etc., are construed as denoting individual events. If 'A' is a genuine singular term, it would seem that the first clause 'A is at least an INUS condition' entails the existence of A, making the second clause requiring the existence of A redundant; a non-existent event cannot be an INUS condition for any event. If, of course, A were taken as a generic event rather than an individual event, good sense could be made of 'A is at least an INUS condition' even in the absence of any individual events falling under A. (But notice that A as a generic event must still exist.) So perhaps $A, B, \ldots$, are best taken as universals, and 'present on the occasion in question' and 'absent on the occasion in question' should be understood in the sense of 'exemplified on the occasion in question' and 'not exemplified on the occasion in question', respectively. In fact, in spite of Mackie's announced aim of analysing singular causal statements, it is doubtful that the entities he is concerned with can consistently be interpreted as spatio-temporally bounded individual events.

To continue a little further in this vein, consider the rule governing the operation of negation on event names. The idea here is that, given an event name 'A', we can construct a compound event name by placing the negation sign over 'A'. But what event does this compound event description '$\bar{A}$' designate? The rule says that it designates that event which necessarily occurs if and only if A does not occur. But if the event A exists, then the event $\bar{A}$ does not exist, and '$\bar{A}$' fails to refer. Thus, the operation of negation as explained is not a well-defined notion; in the usual mathematical sense, it does not qualify as an operation; in this sense it differs from sentential negation, the concept of 'negate' in the calculus of individuals, and set-theoretical complementation. Moreover, given that an event A does not exist, does the event $A \vee B$ just come to B? The scheme we provisionally attributed to Mackie does not entail that it does; in fact, it entails that it does not, unless the occurrence of A is entailed by the occurrence of B. What then is the exact difference in hard cash value between $A \vee B$ and B, when A does not exist? On the other hand, if we adopt a scheme in which $A \vee B$ does not turn out to be identical with B when A does not exist,

Mackie's notion of causation faces an imminent danger of collapse; for suppose A is an INUS condition of P which is also a cause of P. According to Mackie's analysis of 'A caused P', this means that Y in the complex necessary and sufficient condition $AX \vee Y$ or P does not exist (unless it happens to contain a disjunct that contains A as a conjunct), and $AX \vee Y$ reduces to AX, from which it follows that A is no longer an INUS condition.

IV

It should by now be clear that the logical and ontological foundations of Mackie's discussion of causal relations are in urgent need of repair; in fact, 'repair' is too mild a word, since Mackie does not seem aware of the problem of the underlying logic of event talk for his analysis of causation. And the absence of such ontological awareness is not limited to Mackie; it is common to almost all the recent writings on causation and other related problems involving event talk, although, happily, an explicit recognition has lately been given by some philosophers to the importance of the ontological issues in connection with the problem of analysing causation.[9] In this final section, I shall attempt to restate Mackie's theory of causal relations within a framework of events elaborated elsewhere.[10]

The relations of necessity and sufficiency seem best suited for properties and for property-like entities such as generic states and events; and their application to individual events and states seems best explained as being derivative from their application to properties and generic events and states. Typically, we say things like: 'Being an equiangular triangle is a necessary and sufficient condition for being an equilateral triangle,' 'Exposure to sunlight is necessary for the process of photosynthesis,' and so on. Even when we attribute necessity to an 'object', as in 'Oxygen is necessary for combustion', this is easily paraphrased in terms of generic states and events, as 'The presence of oxygen is necessary for combustion.' But since Mackie's chief objective is to analyse singular causal statements, we must have a way of relating the talk of necessity and sufficiency to individual events that are spatio-temporally localized. Thus, we need entities that possess both an element of generality and an element of particularity; the former is necessary for making sense of the relations of necessity and sufficiency, and the latter for making sense of singular causal judgements.

Such entities are ready at hand, however, since realizations of properties

[9] Donald Davidson, 'Causal Relations', *Journal of Philosophy*, 64, no. 21, 1967), 691–703 (reprinted below on pp. 82–95); Zeno Vendler, *Linguistics in Philosophy* (Ithaca, 1967), chs. 5, 6. See also my 'Events and Their Descriptions: Some Considerations' in Nicholas Rescher *et al.*, eds., *Essays in Honor of Carl G. Hempel* (Dordrecht, 1969).

[10] 'Causation, Nomic Subsumption, and the Concept of Event,' forthcoming.

at particular space–time regions or by objects (if one accepts some sort of substance ontology) fill the bill; they are general in that they involve properties, and particular in that they involve particular space–time regions or objects. Thus, we take an event to be the exemplifying of an empirical property by an object at a time (alternatively, at a space–time region, but we shall adopt the former approach); as we use it, the term 'event' must be understood in the wider sense in which it refers to states as well as events in the narrower sense involving changes. The approach being advocated here is well entrenched in the ordinary language: the entities we call 'events' are often those referred to by nominalized sentences of English, especially the gerundial nominalizations; e.g. 'the death of Socrates', 'the sinking of the Titanic', 'Brutus's stabbing Caesar', 'Jack's breaking his leg', and so on. We can take these as singular terms referring to individual events (although of course they must further be supplemented by explicit specification of dates); a bit more formally, we shall use the notation '$[x,P,t]$' to refer to the event of x's exemplifying property P at time t; this is obviously generalizable to yield polyadic events, but this further step is not necessary for the purposes of this paper.

Mackie's 'A', 'B', . . . are best taken as referring to properties—or generic events, i.e. properties whose exemplification by an object is an event. Mackie wants to say that a formula like '$ABC \lor CDF \lor$ . . .' specifies a sufficient condition for an event P and that each disjunct, e.g. 'ABC', specifies a minimal sufficient condition for P. This manner of speaking has certain important disadvantages; for one, it assumes (as Mackie is aware) that there are only finitely many minimal sufficient conditions for P, and, what is more important, it presupposes the compounding of property expressions for which we have nothing like an accepted theory. I think we would do better by talking about *sets* of properties rather than about conjunctive and disjunctive properties. Let us say that a set of properties is *realized* or *exemplified* on a given occasion provided each property in the set is exemplified on that occasion. Assuming, then, that the notions of necessity and sufficiency as applied to properties or generic events are understood, we can capture the import of the statement 'ABC $\lor$ CDF is a necessary and sufficient condition of P' by the statement 'Whenever the set of properties $[A,B,C]$ or the set $[C,D,F]$ is realized, P is realized, and also conversely.' And we say that a set of properties is a minimal sufficient set for P just in case the set is sufficient for P but no proper subset of it is sufficient for P. More generally, we say that a set of properties is sufficient for a property if and only if, whenever the set is realized, the property is also realized; and similarly for necessity. The notion of INUS condition for properties can be explained thus: A is an INUS property of P if and only if there is some unique family S_{AP} of sets s_i of properties such that, for some i, $A \in s_i$; for each i, $s_i \in S_{AP}$ if and only if s_i is minimal sufficient for P; and S_{AP} is a necessary condition of P (by which we mean that if P is realized some member of S_{AP} must also be realized).

We now come to the all-important notion of INUS condition for individual events:

$[x,A,t_1]$ is an INUS condition of $[y,P,t]$ if and only if
  (i) A (x,t_1), $P(y,t)$;
 (ii) A is an INUS property of P;
(iii) some set s_i in S_{AP} containing A and at least one other property is realized on the occasion of $[x,A,t_1]$;
 (iv) S_{AP} contains at least one set other than s_i;
  (v) no set of properties in S_{AP} other than s_i is realized on the occasion of $[y,P,t]$.

The notion of 'at least an INUS condition' is similarly definable. And finally '$[x,A,t_1]$ caused $[y,P,t]$' goes simply into '$[x,A,t_1]$ is at least an INUS condition of $[y,P,t]$'.

There is, however, a gaping hole in the foregoing account which was covered over by the unexplained expression 'on the occasion of'. It should be clear why the proviso 'on the occasion of $[x,A,t_1]$' is necessary in (iii), for the realizations of the properties in s_i in widely separated spatio-temporal regions would be irrelevant; the properties in this set must be 'jointly realized'. Also the import of the qualification 'on the occasion of $[y,P,t]$' in (v) is evident; we do not want to say that these sets are *never* realized; we only want to deny that this particular realization of P followed the realization of one of these sets. This shows that the conditions (i) to (v) are not quite sufficient to capture the definiendum; we must add that $[y,P,t]$ was the realization of P 'on the occasion of' $[x,A,t_1]$; we can think of (i) as modified to incorporate this.[11] So there are two general problems here: first, how do we characterize generally the set of individual events which jointly cause some event? (My striking of the match and the presence of oxygen *in this room*, not my striking of the match and the presence of oxygen in Boise, Idaho, make up such a set.) And, second, how, for each cause event (or set of events), do we generally pick out *its* effect event, and not some other event of the same kind (i.e. whose constitutive property is the same) which happens to occur at the same time? (My striking of the match causes its lighting, not the lighting of Jones's match which he scratched at the same time.)

[11] Recall Mackie's definition of 'A caused P' quoted earlier: '(ii) A was present *on the occasion in question* . . .' (my italics).

These are difficult questions which we cannot discuss here, and I do not know of satisfactory general solutions to them. We can try imposing certain temporal and spatial conditions on causes and effects; [12] we can perhaps try complicating the definition of 'the set s of properties is sufficient for the property P' by incorporating into it appropriate relations relating the realizations of the properties in s and the realization of P. In any case, these are substantive issues in the analysis of causal relations and not peculiar to the particular ontological scheme I have sketched here for such an analysis; and my objective in this paper has been the limited one of clarifying and restructuring the ontological foundation of Mackie's theory of singular causal statements.

[12] For elaboration of this theme as well as a somewhat more detailed discussion of the problems, see my 'Causation, Nomic Subsumption, and the Concept of Event'.

V

CAUSALITY AND DETERMINATION

G. E. M. ANSCOMBE

I

It is often declared or evidently assumed that causality is some kind of necessary connection, or alternatively, that being caused is—non-trivially—instancing some exceptionless generalization saying that such an event always follows such antecedents. Or the two conceptions are combined.

Obviously there can be, and are, a lot of divergent views covered by this account. Any view that it covers nevertheless manifests one particular doctrine or assumption. Namely:

If an effect occurs in one case and a similar effect does not occur in an apparently similar case, there must be a relevant further difference.

Any radically different account of causation, then, by contrast with which all those diverse views will be as one, will deny this assumption. Such a radically opposing view can grant that often—though it is difficult to say generally when—the assumption of relevant difference is a sound principle of investigation. It may grant that there are necessitating causes, but will refuse to identify causation as such with necessitation. It can grant that there are situations in which, given the initial conditions and no interference, only one result will accord with the laws of nature; but it will not see general reason, in advance of discovery, to suppose that any given course of things has been so determined. So it may grant that in many cases difference of issue can rightly convince us of a relevant difference of circumstances; but it will deny that, quite generally, this *must* be so.

The first view is common to many philosophers of the past. It is also, usually but not always in a neo-Humeian form, the prevailing received opinion throughout the currently busy and productive philosophical schools of the English-speaking world, and also in some of the European and Latin American schools where philosophy is pursued in at all the same

An Inaugural Lecture delivered at Cambridge, and published by the Cambridge University Press (1971). Reprinted by permission of the author and publishers.

sort of way; nor is it confined to these schools. So firmly rooted is it that for many even outside pure philosophy, it routinely determines the meaning of "cause", when consciously used as a theoretical term: witness the terminology of the contrast between 'causal' and 'statistical' laws, which is drawn by writers on physics—writers, note, who would not conceive themselves to be addicts of any philosophic school when they use this language to express that contrast.

The truth of this conception is hardly debated. It is, indeed, a bit of *Weltanschauung*: it helps to form a cast of mind which is characteristic of our whole culture.

The association between causation and necessity is old; it occurs for example in Aristotle's *Metaphysics*: "When the agent and patient meet suitably to their powers, the one acts and the other is acted on OF NECESSITY." Only with 'rational powers' an extra feature is needed to determine the result: "What has a rational power [e.g. medical knowledge, which can kill *or* cure] OF NECESSITY does what it has the power to do and as it has the power, when it has the desire."[1]

Overleaping the centuries, we find it an axiom in Spinoza, "Given a determinate cause, the effect follows OF NECESSITY, and without its cause, no effect follows."[2] And in the English philosopher Hobbes: "A cause simply, or an entire cause, is the aggregate of all the accidents both of the agents how many soever they be, and of the patients, put together; which when they are supposed to be present, IT CANNOT BE UNDERSTOOD BUT THAT THE EFFECT IS PRODUCED at the same instant; and if any of them be wanting, IT CANNOT BE UNDERSTOOD BUT THAT THE EFFECT IS NOT PRODUCED."[3]

It was this last view, where the connection between cause and effect is evidently seen as *logical* connection of some sort, that was overthrown by Hume, the most influential of all philosophers on this subject in the English-speaking and allied schools. For he made us see that, given any particular cause—or 'total causal situation' for that matter—and its effect, there is not in general any contradiction in supposing the one to occur and the other not to occur. That is to say, we'd know what was being described—

---

[1] *Metaphysics*, Book IX, Chapter V.
[2] *Ethics*, Book I, Axiom III.
[3] *Elements of Philosophy Concerning Body*, Chapter IX.

what it would be like for it to be true—if it were reported for example that a kettle of water was put, and kept, directly on a hot fire, but the water did not heat up.

Were it not for the preceding philosophers who had made causality out as some species of logical connection, one would wonder at this being called a discovery on Hume's part: for vulgar humanity has always been over-willing to believe in miracles and marvels and *lusus naturae*. Mankind at large saw no contradiction, where Hume worked so hard to show the philosophic world—the Republic of Letters—that there was none.

The discovery was thought to be great. But as touching the equation of causality with necessitation, Hume's thinking did nothing against this but curiously reinforced it. For he himself assumed that NECESSARY CONNECTION is an essential part of the idea of the relation of cause and effect,[4] and he sought for its nature. He thought this could not be found in the situations, objects, or events called "causes" and "effects", but was to be found in the human mind's being determined, by experience of CONSTANT CONJUNCTION, to pass from the sensible impression or memory of one term of the relation to the convinced idea of the other. Thus to say that an event was caused was to say that its occurrence was an instance of some exceptionless generalization connecting such an event with such antecedents as it occurred in. The twist that Hume gave to the topic thus suggested a connection of the notion of causality with that of deterministic laws—i.e. laws such that always, given initial conditions and the laws, a unique result is determined.

The well-known philosophers who have lived after Hume may have aimed at following him and developing at least some of his ideas, or they may have put up a resistance; but in no case, so far as I know,[5] has the resistance called in question the equation of causality with necessitation.

Kant, roused by learning of Hume's discovery, laboured to establish causality as an *a priori* conception and argued that the objective time order consists "in that order of the manifold of appearance according to which, IN CONFORMITY WITH A RULE, the apprehension of that which happens follows upon the apprehension of that which precedes . . . In conformity with such a rule there must be in that which precedes an event the condition of a rule according to which this event INVARIABLY and NECESSARILY

---

[4] *Treatise of Human Nature*, Book I, Part III, Sections II and VI.
[5] My colleague Ian Hacking has pointed out C. S. Peirce to me as an exception to this generalization.

follows."[6] Thus Kant tried to give back to causality the character of a *justified* concept which Hume's considerations had taken away from it. Once again the connection between causation and necessity was reinforced. And this has been the general characteristic of those who have sought to oppose Hume's conception of causality. They have always tried to establish the necessitation that they saw in causality: either *a priori*, or somehow out of experience.

Since Mill it has been fairly common to explain causation one way or another in terms of 'necessary' and 'sufficient' conditions. Now "sufficient condition" is a term of art whose users may therefore lay down its meaning as they please. So they are in their rights to rule out the query: "May not the sufficient conditions of an event be present, and the event yet not take place?" For "sufficient condition" is so used that if the sufficient conditions for X are there, X occurs. But at the same time, the phrase cozens the understanding into not noticing an assumption. For "sufficient condition" sounds like: "enough". And one certainly *can* ask: "May there not be *enough* to have made something happen—and yet it not have happened?"

Russell wrote of the notion of cause, or at any rate of the 'law of causation' (and he seemed to feel the same way about 'cause' itself), that, like the British monarchy, it had been allowed to survive because it had been erroneously thought to do no harm. In a destructive essay of great brilliance he cast doubt on the notion of necessity involved, unless it is explained in terms of universality, and he argued that upon examination the concepts of determination and of invariable succession of like objects upon like turn out to be empty: they do not differentiate between any conceivable course of things and any other. Thus Russell too assumes that necessity or universality is what is in question, and it never occurs to him that there may be any other conception of causality.[7]

Now it's not difficult to shew it prima facie wrong to associate the notion of cause with necessity or universality in this way. For, it being much easier to trace effects back to causes with certainty than to predict effects from causes, we often know a cause without knowing whether there is an exceptionless generalization of the kind envisaged, or whether there is a necessity.

*

---

[6] *Critique of Pure Reason*, Book II, Chapter II, Section III, Second Analogy.
[7] 'The Notion of Cause', in *Mysticism and Logic*.

For example, we have found certain diseases to be contagious. If, then, I have had one and only one contact with someone suffering from such a disease, and I get it myself, we suppose I got it from him. But what if, having had the contact, I ask a doctor whether I will get the disease? He will usually only be able to say, "I don't know—maybe you will, maybe not."

But, it is said, knowledge of causes here is partial; doctors seldom even know any of the conditions under which one invariably gets a disease, let alone all the sets of conditions. This comment betrays the assumption that there is such a thing to know. Suppose there is: still, the question whether there is does not have to be settled before we can know what we mean by speaking of the contact as cause of my getting the disease.

All the same, might it not be like this: knowledge of causes is possible without any satisfactory grasp of what is involved in causation? Compare the possibility of wanting clarification of 'valency' or 'long-run frequency', which yet have been handled by chemists and statisticians without such clarification; and valencies and long-run frequencies, whatever the right way of explaining them, have been known. Thus one of the familiar philosophic analyses of causality, or a new one in the same line, may be correct, though knowledge of it is not necessary for knowledge of causes.

There is something to observe here, that lies under our noses. It is little attended to, and yet still so obvious as to seem trite. It is this: causality consists in the derivativeness of an effect from its causes. This is the core, the common feature, of causality in its various kinds. Effects derive from, arise out of, come of, their causes. For example, everyone will grant that physical parenthood is a causal relation. Here the derivation is material, by fission. Now analysis in terms of necessity or universality does not tell us of this derivedness of the effect; rather it forgets about that. For the necessity will be that of laws of nature; through it *we* shall be able to derive knowledge of the effect from knowledge of the cause, or vice versa, but that does not shew us the cause as source of the effect. Causation, then, is not to be identified with necessitation.

If A comes from B, this does not imply that every A-like thing comes from some B-like thing or set-up or that every B-like thing or set-up has an A-like thing coming from it; or that given B, A had to come from it, or that given A, there had to be B for it to come from. Any of these may be true, but if any is, that will be an additional fact, not comprised in A's coming

from *B*. If we take "coming from" in the sense of travel, this is perfectly
evident.

"But that's because we can observe travel!" The influential Humeian
argument at this point is that we can't similarly observe causality in the
individual case.[8] So the reason why we connect what we call the cause and
what we call the effect as we do must lie elsewhere. It must lie in the fact
that the succession of the latter upon the former is of a kind regularly observed.

There are two things for me to say about this. *First*, as to the statement
that we can never observe causality in the individual case. Someone who
says this is just not going to count anything as 'observation of causality'.
This often happens in philosophy; it is argued that 'all we find' is such-and-
such, and it turns out that the arguer has excluded from his idea of 'finding'
the sort of thing he says we don't 'find'. And when we consider what we
are allowed to say we do 'find', we have the right to turn the tables on Hume,
and say that neither do we perceive bodies, such as billiard balls, approaching one another. When we 'consider the matter with the utmost attention',
we find only an impression of travel made by the successive positions of a
round white patch in our visual fields . . . etc. Now a 'Humeian' account
of causality has to be given in terms of constant conjunction of physical
things, events etc., not of experiences of them. If, then, it must be allowed
that we 'find' bodies in motion, for example, then what theory of perception
can justly disallow the perception of a lot of causality? The truthful—
though unhelpful—answer to the question: How did we come by our primary knowledge of causality? is that in learning to speak we learned the
linguistic representation and application of a host of causal concepts. Very
many of them were represented by transitive and other verbs of action used
in reporting what is observed. Others—a good example is "infect"—form,
not observation statements, but rather expressions of causal hypotheses.
The word "cause" itself is highly general. How does someone show that
he has the concept *cause*? We may wish to say: only by having such a word in
his vocabulary. If so, then the manifest possession of the concept presupposes the mastery of much else in language. I mean: the word "cause" can
be *added* to a language in which are already represented many causal
concepts. A small selection: *scrape*, *push*, *wet*, *carry*, *eat*, *burn*, *knock over*,
keep off, *squash*, *make* (e.g. noises, paper boats), *hurt*. But if we care to
imagine languages in which no special causal concepts are represented,

[8] *Treatise of Human Nature*, Book I, Part III, Section II.

then no description of the use of a word in such languages will be able to present it as meaning *cause*. Nor will it even contain words for natural kinds of stuff, nor yet words equivalent to "body", "wind", or "fire". For learning to use special causal verbs is part and parcel of learning to apply the concepts answering to these, and many other, substantives. As surely as we learned to call people by name or to report from seeing it that the cat was on the table, we also learned to report from having observed it that someone drank up the milk or that the dog made a funny noise or that things were cut or broken by whatever we saw cut or break them.

(I will mention, only to set on one side, one of the roots of Hume's argument, the implicit appeal to Cartesian scepticism. He confidently challenges us to "produce some instance, wherein the efficacy is plainly discoverable to the mind, and its operations obvious to our consciousness or sensation".[9] Nothing easier: is cutting, is drinking, is purring not 'efficacy'? But it is true that the apparent perception of such things may be only apparent: we may be deceived by false appearances. Hume presumably wants us to 'produce an instance' in which *efficacy* is related to sensation as *red* is. It is true that we can't do that; it is not *so* related to sensation. He is also helped, in making his argument that we don't perceive 'efficacy', by his curious belief that "efficacy" means much the same thing as "necessary connection"! But as to the Cartesian-sceptical root of the argument, I will not delay upon it, as my present topic is not the philosophy of perception.)

Second, as to that instancing of a universal generalization, which was supposed to supply what could not be observed in the individual case, the causal relation. the needed examples are none too common. "Motion in one body in all past instances that have fallen under our observation, is follow'd upon impulse by motion in another":[10] so Hume. But, as is always a danger in making large generalizations, he was thinking only of the cases where we do observe this—billiard balls against free-standing billiard balls in an ordinary situation; not billiard balls against stone walls. Neo-Humeians are more cautious. They realize that if you take a case of cause and effect, and relevantly describe the cause A and the effect B, and then construct a universal proposition, "Always, given an A, a B follows" you usually won't get anything true. You have got to describe the absence of circumstances in which an A would not cause a B. But the task of excluding all such circumstances can't be carried out. There is, I suppose,

[9] Ibid., Book I, Part III, Section XIV.
[10] Ibid., Book II, Part III, Section I.

a vague association in people's minds between the universal propositions which would be examples of the required type of generalizations, and scientific laws. But there is no similarity.

Suppose we were to call propositions giving the properties of substances 'laws of nature'. Then there will be a law of nature running "The flash-point of such a substance is . . .", and this will be important in explaining why striking matches usually causes them to light. This law of nature has not the form of a generalization running "Always, if a sample of such a substance is raised to such a temperature, it ignites"; nor is it equivalent to such a generalization, but rather to: "If a sample of such a substance is raised to such a temperature and doesn't ignite, there must be a cause of its not doing so." Leaving aside questions connected with the idea of a pure sample, the point here is that 'normal conditions' is quite properly a vague notion. That fact makes generalizations running "Always . . ." merely fraudulent in such cases; it will always be necessary for them to be hedged about with clauses referring to normal conditions; and we may not know in advance whether conditions are normal or not, or what to count as an abnormal condition. In exemplar analytical practice, I suspect, it will simply be a relevant condition in which the generalization, "Always, if such and such, such and such happens . . .", supplemented with a few obvious conditions that have occurred to the author, turns out to be un-true. Thus the conditional "If it doesn't ignite then there must be some cause" is the better gloss upon the original proposition, for it does not pretend to say specifically, or even disjunctively specifically, what *always* happens. It is probably these facts which make one hesitate to call proposi-tions about the action of substances 'laws of nature'. The law of inertia, for example, would hardly be glossed: "If a body accelerates without any force acting on it, there must be some cause of its doing so." (Though I wonder what the author of *Principia* himself would have thought of that.) On the other hand just such 'laws' as that about a substance's flash-point are connected with the match's igniting because struck.

Returning to the medical example, medicine is of course not interested in the hopeless task of constructing lists of all the sets of conditions under each of which people always get a certain disease. It is interested in finding what that is special, if anything, is always the case when people get a parti-cular disease; and, given such a cause or condition (or in any case), in find-ing circumstances in which people don't get the disease, or tend not to. This is connected with medicine's concern first, and last, with things as they happen in the messy and mixed up conditions of life: only between its first and its last concern can it look for what happens unaffected by un-controlled and inconstant conditions.

II

Yet my argument lies always open to the charge of appealing to ignorance. I must therefore take a different sort of example.

Here is a ball lying on top of some others in a transparent vertical pipe. I know how it got there: it was forcibly ejected with many others out of a certain aperture into the enclosed space above a row of adjacent pipes. The point of the whole construction is to shew how a totality of balls so ejected always build up in rough conformity to the same curve. But I am interested in this one ball. Between its ejection and its getting into this pipe, it kept hitting sides, edges, other balls. If I made a film of it I could run it off in slow motion and tell the impact which produced each stage of the journey. Now was the result necessary? We would probably all have said it was in the time when Newton's mechanics was undisputed for truth. It was the impression made on Hume and later philosophers by that mechanics, that gave them so strong a conviction of the iron necessity with which everything happens, the "absolute fate" by which 'Every object is determin'd to a certain degree and direction of its motion".[11]

Yet no one could have deduced the resting place of the ball—because of the indeterminateness that you get even in the Newtonian mechanics, arising from the finite accuracy of measurements. From exact figures for positions, velocities, directions, spins, and masses you might be able to calculate the result as accurately as you chose. But the minutest inexactitudes will multiply up factor by factor, so that in a short time your information is gone. Assuming a given margin of error in your initial figure, you could assign an associated probability to that ball's falling into each of the pipes. If you want the highest probability you assign to be really high, so that you can take it as practical certainty, it will be a problem to reckon how tiny the permitted margins of inaccuracy must be—analogous to the problem: how small a fraction of a grain of millet must I demand is put on the first square of the chess board, if after doubling up at every square I end up having to pay out only a pound of millet? It would be a figure of such smallness as to have no meaning as a figure for a margin of error.

However, so long as you believed the classical mechanics you might also think there could be no such thing as a figure for a difference that had no

[11] Ibid., Book II, Part III, Section I.

meaning. Then you would think that though it was not feasible for us to find the necessary path of the ball because our margins of error are too great, yet there *was* a necessary path, which could be assigned a sufficient probability for firm acceptance of it, by anyone (not one of us) capable of reducing his limits of accuracy in measurement to a sufficiently small compass. Admittedly, so small a compass that he'd be down among the submicroscopic particles and no longer concerned with the measurements, say, of the ball. And now we can say: with certain degrees of smallness we get to a region where Newton's mechanics is no longer believed.

If the classical mechanics can be used to calculate a certain real result, we may give a sense to, and grant, the 'necessity' of the result, given the antecedents. Here, however, you can't use the mechanics to calculate the result, but at most to give yourself a belief in its necessity. For this to be reasonable the system has got to be acknowledged as true. Not, indeed, that that would be enough; but if so much were secured, then it would be worth while to discuss the metaphysics of absolute measures of continuous quantities.

The point needs some labouring precisely because 'the system does apply to such bodies'—that is, to moderately massive balls. After all, it's Newton we use to calculate Sputniks! "The system applies to these bodies" is true only in the sense and to the extent that it yields sufficient results of calculations about these bodies. It does not mean: in respect of these bodies the system is the truth, so that it just doesn't matter that we can't use it to calculate such a result in such a case. I am not saying that a deterministic system involves individual predictability: it evidently does not. But in default of predictability the determinedness declared by the deterministic system has got to be believed because the system itself is believed.

I conclude that we have no ground for calling the path of the ball determined—at least, until it has taken its path—but, it may be objected, is not each state of its path determined, even though we cannot determine it? My argument has partly relied on loss of information through multiplicity of impacts. But from one impact to the next the path is surely determined, and so the whole path is so after all.

It sounds plausible to say: each stage is determined and so the whole is. But what does "determined" mean? The word is a curious one (with a curious history); in this sort of context it is often used as if it *meant* "caused". Or perhaps "caused" is used as if it meant "determined". But there is at any rate one important difference—a thing hasn't been caused until it has happened; but it may be determined before it happens.

(It is important here to distinguish between being *determined* and being *determinate*. In indeterministic physics there is an apparent failure of both. I am concerned only with the former.)

When we call a result determined we are implicitly relating it to an antecedent range of possibilities and saying that all but one of these is disallowed. What disallows them is not the result itself but something antecedent to the result. The antecedences may be logical or temporal or in the order of knowledge. Of the many—antecedent—possibilities, *now* only one is—antecedently—possible.

Mathematical formulae and human decisions are limiting cases; the former because of the obscurity of the notion of antecedent possibilities, and the latter because decisions can be retrieved.

In a chess-game, the antecedent possibilities are, say, the powers of the pieces. By the rules, a certain position excludes all but one of the various moves that were in that sense antecedently possible. This is logical antecedence. The next move is determined.

In the zygote, sex and eye-colour are already determined. Here the antecedent possibilities are the possibilities for sex and eye-colour for a child; or more narrowly: for a child of these parents. *Now*, given the combination of this ovum and this spermatozoon, all but one of these antecedent possibilities is excluded.

It might be said that anything was determined once it had happened. There is now no possibility open: it *has* taken place! It was in this sense that Aristotle said that past and present were necessary. But this does not concern us: what interests us is *pre*-determination.

Then "each stage of the ball's path is determined" must mean "Upon any impact, there is only one path possible for the ball up to the next impact (and assuming no air currents, etc.)." But what ground could one have for believing this, if one does not believe in some system of which it is a consequence? Consider a steel ball dropping between two pins on a Galton board to hit the pin centred under the gap between them. That it should balance on this pin is not to be expected. It has two possibilities; to go to the right or to the left. If you have a system which forces this on you, you can say: "There has to be a determining factor; otherwise, like Buridan's ass, the ball must balance." But if you have not, then you should say that the ball may be undetermined until it does move to the right or the left. Here the ball had only two significant possibilities and was perhaps unpredetermined between them. This was because it cannot be called determined —no reasonable account can be given of insisting that it is so—within a small range of possibility, actualization within which will lead on to its falling either to the right or to the left. With our flying ball there will also be such a small range of possibility. The further consequences of the path it may take are not tied down to just two significant possibilities, as with one step down the Galton board: the range of further possibility gets wider as we consider the paths it may take. Otherwise, the two cases are similar.

We see that to give content to the idea of something's being determined, we have to have a set of possibilities, which something narrows down to one—before the event.

This accords well with our understanding of part of the dissatisfaction of some physicists with the quantum theory. They did not like the undeterminedness of individual quantum phenomena. Such a physicist might express himself by saying "I believe in causality!" He meant: I believe that the real physical laws and the initial conditions must entail uniqueness of result. Of course, within a range of co-ordinate and mutually exclusive identifiable possible results, only one happens: he means that the result that happens ought to be understood as the only one that was possible before it happened.

Must such a physicist be a 'determinist'? That is, must he believe that the whole universe is a system such that, if its total states at t and t' are thus and so, the laws of nature are such as then to allow only one possibility for its total state at any other time? No. He may not think that the idea of a total state of the universe at a time is one he can do anything with. He may even have no views on the uniqueness of possible results for whatever may be going on in any arbitrary volume of space. For "Our theory should be such that only the actual result was possible for that experiment" doesn't mean "Our theory should have excluded the experiment's being muffed or someone's throwing a boot, so that we didn't get the result", but rather: "Our theory should be such that only this result was possible as *the result of the experiment*." He hates a theory, even if he has to put up with it for the time being, that essentially assigns only probability to a result, essentially allows of a range of possible results, never narrowed down to one until the event itself.

It must be admitted that such dissatisfied physicists very often have been determinists. Witness Schrödinger's account of the 'principle of causality': "The exact physical situation at *any* point P at a given moment t is unambiguously determined by the exact physical situation within a certain surrounding of P at any previous time, say $t - \tau$. If τ is large, that is if that previous time lies far back, it may be necessary to know the previous situation for a wide domain around P."[12] Or Einstein's more modest version of a notorious earlier claim: if you knew all about the contents of a sphere of radius 186,000 miles, and knew the laws, you would be able to know for sure what would happen at the centre for the next second. Schrödinger says: *any* point P; and *a* means *any* sphere of that radius. So their view of causality was not that of my hypothetical physicist, who I said may not have views on the uniqueness of possible results for whatever may be going on in any arbitrary volume of space. My physicist restricts his demand for uniqueness of result to situations in which he has got certain processes going in isolation from inconstant external influences, or where they do not matter, as the weather on a planet does not matter for predicting its course round the sun.

The high success of Newton's astronomy was in one way an intellectual disaster: it produced an illusion from which we tend still to suffer. This illusion was created by the circumstance that Newton's mechanics *had a good model in the solar system*. For this gave the impression that we had here an ideal of scientific explanation; whereas the truth was, it was mere obligingness on the part of the solar system, by having had so peaceful a history in recorded time, to provide such a model. For suppose that some planet had at some time erupted with such violence that its shell was propelled rocket-like out of the solar system. Such an event would not have violated Newton's laws; on the contrary, it would have illustrated them. But also it would not have been calculable as the past and future motions of the planets are presently calculated on the assumption that they can be treated as the simple 'bodies' of his mechnics, with no relevant

[12] *Science and Humanism.*

properties but mass, position, and velocity and no forces mattering except gravity.

Let us pretend that Newton's laws were still to be accepted without qualification: no reserve in applying them in electrodynamics; no restriction to bodies travelling a good deal slower than light; and no quantum phenomena. Newton's mechanics is a deterministic system; but this does not mean that believing them commits us to determinism. We could say: Of course nothing violates those axioms or the laws of the force of gravity. But animals, for example, run about the world in all sorts of paths and no path is dictated for them by those laws, as it is for planets. Thus in relation to the solar system (apart from questions like whether in the past some planet has blown up), the laws are like the rules of an infantile card game: once the cards are dealt we turn them up in turn, and make two piles each, one red, one black; the winner has the biggest pile of red ones. So once the cards are dealt the game is determined, and from any position in it you can derive all others back to the deal and forward to win or draw. But in relation to what happens on and inside a planet the laws are, rather, like the rules of chess; the play is seldom determined, though nobody breaks the rules.[13]

Why this difference? A natural answer is: the mechanics does not give the special laws of all the forces. Not, for example, for thermal, nuclear, electrical, chemical, muscular forces. And now the Newtonian model suggests the picture: given the laws of all the forces, then there is total coverage of what happens and then the whole game of motion is determined; for, by the first law, any acceleration implies a force of some kind, and must not forces have laws? My hypothetical physicist at least would think so; and would demand that they be deterministic. Nevertheless he still does not have to be a 'determinist'; for many forces, unlike gravity, can be switched on and off, are generated, and also shields can be put up against them. It is one thing to hold that in a clear-cut situation—an astronomical or a well-contrived experimental one designed to discover laws—'the result' should be determined: and quite another to say that in the hurly-burly of many crossing contingencies whatever happens next must be determined; or to say that the generation of forces (by human experimental procedures, among other things) is always determined in advance of the generating procedure; or to say that there is always a law of composition,

---

[13] I should have made acknowledgements to Gilbert Ryle (*Concept of Mind*, p. 77) for this comparison. But his use of the openness of chess is somewhat ambiguous and is not the same as mine. For the contrast with a closed card game I was indebted to A. J. P. Kenny.

of such a kind that the combined effect of a set of forces is determined in every situation.

Someone who is inclined to say those things, or implicitly to assume them, has almost certainly been affected by the impressive relation between Newton's mechanics and the solar system.

We remember how it was in mechanics. By knowing the position and velocity of a particle at one single instant, by knowing the acting forces, the whole future path of the particle could be foreseen. In Maxwell's theory, if we know the field at one instant only, we can deduce from the equations of the theory how the whole field will change in space and time. Maxwell's equations enable us to follow the history of the field, just as the mechanical equations enabled us to follow the history of material particles . . . With the help of Newton's laws we can deduce the motion of the earth from the force acting between the sun and the earth.[14]

"By knowing the acting forces"—that must of course include the *future* acting forces, not merely the present ones. And similarly for the equations which enable us to follow the history of the field; a change may be produced by an external influence. In reading both Newton and later writers one is often led to ponder that word "external". Of course, to be given 'the acting forces' is to be given the external forces too and any new forces that may later be introduced into the situation. Thus those first sentences are true, if true, without the special favour of fate, being general truths of mechanics and physics, but the last one is true by favour, by the brute fact that only the force acting between earth and sun matters for the desired deductions.

The concept of necessity, as it is connected with causation, can be explained as follows: a cause C is a necessitating cause of an effect E *when* (I mean: on the occasions when) if C occurs it is certain to cause E unless something prevents it. C and E are to be understood as general expressions, not singular terms. If 'certainty' should seem too epistemological a notion: a necessitating cause C of a given kind of effect E is such that it *is* not possible (on the occasion) that C should occur and should not cause an E, nor should there be anything that prevents an E from occurring. A non-necessitating cause is then one that can fail of its effect without the intervention of anything to frustrate it. We may discover *types* of necessitating and non-necessitating cause; e.g. rabies is a necessitating cause of death, because it is not possible for one who has rabies to survive without treat-

---

[14] Albert Einstein and Leopold Infeld, *The Evolution of Physics*, Simon and Schuster, New York, 1938; (paperback edn., 1967), p. 146.

ment. We don't have to tie it to the occasion. An example of a non-necessitating cause is mentioned by Feynman: a bomb is connected with a Geiger counter, so that it will go off if the Geiger counter registers a certain reading; whether it will or not is not determined, for it is so placed near some radioactive material that it may or may not register that reading.

There would be no doubt of the cause of the reading or of the explosion if the bomb did go off. Max Born is one of the people who has been willing to dissociate causality from determinism: he explicates cause and effect in terms of dependence of the effect on the cause. It is not quite clear what 'dependence' is supposed to be, but at least it seems to imply that you would not get the effect without the cause. The trouble about this is that you might —from some other cause. That this effect was produced by this cause does not at all shew that it could not, or would not, have been produced by something else in the absence of this cause.

Indeterminism is not a possibility unconsidered by philosophers. C. D. Broad, in his inaugural lecture, given in 1934, described it as a possibility; but added that whatever happened without being determined was accidental. He did not explain what he meant by being accidental; he must have meant more than not being necessary. He may have meant being uncaused; but, if I am right, not being determined does not imply not being caused. Indeed, I should explain indeterminism as the thesis that not all physical effects are necessitated by their causes. But if we think of Feynman's bomb, we get some idea of what is meant by "accidental". It was random: it 'merely happened' that the radio-active material emitted particles in such a way as to activate the Geiger counter enough to set off the bomb. Certainly the motion of the Geiger counter's needle is caused; and the actual emission is caused too; it occurs because there is this mass of radioactive material here. (I have already indicated that, contrary to the opinion of Hume, there are many different sorts of causality.) But all the same the *causation* itself is, one could say, *mere hap*. It is difficult to explain this idea any further.

Broad used the idea to argue that indeterminism, if applied to human action, meant that human actions are 'accidental'. Now he had a picture of choices as being determining causes, analogous to determining physical causes, and of choices in their turn being either determined or accidental. To regard a choice as such—i.e. any case of choice—as a predetermining causal event, now appears as a naïve mistake in the philosophy of mind, though that is a story I cannot tell here.

It was natural that when physics went indeterministic, some thinkers should have seized on this indeterminism as being just what was wanted for defending the freedom of the will. They received severe criticism on two counts: one, that this 'mere hap' is the very last thing to be invoked as the physical correlate of 'man's ethical behaviour'; the other, that quantum laws predict statistics of events when situations are repeated; interference with these, by the *will*'s determining individual events which the laws of nature leave undetermined, would be as much a violation of natural law as would have been interference which falsified a deterministic mechanical law.

Ever since Kant it has been a familiar claim among philosophers, that one can believe in both physical determinism and 'ethical' freedom. The reconciliations have always seemed to me to be either so much gobbledegook, or to make the alleged freedom of action quite unreal. My actions are mostly physical movements; if these physical movements are physically predetermined by processes which I do not control, then my freedom is perfectly illusory. The truth of physical indeterminism is thus indispensable if we are to make anything of the claim to freedom. But certainly it is insufficient. The physically undetermined is not thereby 'free'. For freedom at least involves the power of acting according to an idea, and no such thing is ascribed to whatever is the subject (what would be the relevant subject?) of unpredetermination in indeterministic physics. Nevertheless, there is nothing unacceptable about the idea that that 'physical haphazard' should be the only physical correlate of human freedom of action; and perhaps also of the voluntariness and intentionalness in the conduct of other animals which we do not call 'free'. The freedom, intentionalness and voluntariness are not to be analysed as the same thing as, or as produced by, the physical haphazard. Different sorts of pattern altogether are being spoken of when we mention them, from those involved in describing elementary processes of physical causality.

The other objection is, I think, more to the point. Certainly if we have a statistical law, but undetermined individual events, and then enough of these are supposed to be pushed by will in one direction to falsify the statistical law, we have again a supposition that puts will into conflict with natural laws. But it is not at all clear that the same train of minute physical events should have to be the regular correlate of the same action; in fact, that suggestion looks immensely implausible. It is, however, required by the objection.

Let me construct an analogy to illustrate this point. Suppose that we have a large glass box full of millions of extremely minute coloured particles, and the box is constantly shaken. Study of the box and particles leads to statistical laws, including laws for the random generation of small unit patches of uniform colour. Now the box is remarkable for also presenting the following phenomenon: the word "Coca-Cola" formed like a mosaic, can always be read when one looks at one of the sides. It is not always the same shape in the formation of its letters, not always the same size or in the same position, it varies in its colours; but there it always is. It is not at all clear that those statistical laws concerning the random motion of the particles and their formation of small unit patches of colour would have to be supposed violated by the operation of a cause for this phenomenon which did not derive it from the statistical laws.

It has taken the inventions of indeterministic physics to shake the rather common dogmatic conviction that determinism is a presupposition or perhaps a conclusion, of scientific knowledge. Not that that conviction has been very much shaken even so. Of course, the belief that the laws of nature are deterministic has been shaken. But I believe it has often been supposed that this makes little difference to the assumption of macroscopic determinism: as if undeterminedness were always encapsulated in systems whose internal workings could be described only by statistical laws, but where the total upshot, and in particular the outward effect, was as near as makes no difference always the same. What difference does it make, after all, that the scintillations, whereby my watch dial is luminous, follow only a statistical law—so long as the gross manifest effect is sufficiently guaranteed by the statistical law? Feynman's example of the bomb and Geiger counter smashes this conception; but as far as I can judge it takes time for the lesson to be learned. I find deterministic assumptions more common now among people at large, and among philosophers, than when I was an undergraduate.

The lesson is welcome, but indeterministic physics (if it succeeds in giving the lesson) is only culturally, not logically, required to make the deterministic picture doubtful. For it was always a mere extravagant fancy, encouraged in the 'age of science' by the happy relation of Newtonian mechanics to the solar system. It ought not to have mattered whether the laws of nature were or were not deterministic. For them to be deterministic is for them, together with the description of the situation, to entail unique results in situations defined by certain relevant objects and measures, and where no part is played by inconstant factors external to such definition. If that is right, the laws' being deterministic does not tell us whether 'determinism' is true. It is the total coverage of every motion that happens, that is a fanciful claim. But I do not mean that any motions lie outside the scope of physical laws, or that one cannot say, in any given context, that certain motions would be violations of physical law. Remember the contrast between chess and the infantile card game.

Meanwhile in non-experimental philosophy it is clear enough what are the dogmatic slumbers of the day. It is over and over again assumed that any singular causal proposition implies a universal statement running "Always when this, then that"; often assumed that true singular causal statements are derived from such 'inductively believed' universalities. Examples indeed are recalcitrant, but that does not seem to disturb. Even a philosopher acute enough to be conscious of this, such as Davidson, will say, without offering any reason at all for saying it, that a singular causal statement implies *that there is* such a true universal proposition [15]—though perhaps we can never have knowledge of it. Such a thesis needs some reason for believing it! 'Regularities in nature': that is not a reason. The most neglected of the key topics in this subject are: interference and prevention.

[15] 'Causal Relations', *Journal of Philosophy*, 64 (November 1967), [VI in this volume].

VI

CAUSAL RELATIONS

DONALD DAVIDSON

WHAT is the logical form of singular causal statements like: 'The flood caused the famine,' 'The stabbing caused Caesar's death,' 'The burning of the house caused the roasting of the pig'? This question is more modest than the question how we know such statements are true, and the question whether they can be analysed in terms of, say, constant conjunction. The request for the logical form is modest because it is answered when we have identified the logical or grammatical roles of the words (or other significant stretches) in the sentences under scrutiny. It goes beyond this to define, analyse, or set down axioms governing, particular words or expressions.

I

According to Hume, 'we may define a cause to be an object, followed by another, and where all the objects similar to the first are followed by objects similar to the second.' This definition pretty clearly suggests that causes and effects are entities that can be named or described by singular terms; probably events, since one can follow another. But in the *Treatise*, under 'rules by which to judge of causes and effects', Hume says that 'where several different objects produce the same effect, it must be by means of some quality, which we discover to be common among them. For as like effects imply like causes, we must always ascribe the causation to the circumstances wherein we discover the resemblance.' Here it seems to be the 'quality' or 'circumstances' of an event that is the cause rather than the event itself, for the event itself is the same as others in some respects and different in other respects. The suspicion that it is not events, but something more closely tied to the descriptions of events, that Hume holds to be causes, is fortified by Hume's claim that causal statements are never

From *Journal of Philosophy*, 64 (1967), 691–703. Reprinted by permission of the author and the editor of the journal.

I am indebted to Harry Lewis and David Nivison, as well as to other members of seminars at Stanford University to whom I presented the ideas in this paper during 1966–7, for many helpful comments. I have profited greatly from discussion with John Wallace of the questions raised here; he may or may not agree with my answers. My research was supported in part by the National Science Foundation.

necessary. For if events were causes, then a true description of some event would be 'the cause of *b*', and, given that such an event exists, it follows logically that the cause of *b* caused *b*.

Mill said that the cause 'is the sum total of the conditions positive and negative taken together . . . which being realized, the consequent invariably follows'. Many discussions of causality have concentrated on the question whether Mill was right in insisting that the 'real Cause' must include all the antecedent conditions that jointly were sufficient for the effect, and much ingenuity has been spent on discovering factors, pragmatic or otherwise, that guide and justify our choice of some 'part' of the conditions as the cause. There has been general agreement that the notion of cause may be at least partly characterized in terms of sufficient and (or) necessary conditions.[1] Yet it seems to me we do not understand how such characterizations are to be applied to particular causes.

Take one of Mill's examples: some man, say Smith, dies, and the cause of his death is said to be that his foot slipped in climbing a ladder. Mill would say we have not given the whole cause, since having a foot slip in climbing a ladder is not always followed by death. What we were after, however, was not the cause of death in general but the cause of Smith's death: does it make sense to ask under what conditions Smith's death invariably follows? Mill suggests that part of the cause of Smith's death is 'the circumstance of his weight', perhaps because if Smith had been light as a feather his slip might not have injured him. Mill's explanation of why we don't bother to mention this circumstance is that it is too obvious to bear mention, but it seems to me that if it was Smith's fall that killed him, and Smith weighed twelve stone, then Smith's fall was the fall of a man who weighed twelve stone, whether or not we know it or mention it. How could Smith's actual fall, with Smith weighing, as he did, twelve stone, be any more efficacious in killing him than Smith's actual fall?

The difficulty has nothing to do with Mill's sweeping view of the cause, but attends any attempt of this kind to treat particular causes as necessary or sufficient conditions. Thus Mackie asks, 'What is the exact force of [the statement of some experts] that this short-circuit caused this fire?' And he answers, 'Clearly the experts are not saying that the short-circuit was a necessary condition for this house's catching fire at this time; they know perfectly well that a short-circuit somewhere else, or the overturning of a lighted oil stove . . . might, if it had occurred, have set the house on fire' (ibid., p. 245). Suppose the experts know what they are said to; how does

---

[1] For a recent example, with reference to many others, see J. L. Mackie, 'Causes and Conditions', *American Philosophical Quarterly*, 2.4 (October 1965), 245–64 [reprinted above, pp. 15–38].

this bear on the question whether the short circuit was a necessary condition of this particular fire? For a short-circuit elsewhere could not have caused *this* fire, nor could the overturning of a lighted oil stove.

To talk of particular events as conditions is bewildering, but perhaps causes aren't events (like the short-circuit, or Smith's fall from the ladder), but correspond rather to sentences (perhaps like the fact that this short-circuit occurred, or the fact that Smith fell from the ladder). Sentences can express conditions of truth for others—hence the word 'conditional'.

If causes correspond to sentences rather than singular terms, the logical form of a sentence like:

(1) The short-circuit caused the fire.

would be given more accurately by:

(2) *The fact that* there was a short-circuit *caused it to be the case that* there was a fire.

In (2) the italicized words constitute a sentential connective like 'and' or 'if . . . then . . .' This approach no doubt receives support from the idea that causal laws are universal conditionals, and singular causal statements ought to be instances of them. Yet the idea is not easily implemented. Suppose, first that a causal law is (as it is usually said Hume taught) nothing but a universally quantified material conditional. If (2) is an instance of such, the italicized words have just the meaning of the material conditional, 'If there was a short-circuit, then there was a fire.' No doubt (2) entails this, but not conversely, since (2) entails something stronger, namely the conjunction 'There was a short-circuit *and* there was a fire.' We might try treating (2) as the conjunction of the appropriate law and 'There was a short-circuit and there was a fire'—indeed this seems a possible interpretation of Hume's definition of cause quoted above—but then (2) would no longer be an instance of the law. And aside from the inherent implausibility of this suggestion as giving the logical form of (2) (in contrast, say, to giving the grounds on which it might be asserted) there is also the oddity that an inference from the fact that there was a short-circuit and there was a fire, and the law, to (2) would turn out to be no more than a conjoining of the premises.

Suppose, then, that there is a non-truth-functional causal connective, as has been proposed by many.[2] In line with the concept of a cause

---

[2] For example by: Mackie, op. cit., p. 254; Arthur Burks, 'The Logic of Causal Propositions', *Mind*, 60, 239 (July 1951), 363–82; and Arthur Pap, 'Disposition Concepts and Extensional Logic', in *Minnesota Studies in the Philosophy of Science*, ii, ed. H. Feigl, M. Scriven, and G. Maxwell (Minneapolis, 1958), pp. 196–224.

as a condition, the causal connective is conceived as a conditional, though stronger than the truth-functional conditional. Thus Arthur Pap writes, 'The distinctive property of causal implication as compared with material implication is just that the falsity of the antecedent is no ground for inferring the truth of the causal implication' (p. 212). If the connective Pap had in mind were that of (2), this remark would be strange, for it is a property of the connective in (2) that the falsity of either the 'antecedent' or the 'consequent' is a ground for inferring the falsity of (2). That treating the causal connective as a kind of conditional unsuits it for the work of (1) or (2) is perhaps even more evident from Burks's remark that 'p is causally sufficient for q is logically equivalent to $\sim q$ is causally sufficient for $\sim p$' (p. 369). Indeed, this shows not only that Burks's connective is not that of (2), but also that it is not the subjunctive causal connective 'would cause'. My tickling Jones would cause him to laugh, but his not laughing would not cause it to be the case that I didn't tickle him.

These considerations show that the connective of (2), and hence by hypothesis of (1), cannot, as is often assumed, be a conditional of any sort, but they do not show that (2) does not give the logical form of singular causal statements. To show this needs a stronger argument, and I think there is one, as follows.

It is obvious that the connective in (2) is not truth-functional, since (2) may change from true to false if the contained sentences are switched. Nevertheless, substitution of singular terms for others with the same extension in sentences like (1) and (2) does not touch their truth value. If Smith's death was caused by the fall from the ladder and Smith was the first man to land on the moon, then the fall from the ladder was the cause of the death of the first man to land on the moon. And if the fact that there was a fire in Jones's house caused it to be the case that the pig was roasted, and Jones's house is the oldest building on Elm street, then the fact that there was a fire in the oldest building on Elm street caused it to be the case that the pig was roasted. We must accept the principle of extensional substitution, then. Surely also we cannot change the truth value of the likes of (2) by substituting logically equivalent sentences for sentences in it. Thus (2) retains its truth if for 'there was a fire' we substitute the logically equivalent '$\hat{x}(x = x \ \& \ \text{there was a fire}) = \hat{x}(x = x)$'; retains it still if for the left side of this identity we write the coextensive singular term '$\hat{x}(x = x \ \& \ \text{Nero fiddled})$'; and still retains it if we replace '$\hat{x}(x = x \ \& \ \text{Nero fiddled}) = \hat{x}(x = x)$' by the logically equivalent 'Nero fiddled'. Since the only aspect of 'there was a fire' and 'Nero fiddled' that matters to this chain of reasoning is the fact of their material equivalence, it appears that our assumed principles have led to the conclusion that the main connective of (2) is, contrary to what we supposed, truth-functional.[3]

Having already seen that the connective of (2) cannot be truth-functional, it is tempting to try to escape the dilemma by tampering with the principles of substitution that led to it. But there is another, and, I think, wholly preferable way out: we may reject the hypothesis that (2) gives the logical form of (1), and with it the ideas that the 'caused' of (1) is a more or less concealed sentential connective, and that causes are fully expressed only by sentences.

II

Consider these six sentences:

(3) *It is a fact that* Jack fell down.
(4) Jack fell down *and* Jack broke his crown.
(5) Jack fell down *before* Jack broke his crown.
(6) Jack fell down, *which caused it to be the case that* Jack broke his crown.
(7) *Jones forgot the fact that* Jack fell down.
(8) *That* Jack fell down *explains the fact that* Jack broke his crown.

Substitution of equivalent sentences for, or substitution of coextensive singular terms or predicates in, the contained sentences, will not alter the truth value of (3) or (4): here extensionality reigns. In (7) and (8), intensionality reigns, in that similar substitution in or for the contained sentences is not guaranteed to save truth. (5) and (6) seem to fall in between; for in them substitution of coextensive singular terms preserves truth, whereas substitution of equivalent sentences does not. However this last is, as we just saw with respect to (2), and hence also (6), untenable middle ground.

Our recent argument would apply equally against taking the 'before' of (5) as the sentential connective it appears to be. And of course we don't interpret 'before' as a sentential connective, but rather as an ordinary two-place relation true of ordered pairs of times; this is made to work by introducing an extra place into the predicates ('x fell down' becoming x fell down at t') and an ontology of times to suit. The logical form of (5) is made perspicuous, then, by:

[3] This argument is closely related to one spelled out by Dagfinn Føllesdal, 'Quantification into Causal Contexts', in *Boston Studies in the Philosophy of Science*, ii, ed. R. S. Cohen and M. W. Wartofsky (New York, 1966), pp. 263–74, to show that unrestricted quantification into causal contexts leads to difficulties. His argument is in turn a direct adaptation of Quine's (*Word and Object* (Cambridge, Mass., 1960), pp. 197–8) to show that (logical) modal distinctions collapse under certain natural assumptions. My argument derives directly from Frege.

(5) There exist times t and t' such that Jack fell down at t, Jack broke his crown at t', and t preceded t'.

This standard way of dealing with (5) seems to me essentially correct, and I propose to apply the same strategy to (6), which then comes out:

(6) There exists events e and e' such that e is a falling down of Jack, e' is a breaking of his crown by Jack, and e caused e'.

Once events are on hand, an obvious economy suggests itself: (5) may as well be construed as about events rather than times. With this, the canonical version of (5) becomes just (6'), with 'preceded' replacing 'caused'. Indeed, it would be difficult to make sense of the claim that causes precede, or at least do not follow, their effects if (5) and (6) did not thus have parallel structures. We will still want to be able to say when an event occurred, but with events this requires an ontology of pure numbers only. So 'Jack fell down at 3 p.m.' says that there is an event e that is a falling down of Jack, and the time of e, measured in hours after noon, is three; more briefly, $(\exists e)$ $(F(\text{Jack}, e)$ & $t(e) = 3)$.

On the present plan, (6) means some fall of Jack's caused some breaking of Jack's crown; so (6) is not false if Jack fell more than once, broke his crown more than once, or had a crown-breaking fall more than once. Nor, if such repetitions turned out to be the case, would we have grounds for saying that (6) referred to one rather than another of the fracturings. The same does not go for 'The short-circuit caused the fire' or 'The flood caused the famine' or 'Jack's fall caused the breaking of Jack's crown'; here singularity is imputed. ('Jack's fall', like 'the day after tomorrow', is no less a singular term because it may refer to different entities on different occasions.) To do justice to 'Jack's fall caused the breaking of Jack's crown' what we need is something like 'The one and only falling down of Jack caused the one and only breaking of his crown by Jack'; in some symbols of the trade, '$(\imath e)$ $F(\text{Jack}, e)$ caused $(\imath e)$ $B(\text{Jack's crown}, e)$'.

Evidently (1) and (2) do not have the same logical form. If we think in terms of standard notations for first-order languages, it is (1) that more or less wears its form on its face; (2), like many existentially quantified sentences, does not (witness 'Somebody loves somebody'). The relation between (1) and (2) remains obvious and close: (1) entails (2), but not conversely.[4]

---

[4] A familiar device I use for testing hypotheses about logical grammar is translation into standard quantificational form; since the semantics of such languages is transparent, translation into them is a way of providing a semantic theory (a theory of the logical form) for what is translated. In this employment, canonical notation is not to be conceived as an improvement on the vernacular, but as a comment on it.

III

The salient point that emerges so far is that we must distinguish firmly between causes and the features we hit on for describing them, and hence between the question whether a statement says truly that one event caused another and the further question whether the events are characterized in such a way that we can deduce, or otherwise infer, from laws or other causal lore, that the relation was causal. 'The cause of this match's lighting is that it was struck.—Yes, but that was only *part* of the cause; it had to be a dry match, there had to be adequate oxygen in the atmosphere, it had to be struck hard enough, etc.' We ought now to appreciate that the 'Yes, but' comment does not have the force we thought. It cannot be that the striking of this match was only part of the cause, for this match was in fact dry, in adequate oxygen, and the striking was hard enough. What is partial in the sentence 'The cause of this match's lighting is that it was struck' is the *description* of the cause; as we add to the description of the cause, we may approach the point where we can deduce, from this description and laws, that an effect of the kind described would follow.

If Flora dried herself with a coarse towel, she dried herself with a towel. This is an inference we know how to articulate, and the articulation depends in an obvious way on reflecting in language an ontology that includes such things as towels: if there is a towel that is coarse and was used by Flora in her drying, there is a towel that was used by Flora in her drying. The usual way of doing things does not, however, give similar expression to the similar inference from 'Flora dried herself with a towel on the beach at noon' to 'Flora dried herself with a towel', or for that matter, from the last to 'Flora dried herself'. But if, as I suggest, we render 'Flora dried herself' as about an event, as well as about Flora, these inferences turn out to be quite parallel to the more familiar ones. Thus if there was an event that was by Flora of herself and that was done with a towel, on the beach, at noon, then clearly there was an event that was a drying by Flora of herself— and so on.

The mode of inference carries over directly to causal statements. If it was a drying she gave herself with a coarse towel on the beach at noon that caused those awful splotches to appear on Flora's skin, then it was a drying she gave herself that did it; we may also conclude that it was something that happened on the beach, something that took place at noon, and something that was done with a towel, that caused the tragedy. These

---

For elaboration and defense of the view of events sketched in this section, see my 'The Logical Form of Action Sentences', in *The Logic of Action and Preference*, ed. Nicholas Rescher (Pittsburgh, 1967).

little pieces of reasoning seem all to be endorsed by intuition, and it speaks well for the analysis of causal statements in terms of events that on that analysis the arguments are transparently valid.

Mill, we are now in a better position to see, was wrong in thinking we have not specified the whole cause of an event when we have not wholly specified it. And there is not, as Mill and others have maintained, anything elliptical in the claim that a certain man's death was caused by his eating a particular dish, even though death resulted only because the man had a particular bodily constitution, a particular state of present health, and so on. On the other hand Mill was, I think quite right in saying that 'there certainly is, among the circumstances that took place, some combination or other on which death is invariably consequent . . . the whole of which circumstances perhaps constituted in this particular case the conditions of the phenomenon . . .' (*A System of Logic*, book III, chap. v, § 3.) Mill's critics are no doubt justified in contending that we may correctly give the cause without saying enough about it to demonstrate that it was sufficient; but they share Mill's confusion if they think every deletion from the description of an event represents something deleted from the event described.

The relation between a singular causal statement like 'The short-circuit caused the fire' and necessary and sufficient conditions seems, in brief, to be this. The fuller we make the description of the cause, the better our chances of demonstrating that it was sufficient (as described) to produce the effect, and the worse our chances of demonstrating that it was necessary; the fuller we make the description of the effect, the better our chances of demonstrating that the cause (as described) was necessary, and the worse our chances of demonstrating that it was sufficient. The symmetry of these remarks strongly suggests that in whatever sense causes are correctly said to be (described as) sufficient, they are as correctly said to be necessary. Here is an example. We may suppose there is some predicate '$P(x,y,e)$' true of Brutus, Caesar, and Brutus's stabbing of Caesar and such that any stab (by anyone of anyone) that is P is followed by the death of the stabbed. And let us suppose further that this law meets Mill's requirements of being *unconditional*—it supports counterfactuals of the form 'If Cleopatra had received a stab that was P, she would have died.' Now we can prove (assuming a man dies only once) that Brutus's stab was sufficient for Caesar's death. Yet it was not the cause of Caesar's death, for Caesar's death was the death of a man with more wounds than Brutus inflicted, and such a death could not have been caused by an event that was P ('P' was chosen to apply only to stabbings administered by a single hand). The trouble here is not that the description of the cause is partial, but that the event described was literally (spatio-temporally) only part of the cause.

Can we then analyse '*a* caused *b*' as meaning that *a* and *b* may be described in such a way that the existence of each could be demonstrated, in the light of causal laws, to be a necessary and sufficient condition of the existence of the other? One objection, foreshadowed in previous discussion, is that the analysandum does, but the analysans does not, entail the existence of *a* and *b*. Suppose we add, in remedy, the condition that either *a* or *b* as described, exists. Then on the proposed analysis one can show that the causal relation holds between any two events. To apply the point in the direction of sufficiency, imagine some description '$(\imath x)Fx$' under which the existence of an event *a* may be shown sufficient for the existence of *b*. Then the existence of an arbitrary event *c* may equally be shown sufficient for the existence of *b*: just take as the description of *c* the following: '$(\imath y)(y = c \ \& \ (\exists !x)Fx)$'.[5] It seems unlikely that any simple and natural restrictions on the form of allowable descriptions would meet this difficulty, but since I have abjured the analysis of the causal relation, I shall not pursue the matter here.

There remains a legitimate question concerning the relation between causal laws and singular causal statements that may be raised independently. Setting aside the abbreviations successful analysis might authorize, what form are causal laws apt to have if from them, and a premise to the effect that an event of a certain (acceptable) description exists, we are to infer a singular causal statement saying that the event caused, or was caused by, another? A possibility I find attractive is that a full-fledged causal law has the form of a conjunction:

(L) $\begin{cases} \text{(S)} \quad (e)(n)((Fe \ \& \ t(e) = n) \to \\ \qquad\qquad\qquad\qquad (\exists !f)(Gf \ \& \ t(f) = n + \in \ \& \ C(e,f))) \ and \\ \text{(N)} \quad (e)(n)((Ge \ \& \ t(e) = n + \in) \to \\ \qquad\qquad\qquad\qquad (\exists !f)(Ff \ \& \ t(f) = n \ \& \ C(f,e))). \end{cases}$

Here the variables '*e*' and '*f*' range over events, '*n*' ranges over numbers, *F* and *G* are properties of events, '$C(e,f)$' is read '*e* causes *f*', and '*t*' is a function that assigns a number to an event to mark the time the event occurs. Now, given the premise:

(P) $\qquad\qquad\qquad\qquad (\exists !e)(Fe \ \& \ t(e) = 3)$

(C) $\qquad\qquad (\imath e)(Fe \ \& \ t(e) = 3) \ caused \ (\imath e)(Ge \ \& \ t(e) = 3 + \in).$

It is worth remarking that part (N) of (L) is as necessary to the proof of (C) from (P) as it is to the proof of (C) from the premise '$(\exists !e)(Ge \ \& \ t(e) =$

[5] Here I am indebted to Professor Carl Hempel, and in the next sentence to John Wallace.

$3 + \in))$'. This is perhaps more reason for holding that causes are, in the sense discussed above, necessary as well as sufficient conditions.

Explaining 'why an event occurred', on this account of laws, may take an instructively large number of forms, even if we limit explanation to the resources of deduction. Suppose, for example, we want to explain the fact that there was a fire in the house at 3.01 p.m. Armed with appropriate premises in the form of (P) and (L), we may deduce: that there was a fire in the house at 3.01 p.m.; that it was caused by a short-circuit at 3.00 p.m.; that there was only one fire in the house at 3.01 p.m.; that this fire was caused by the one and only short-circuit that occurred at 3.00 p.m. Some of these explanations fall short of using all that is given by the premises; and this is lucky, since we often know less. Given only (S) and (P), for example, we cannot prove there was only one fire in the house at 3.01 p.m., though we can prove there was exactly one fire in the house at 3.01 p.m. that was caused by the short-circuit. An interesting case is where we know a law in the form of (N), but not the corresponding (S). Then we may show that, given that an event of a particular sort occurred, there must have been a cause answering to a certain description, but, given the same description of the cause, we could not have predicted the effect. An example might be where the effect is getting pregnant.

If we explain why it is that a particular event occurred by deducting ~~deducing~~ a statement that there is such an event (under a particular description) from a premise known to be true, then a simple way of explaining an event, for example the fire in the house at 3.01 p.m., consists in producing a statement of the form of (C); and this explanation makes no use of laws. The explanation will be greatly enhanced by whatever we can say in favour of the truth of (C); needless to say, producing the likes of (L) and (P), if they are known true, clinches the matter. In most cases, however, the request for explanation will describe the event in terms that fall under no full-fledged law. The device to which we will then resort, if we can, is apt to be re-description of the event. For we can explain the occurrence of any event a if we know (L), (P), and the further fact that $a = (\iota e)(Ge \ \& \ t(e) = 3 + \in)$. Analogous remarks apply to the redescription of the cause, and to cases where all we want, or can, explain is the fact that there was *an* event of a certain sort.

The great majority of singular causal statements are not backed, we may be sure, by laws in the way (C) is backed by (L). The relation in general is rather this: if 'a caused b' is true, then there are descriptions of a and b such that the result of substituting them for 'a' and 'b' in 'a caused b' is entailed by true premises of the form of (L) and (P); and the converse holds if suitable restrictions are put on the descriptions.[6] If this is correct, it does not follow that we must be able to dredge up a law if we know a singular causal statement to be true; all that follows is that we know there must be a covering law. And very often, I think, our justification for accepting a singular causal statement is that we have reason to believe an appropriate causal law exists, though we do not know what it is. Generalizations like 'If you strike a well-made match hard enough against a properly prepared surface, then, other conditions being favourable, it will light' owe their importance not to the fact that we can hope eventually to render them untendentious and exceptionless, but rather to the fact that they summarize much of our evidence for believing that full-fledged causal laws exist covering events we wish to explain.[7]

If the story I have told is true, it is possible to reconcile, within limits, two accounts thought by their champions to be opposed. One account agrees with Hume and Mill to this extent: it says that a singular causal statement '*a* caused *b*' entails that there is a law to the effect that 'all the objects similar to *a* are followed by objects similar to *b*' and that we have reason to believe the singular statement only in so far as we have reason to believe there is such a law. The second account (persuasively argued by C. J. Ducasse)[8] maintains that singular causal statements entail no law and that we can know them to be true without knowing any relevant law. Both of these accounts are entailed, I think, by the account I have given, and they are consistent (I therefore hope) with each other. The reconciliation depends, of course, on the distinction between knowing there is a law 'covering' two events and knowing what the law is: in my view, Ducasse is right that singular causal statements entail no law; Hume is right that they entail there is a law.

IV

Much of what philosophers have said of causes and causal relations is intelligible only on the assumption (often enough explicit) that causes are

[6] Clearly this account cannot be taken as a definition of the causal relation. Not only is there the inherently vague quantification over expressions (of what language?), but there is also the problem of spelling out the 'suitable restrictions'.

[7] The thought in these paragraphs, like much more that appears here, was first adumbrated in my 'Actions, Reasons, and Causes', *Journal of Philosophy*, 60 (1963), 685–700, especially pp. 696–9; reprinted in *Free Will and Determinism*, ed. Bernard Berofsky (New York, 1966). This conception of causality was subsequently discussed and, with various modifications, employed by Samuel Gorovitz, 'Causal Judgments and Causal Explanations', *Journal of Philosophy*, 62 (1965), 695–711, and by Bernard Berofsky, 'Causality and General Laws', ibid., 63 (1966), 148–57.

[8] See his 'Critique of Hume's Conception of Causality', *Journal of Philosophy*, 63 (1966), 141–8; *Causation and the Types of Necessity* (Seattle, 1924); *Nature, Mind, and Death* (La Salle, Ill., Open Court, 1951), part II. I have omitted from my 'second account' much that Ducasse says that is not consistent with Hume.

individual events, and causal relations hold between events. Yet, through failure to connect this basic *aperçu* with the grammar of singular causal judgements, these same philosophers have found themselves pressed especially when trying to put causal statements into quantificational form, into trying to express the relation of cause to effect by a sentential connective. Hence the popularity of the utterly misleading question: can causal relations be expressed by the purely extensional material conditional, or is some stronger (non-Humean) connection involved? The question is misleading because it confuses two separate matters: the logical form of causal statements and the analysis of causality. So far as form is concerned, the issue of nonextensionality does not arise, since the relation of causality between events can be expressed (no matter how 'strong' or 'weak' it is) by an ordinary two-place predicate in an ordinary, extensional first-order language. These plain resources will perhaps be outrun by an adequate account of the form of causal laws, subjunctives, and counterfactual conditionals, to which most attempts to analyse the causal relation turn. But this is, I have urged, another question.

This is not to say there are no causal idioms that directly raise the issue of apparently non-truth-functional connectives. On the contrary, a host of statement forms, many of them strikingly similar, at least at first view, to those we have considered, challenge the account just given. Here are samples: 'The failure of the sprinkling system caused the fire,' 'The slowness with which controls were applied caused the rapidity with which the inflation developed,' 'The collapse was caused, not by the fact that the bolt gave way, but by the fact that it gave way so suddenly and unexpectedly,' 'The fact that the dam did not hold caused the flood.' Some of these sentences may yield to the methods I have prescribed, especially if failures are counted among events, but others remain recalcitrant. What we must say in such cases is that in addition to, or in place of, giving what Mill calls the 'producing cause', such sentences tell, or suggest, a causal story. They are, in other words, rudimentary causal explanations. Explanations typically relate statements, not events. I suggest therefore that the 'caused' of the sample sentences in this paragraph is not the 'caused' of straightforward singular causal statements, but is best expressed by the words 'causally explains'.[9]

[9] Zeno Vendler has ingeniously marshalled the linguistic evidence for a deep distinction, in our use of 'cause', 'effect', and related words, between occurrences of verb-nominalizations that are fact-like or propositional, and occurrences that are event-like. See Zeno Vendler, 'Effects, Results and Consequences', in *Analytic Philosophy*, ed. R. J. Butler (New York, Barnes & Noble, 1962), pp. 1–15. Vendler concludes that the 'caused' of 'John's action caused the disturbance' is always flanked by expressions used in the propositional or fact-like sense, whereas 'was an effect of' or 'was due to' in 'The

A final remark. It is often said that events can be explained and predicted only in so far as they have repeatable characteristics, but not in so far as they are particulars. No doubt there is a clear and trivial sense in which this is true, but we ought not to lose sight of the less obvious point that there is an important difference between explaining the fact that there was *an* explosion in the broom closet and explaining the occurrence of *the* explosion in the broom closet. Explanation of the second sort touches the particular event as closely as language can ever touch any particular. Of course this claim is persuasive only if there are such things as events to which singular terms, especially definite descriptions, may refer. But the assumption, ontological and metaphysical, that there are events, is one without which we cannot make sense of much of our most common talk; or so, at any rate, I have been arguing. I do not know any better, or further, way of showing what there is.

---

shaking of the earth was an effect of (was due to) the explosion' is flanked by expressions in the event-like sense. My distinction between essentially sentential expressions and the expressions that refer to events is much the same as Vendler's and owes much to him, though I have used more traditional semantic tools and have interpreted the evidence differently.

My suggestion that 'caused' is sometimes a relation, sometimes a connective, with corresponding changes in the interpretation of the expressions flanking it, has much in common with the thesis of J. M. Shorter's 'Causality, and a Method of Analysis', in *Analytic Philosophy*, ii (1965), pp. 145–57.

ON THE LOGIC AND EPISTEMOLOGY OF THE CAUSAL RELATION

G. H. VON WRIGHT

1. The aim of my paper is threefold. First, I shall discuss some uses of formal logic to clarify the nature of causal relationships. Second, I shall examine the epistemological foundations of the concepts used in this formal analysis. Third, in the light of these formal and epistemological considerations, I shall discuss the place of causation and of causal categories in the philosophy of science.

It goes without saying that the discussion of such vast topics within the scope of a relatively brief paper must be very sketchy indeed. It can do little more than outline a conceptual framework and try to place some of the traditional problems of causation in the new frame. It is my hope that this approach may stimulate further discussion within this frame or challenge criticism of the framework itself. If it had the one or the other effect, or both, some light might be thrown on what is notoriously one of the most entangled problem-bundles in the whole of philosophy.

2. It has been thought that the notion of causality ought to be expurgated from the philosophy of science on the ground either that it is too heavily loaded metaphysically or that it is too imprecise logically to have a place in exact thinking. People who have thought thus have sometimes supported their view by alleging that the role of causation has grown progressively smaller as science has advanced. So, for example, Bertrand Russell in a famous and influential essay written at the beginning of the century.[1] Thinking in terms of cause and effect, it is said, is being replaced by thinking in terms of functional relationships and probabilistic correlations or in terms of conditionship relations between events or states of affairs. This may be a true description of current trends. But their significance to the philosophic problems of causality is not that they make these problems

From *Logic, Methodology and Philosophy of Science IV*, ed. P. Suppes *et al*. (Amsterdam: North-Holland, 1973), pp. 293–312. © North-Holland Publishing Company, 1973. Reprinted by permission of the author and the publishers.
[1] 'On the Notion of Cause', *Proceedings of the Aristotelian Society*, 13 (1912–13), 1–26.

obsolete, but rather that they enable us to present them with an increased degree of clarity and precision.

There can be little doubt about the usefulness, not least for purposes of logic, of analysing causal relationships in terms of conditions. By means of these analytic tools one can make a number of distinctions which, as long as one speaks loosely about 'causes' and 'effects' only, remain blurred or cannot be made at all. Thus, for example, causal factors which are necessary conditions of given effects behave logically rather differently from causal factors which are sufficient conditions. Failure to observe these differences has been responsible for disastrous confusions in traditional inductive logic. For this branch of logical study, the theory of conditions has therefore opened new prospects which are only beginning to be explored.

Condition concepts, however, cannot be regarded as logical primitives. They must be analysed in the terms of some other concepts and their theory thus incorporated into more 'standard' branches of logic. What are these other concepts? Here, two answers seem possible.

One analysis is in terms of quantifiers. If p and q are two (generic) states of affairs, then that (the obtaining of) p is a sufficient condition of (the obtaining of) q might mean that *whenever p* is the case, then q is the case too. The notion of 'whenever' is a temporal or tense-logical quantifier.

The other analysis is in terms of modal concepts. That p is a sufficient condition of q would then mean something like this: it is *necessary* that q obtains, if p obtains.

I shall call the first analysis of condition concepts extensional, the second intensional. In the extensional view, the 'groundform' of a conditionship and therewith also of a causal relation is that of a universal implication. In the intensional view, the groundform is that of a strict (necessary) implication.

That an extensional analysis may appear inadequate, and an intensional analysis needful, is perhaps best shown by the following observation: Let p be a (causally) sufficient condition of q. This, it would normally be thought, entitles us to maintain that had p obtained on any given occasion when in fact it did *not* obtain, then q too would have obtained on that occasion. A causal relation should provide a valid basis for so-called contrary-to-fact conditional assertions. The accidental uniformity that q is always there with p cannot by itself provide this basis. Must we not therefore assume a 'nomic necessity' connecting p and q, if counterfactual conditionals are to be extracted from their connection? Some, but by no means all philosophical logicians think that the correct answer to this question will commit us to what I have called here an intensional analysis of causal relationships.

Both an extensional and an intensional analysis of conditions leave unsolved the following problem:

To say that whenever p is the case q is the case too is equivalent to saying that whenever q is not the case p is not the case either. And to say that necessarily, if p then q, is equivalent to saying that necessarily, if not-q then not-p. It would then, on either analysis of the notion of a sufficient condition, follow that p is a sufficient condition of q if and only if not-q is a sufficient condition of not-p. This, as such, need not be thought objectionable. But if a relation of sufficient conditionship is thought of as a causal relation, the fact just mentioned is bound to worry us. For to say that p is a cause of q and to say that not-q causes not-p can hardly mean the same. Heavy rainfall may be the cause of flooding, but we should not normally regard the fact that no flooding occurs as a *cause* of the absence of rain. Causal relations have an *asymmetry* which their analysis in terms of condition concepts seems incapable, by itself, of capturing. I shall refer to the puzzle here as the Problem of Asymmetry of Cause and Effect.

It may be thought that the problem is solved if we add to the definition of causal relations in terms of conditionship a temporal qualification separating the conditioning from the conditioned terms of the relations. For example, we could stipulate that, on an instantiation of the causal relation, the conditioning or cause-factor must materialize before, or at least not later than, the conditioned or effect-factor.

I am not sure, however, that the attempts to distinguish between cause and effect on the basis of temporality and condition concepts alone will be successful. I incline to think that they will not, and shall later give reasons for this opinion.

3. The tools which I am going to use in the formal analysis are exceedingly simple. They consist of 'ordinary' propositional logic, a propositional modal logic, and a propositional tense-logic.

As modal primitive I shall use the notion of possibility. Its symbol will be M. As a symbol for necessity I shall use N, which is an abbreviation for the complex sign $\sim M \sim$.

The tense-logic concerned has two primitives. One is a binary connective. Its symbol will be T and can be read 'and next'. The other is a temporal quantifier. Its symbol $\vee$ is read 'sometime (in the future)'. As an abbreviation for the complex $\sim \vee \sim$ we shall use $\wedge$; it means 'always (in the future)'.

The logic of the connective T may be characterized as the logic of changes among states of affairs over a finite succession of discrete temporal occasions. It can easily be axiomatized and shown to be semantically complete with regard to a criterion of logical truth which is substantially that of a truth-functional tautology.

The logic of the quantifiers is structurally isomorphic with a weakened version of the modal system S4.3. When the logic of $\vee$ is combined with that of T, some additional principles of an axiomatic character are needed to cater for the peculiarities of quantification in a *discrete* time-medium.

I need not here discuss further the problems of tense-logic. The tense-logic involved in our analysis of causality does not embody anything over and above things already known from the literature.[2] As to the modal logic involved some comments will be made on this later.

4. Let us entertain here the following picture of the logical build of the world:

We assume that the total state of the world at any given point in time (I shall also call it 'occasion') can be completely described by telling, for any one of the members of a set of states of affairs $p, q, \ldots$, whether this state obtains or not on that occasion. If the set is finite and has n logically independent members, the number of possible total states of the world is 2^n and the number of possible successions of total states on m occasions is 2^{mn}. We shall call any such succession a possible *history* of the world of length m.

If the world at a given stage of its history is in a certain state, it can, as far as logic is concerned, at the next stage be in any one of the (2^n) logically possible different states. But this 'logical freedom' of development can, for non-logical reasons, be restricted. I shall call these non-logical reasons (restrictions) 'causal'. Thus the number of causally possible histories of length m of the world, starting from a given initial world state, may be less than the number 2^{mn} of logically possible histories. We can picture these possibilities of world developments in a topological figure ('tree'). (See picture on p. 99.)

In this picture circles represent total states of the world. The circle to the extreme left is the state on the first occasion. A progression of circles from the left to the right represents a possible history of the world. The bifurcations after any given circle indicate the various alternative developments which are immediately open to the world represented by that circle.

Looking towards the future from any given circle in the figure, there are so many possible histories ahead of us. We do not know in advance which

---

[2] Cf. von Wright, 'And Next', *Acta Philosophica Fennica*, 18 (1965), 293–304; 'And Then', *Commentationes Physico-mathematicae, Societas Scientiarum Fennica*, 32 (1966), 1–11; 'Always', *Theoria*, 34 (1968), 208–21; H. Kamp, review of 'And Next' and 'And Then', *Journal of Symbolic Logic*, 35 (1970), 459–60.

of the possible histories would be the actual history of the world if the circle in question happened to represent the actual total state of the world at that stage in its development. But we know that *one* of the possible histories would come true. I shall call this singular history the *natural* development of the world after the state in question. (An important addition will shortly be made to our definition of this notion of a 'natural' development or history of the world. See below Section 7.) We shall adopt the convention that the natural development after any given circle is always represented by the topmost layer of circles in the branch of the tree which has the given circle as its apex. Thus, in our figure, the horizontal strings of circles represent the various possible natural developments.

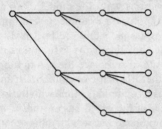

Let there be k alternative developments immediately after a given circle. The fraction $\frac{k-1}{2^n - 1}$ can then be said to measure the degree of freedom (or of determinism) which the world, at that given point of its history, enjoys as far as its immediate development is concerned. If $k = 1$ and the fraction $= 0$, this freedom is nil. The course of the world from that given state to the next is completely determined. If k equals the maximum 2^n, the fraction has the value 1, which means that the course of world development at this point is completely undetermined. (The various alternatives may also be correlated with probabilities, adding up to 1, but this case will not be considered by us here.)

The picture which we have been entertaining concerning the logical build of the world is a version of the position called *logical atomism*. All of its basic assumptions may be questioned. Is the total state of the world a truth-functional compound of logically independent atomic states of affairs? Is its history a succession of logically independent total states? Is time a discrete flow of successive occasions? Is the number of atomic states a finite constant? Has the world a beginning in time?

Some of these questions may have an affirmative and others a negative answer. I shall not attempt to answer any of them here. (But this does not mean that I regard them as unimportant in themselves or irrelevant to the problems of causality.) I shall regard the logico-atomistic structure, which we have just characterized, as being a 'fiction' or 'model' of what a world might be like, logically speaking. My primary interest is to define and study causal relations in this model. This will give us a *sharp* picture of causality. With it may be compared the more or less *blurred* pictures of causality which are employed in scientific practice and underlie the causal talk of natural and social scientists and historians. As a consequence of this comparison, we may come to a better appreciation also of the claims philosophers have made regarding the limitations and scope of causal explanations and regarding the operations of causality in the web of facts constituting reality.

One can relax in various ways the model of an atomistic world which we are building. One could, for example, give up the assumption that the members of the set of atomic states are invariably the same and/or that their number is finite, but retain the assumption that they are logically independent. One could also replace the assumption that time is discrete with the assumption that it is dense or continuous, and replace the assumption that the world has a beginning in time with the assumption that neither the past nor the future of the world has an end. It would be of interest to inquire how these modifications would influence the causal notions as defined for the stricter model. As the core of the notion of an atomistic world model, I should regard the logical independence of the atomic components of the world states on the one hand, and of the temporally separated total states of the world on the other hand. But these requirements of independence too could be 'relaxed' and the consequences of this relaxation for the causal notions studied.

5. What does it mean that on a certain occasion a certain state p is (causally) possible? Which is the modal logic of our topological tree?

These questions have no univocal answer. I shall here mention two ways of answering them. They are not the only ones, but they are of particular relevance to our problems.

That 'Mp' is true of a given world (circle in our figure) can mean that the generic state p, e.g. that it is raining, obtains in at least one of the worlds which are possible immediately after the given world. But it can also mean that p obtains in at least one of the worlds which are possible either immediately after the given world, or at some later time.

On both interpretations, possibility is, so to speak, a forward-looking idea. It is a 'potency' inherent in a world to develop into a world of which a certain feature is true. On the first interpretation this potency has to manifest itself immediately, if at all. This feature of the interpretation can be modified by replacing the word 'immediately' with the phrase 'on one of the next n occasions'.

The two interpretations yield different systems of modal logic. In neither system does the *ab esse ad posse* principle, or $p \rightarrow Mp$, hold true. But in both the principle holds that if p is true of the world on the next occasion, then p is a possibility in the world now. In symbols: $tTp \rightarrow Mp$, where t stands for an arbitrary tautology of propositional logic.

This failure of the *ab esse ad posse* principle, incidentally, should not be regarded as an oddity. It is in fact not very natural to say of that which is true that it is also possible. It is in better accord with ordinary usage to say that the obtaining of a state of affairs in the world proves that this was a possible world development. What *is* true *was* possible—but whether it still is a potency of the world is not certain.

On both interpretations the usual distribution principles for the modal operators hold true. Possibility distributes disjunctively, according to the equivalence $M(p \vee q) \leftrightarrow Mp \vee Mq$; necessity conjunctively according to the dual formula $N(p \ \& \ q) \leftrightarrow Np \ \& \ Nq$.

On the first interpretation, the second-order possibility MMp means the following thing: At least one world immediately after the world of which MMp is true has the potency Mp of becoming a world of which p is true. In other words: p is true of some world which may come true two steps from now. The truth of this statement obviously does not entail the truth of Mp or that p is true of some world which may come true at the very next moment.

On the second interpretation, MMp means that p obtains in some world which is possible after some world which is possible after the world of which MMp is true. This clearly entails the truth of Mp or that p is true of some world which is possible after the world of which Mp is true. $MMp \rightarrow Mp$ thus holds under this interpretation. On this ground I shall call it S4-like.

It is easy to convince oneself that none of the modal principles $MNp \rightarrow NMp$ or $MNp \rightarrow p$ or $MNp \rightarrow Np$ holds on either interpretation.

Consider the interpretation of $M(tTp)$ or the formula which says that a given world may develop into a world which a moment later will be a p-world. On the first interpretation this entails that p is true in some world which it is possible to reach in two steps from the given world, i.e. it entails MMp. On the second interpretation, it entails that p is true in some world after the given world, i.e. it entails Mp. Thus, under the first interpretation, the formula $M(tTp) \rightarrow MMp$ holds; and under the second, the formula $M(tTp) \rightarrow Mp$.

It should be observed that neither one of these last implications can be reversed. Assume that $M(tTp)$ is true. Then there is some world—either immediately after the given world or somewhere later in the tree of possible histories—such that p obtains in the world which *will* come true immediately after this world. And this is a stronger statement than to say merely that p obtains in some world which *may* come true immediately after the world in question, i.e. it is a stronger statement than either MMp or Mp.

Consider finally the formula $\lor p$. It says that on some later occasion p will obtain in the world. If this is true, then, on our second interpretation of possibility, Mp will be true too, i.e. p will be true of some possible future world. Thus we have $\lor p \to Mp$. By contraposition, and substituting $\sim p$ for p we can also write this entailment in the form $Np \to \land p$, which says that if p is necessary, in the sense of the second interpretation, then it is true for all the future. The causally necessary is also universally true, one could say. But universal truth is weaker than causally necessary truth.

Together with the axioms of propositional logic and of the quantified tense-logic for discrete time, the principles which we have been elucidating constitute, as far as I can see, a sufficient axiomatic basis for the modal logic of causally possible world segments under the two alternative interpretations of possibility. We can write down the axioms in a table:

Interpretation I

A1. $(tTp) \to Mp$ $\qquad\qquad (Np \to (tTp))$
A2. $M(tTp) \to MMp$ $\qquad (NNp \to N(tTp))$
A3. $M(p \lor q) \to Mp \lor Mq$ $\qquad (N(p \& q) \leftrightarrow Np \& Nq)$

Interpretation II

B1. $M(tTp) \to Mp$ $\qquad\qquad (Np \to N(tTp))$
B2. $MMp \to Mp$ $\qquad\qquad (Np \to NNp)$
B3. $M(p \lor q) \to Mp \lor Mq$ $\qquad (N(p \& q) \leftrightarrow Np \& Nq)$
B4. $\lor p \to Mp$ $\qquad\qquad\qquad (Np \to \land p)$

We shall not here prove theorems. Be it only noted that from B4 we immediately get the formula $(tTp) \to Mp$, which we said was valid also for the second interpretation.

Since we have given two interpretations, someone may raise the question as to which of them yields an *adequate* logic of the causal modalities. The answer is that both the interpretations which we have mentioned, and some others which we have not mentioned here, are relevant to the logical study of causal relationships—but also that it is the second, S4-like interpretation that is of prime importance to our topic.

6. The proposition that p is a cause of q is often equated with the proposition that p, by itself, is a sufficient condition of q. This is a great, but nevertheless useful, oversimplification.

As regards the proposition that p is a sufficient condition of q we can, moreover, distinguish several cases, depending upon how p and q are thought to be related in time. The two factors and the relationship between them may obtain on one and the same occasion, or the conditioning factor p may obtain on a given occasion and the conditioned factor q on the next, or p may obtain on a given occasion and q on *some* occasion after that. (I shall here omit altogether from consideration the possibility that p may obtain after q and yet be said to condition it causally.)

In 'formalizing' the relation, we begin with the second case. Since we have found that in the S4-like interpretation of the causal modalities Np entails $\wedge p$, we can conveniently read the formula $N(p \rightarrow tTq)$ as saying that necessarily, whenever p is the case, q immediately follows. And this we may, for present purposes, equate with a statement to the effect that p is a causally sufficient condition of q.

When p and q are simultaneous and the conditionship relation holds between them, the above formula becomes $N(p \rightarrow q)$. When p is supposed to be followed by q on *some* later occasion, the formula will be $N(p \rightarrow \vee q)$. We may regard as standard the case when the effect follows immediately in time upon the cause.

As regards the proposition that p is a necessary condition of q one can similarly distinguish several cases. We may regard as standard the case, when q cannot obtain unless p was there on the immediately preceding occasion, or in symbols: $N(tTq \rightarrow p)$. The implication can of course be contraposited to $N(\sim p \rightarrow (tT \sim q))$. From this it is seen that the proposition that p is a necessary condition of q is equivalent to the proposition that not-p is a sufficient condition of not-q. In *this* way the two types of condition are, incontestably, interdefinable.

$N(p \rightarrow (tTq))$ is not equivalent to $N(\sim q \rightarrow (tT \sim p))$. That p is a sufficient condition of q is thus not (generally) equivalent to the proposition that q is a necessary condition of p. The two types of condition are not interdefinable by means of such an equivalence.

7. I now turn to the epistemological aspect of our problem. How, if at all, can we come to know that p is the sufficient cause of q? Let us confine ourselves here to the case when q is supposed to be there immediately after p.

$N(p \rightarrow tTq)$ entails the generalization $\wedge (p \rightarrow tTq)$. The truth of contingent generalizations, it is universally agreed, we cannot, in a strict sense, come to *know* at all. But we may have observed numerous instances when p was followed by q, and no counter-instances, and then generalized the observed regular sequence. We may feel very confident of the truth of the generalization, so confident of it that we are willing to stake that on any occasion when p was *not* there, q would have followed had p been there. Then our confidence is that the generalization reflects ('flows from') a natural necessity ($N(p \rightarrow tTq)$) and that p is a *cause* of q and not merely an accidental, though regular, antecedent.

Our question now is: What can give us this eminent degree of confidence here? Continued observation may induce us to advance a *hypothesis* that the regularity reflects a causal connection. What we are in search of is something that would confirm us in *this* belief *as distinct from* the belief in the universal nature of the regularity.

Continued observation will never satisfy this craving. It is tied to the 'surface of reality' so to speak. What is required is a peep under this surface, somehow; a dive into the depths of unactualized possibilities for the sake of making sure that even if the actual course of events had been different from what it was, whenever p might have obtained, q would have followed.

There is also another way of expressing what I take to be substantially the same craving or requirement: We want to 'substitute' for a given world in which p is *not* the case another world in which p is the case, so as to be able to show that had p been true of the given world, q would be true of the following one.

But is it not obvious that we are asking for the moon here? In some sense this is certainly so. There is no substituting for a world which is or was, another world where different states obtain. Nor can one step back in our topological tree and make a fresh start along a different branch. With the future, however, the case is different.

Is it then not so that *che sarà, sarà* as the saying goes? I shall maintain that in a logically interesting and philosophically important sense this is *not* so.

At any given point in our topological tree there are alternative histories ahead of us. We do not know *which* one will come true—only that *some* one will be true. And we decided that the branches should be so drawn that the topmost progression of circles after any given circle pictures that history which would be the true one, if the given circle were to picture the true world. The phrase 'would be true' I shall now qualify by the following addition 'unless interference with the course of nature takes place'. What the topmost branches picture is thus the course of future developments if nature is 'left alone', 'untouched', 'to itself', to continue its course from any given point. It may have come to this point either 'of itself', from some previous point in the same 'natural' history, or thanks to some act of interference. This last means that the development from some point in another history was 'deflected' so as to become the starting point of a new history. Such deflections can happen, in principle, at any point in any of the natural histories. They could also be called 'shifts of reality'. They are by no means impossible, nor even uncommon happenings. They occur whenever agents act.

In order to see clearly what all this amounts to, we must inspect somewhat more closely the logic of action. Assume that a certain world obtains and in it a state of affairs $\sim p$. We feel confident—presumably on the basis of past experience, or for some other reason—that p will continue to be absent from the world on the next occasion unless we produce it, i.e., change the world into one that contains the state p. We feel confident, moreover, that we can do this, say, because we have *learnt* (been taught) how to do it.

But, you will ask, what is this confidence worth? Can we not be mistaken in thinking that p will not come about 'of itself', but only if we produce it? And may we not be mistaken in thinking that we *can* make p come about? Certainly! Unexpected changes sometimes occur in nature 'of themselves' and unexpected disabilities sometimes befall a man. But, by and large, the type of confidence to which I am here referring is trustworthy. Were it not so, *action* would not be possible. It is a conceptual feature of the utmost importance of that which we call action that certain changes in nature would not have occurred had we not produced them—or would have happened had we not prevented them. (One can refer to this as the *counterfactual element* involved in every action.)

Now imagine that we do interfere in the above situation and make a p-world out of a world which would otherwise have remained in the state not-p. We let this newly created world continue without touching it and find that it immediately changes to a q-world. This operation will, usually, 'impress' us strongly and confirm the surmise, if we had made it, that the regular sequence of p and q in the past was no mere accident but signified a causal tie between the two factors.

But perhaps q would have come into being even if we had refrained from interference and let the initial world continue as a $\sim p$-world. This we cannot check *post hoc*. But we can wait for, or perhaps ourselves produce, a new situation in which p is not there and will remain absent unless we interfere and *then* abstain from interfering. If now q is *not* there immediately after—or at least is not always there on such-like occasions—this further strengthens our belief in the causal connection.

Of these two operations, viz. that of producing p and always finding q

on the next occasion and that of letting p remain absent and not always finding q on the next occasion, I shall say that they come 'as near as is logically conceivable' to the verification of the counterfactual statement that on the past occasions when p was not there, q would have immediately followed had p been there. It is no proof, of course, that the counterfactual is true. But it is what makes us believe this. It confirms our belief that an observed regularity amounts to a causal or nomic connection.

Granted that these operations have this influence on our causal beliefs and hypotheses, we may raise the question of *why* they should have it. This is, at least partly, a question pertaining to the *logic* of the case. There seem to be two reasons why the observations which I described should have the effect which I attributed to them.

As long as we restrict ourselves to observing the regular sequence of q upon p, two possibilities will forever remain open which, if true, would make us withdraw the statement that p is the cause of q. One is that p and q have a *common cause*, i.e. that there is some factor which causes the succession pTq invariably to take place. If such a common cause were found one would not say that there is a causal tie *between p* and q. The other possibility is that q has some more remote cause, so that q would have been there in any case, whether or not p happened to 'pop up' immediately before it. If this turned out to be the case, we should again not say that it was p which caused q.

Now, the first of these possibilities, viz. that of a common cause, is eliminated by the experiment in which we shifted to a new succession of natural developments. For, at the point where the shift took place, the world would, we feel confident, have continued to be in the state not-p had we not 'steered' it to the state p, and this possibility of 'steering' the world rules out the existence of an antecedent cause which would have taken the world to p, i.e. produced p, and thereby also rules out the possibility of a cause responsible for the succession of q upon p.

Again the second possibility, viz. that the effect-factor would have occurred in any case and that the alleged cause-factor had no share in bringing it about, is excluded by the simple observation that when we refrain from producing the cause we also, on the whole, lose the effect. It is essential to say here 'on the whole' or 'generally' and not to insist on 'always'. For we do not, of course, wish to rule out the possibility that there may exist other causes of q beside p and that some of them happen to operate when p is not there. We must only make sure that such a cause is not constantly operating when p can be experimentally introduced. For otherwise, we should have no indication of the independent causal efficacy of p.

I have tried to argue that what confers on observed regularities the character of causal or nomic connections is the possibility of subjecting cause-factors to experimental test by interfering with the 'natural' course of events. In an important sense, therefore, the causal relation can be said to be dependent upon the concept of (human) *action*. This dependence is *epistemological*, rather than ontological, because it has to do with the way causal relations are established and distinguished from accidental regularities. But this dependence is also, in a sense which I have tried to make as precise as possible, *logical*, because it is connected with features which are peculiar to the *concept* of action.

The conceptual relationships in this region are complex and intricate and I am afraid that the view of causality which I have put forward can easily be misunderstood. I shall here give warning of two of the many possible misunderstandings:

The characteristic procedures whereby causal ties are tested do not by any means amount to a verification of nomic connections. Calling causal connections natural necessities may be convenient, but it does not mean that causal laws are *a priori* any more than ordinary inductive generalizations are. Their truth is a matter of future experience which can never be exhausted, and they share with inductive generalizations the characteristic asymmetry with regard to verifiability and falsifiability.

The second misunderstanding is a confusion between the epistemic and the ontic aspect. By no means have I wanted to maintain that the operation of a cause always results from action. Causation, needless to say, operates throughout nature independently of agency, also in regions of the world forever inaccessible to human interference. But the test-procedures characteristic of causal laws, including those whose operation is far removed from us in space or time, belong to the scientists' laboratories—and they belong there *essentially*, because of their conceptual connection with the mode of action we call experiment.

8. We have now a clue to answering what I called the *asymmetry problem*. This was the question of what distinguishes cause from effect, the conditioning from the conditioned factor in a nomic relationship. What makes p a cause-factor relative to the effect-factor q is, I shall maintain, the fact that by *manipulating p*, i.e. by producing changes in it 'at will' as we say, we could bring about changes in q. This applies both to cause-factors which are sufficient and those which are necessary conditions of the corresponding effect-factor.

In the normal cases, the effect brought about by the operation of the cause occurs later. In such cases time has already provided the distinction.

More problematic is the case when cause and effect are supposed to be simultaneous. Those who think of the cause–effect distinction in terms of temporality alone will be at a loss here. But when the distinction is made in terms of manipulability, the difficulty can be solved.

Consider the following example. There is a container with two valves. On a given occasion, one valve is open: this state of affairs I shall call not-p, the other valve is shut: this I shall symbolize by q. If the first valve is being closed, the second will at the very same time open. If, again, the second valve is being opened, the first will at the very same time close. In the first case we should say that (the coming into being of) p causes not-q, i.e. causes q to cease to be. In the second case we would say that not-q caused p (to come about). If the states which obtain are p and not-q and we do not know how this situation came to be, we could not tell whether the first valve is shut because the second is open, or whether the second is open because the first is shut. But whether or not one of the two states, when they obtain, can be singled out as cause and the other as effect, the two states can quite correctly be said to be *causally connected*. That they are causally connected means that we can influence the one by manipulating the other. (We must not say that *because* they are causally connected we can influence the one by manipulating the other.)

This observation is relevant to the question of the relation of causal laws to functional laws. Functional laws such as the Gas Law or Ohm's Law can quite appropriately be said to express *causal relationships*. But this does not mean that functional laws relate factors as causes and effects. Therefore there is good reason for not calling them 'causal laws'. What is causal about the relationship is that by manipulating one term one can induce changes in other terms. And when such manipulation takes place, one can distinguish cause from effect—even in cases when the changes occur simultaneously. The cause–effect distinction refers to the history of an individual occasion, one could say, and does not reside in the relation between the generic factors themselves.

Sometimes not all the factors in a functional relationship are manipulable. Then the non-manipulable factors can only assume the role of effects, never that of causes. Assume, for example, that there is no other way of changing the volume of a gas than by changing either pressure or temperature. Then changes in volume are always effects and never causes. And it is for a similar reason that the absence of flooding is not a *cause* of the absence of rain, although rain may cause flooding and therefore from the non-occurrence of flooding we can conclude to the non-occurrence of rain by virtue of that causal relation. We can, given our present knowledge of the laws of nature, imagine ways of controlling floods by controlling rainfall, but not the other way round. That it should be so, however, is contingent.

9. The idea of causation which I have been discussing could be termed *manipulative* or *experimentalist* causation. It is an idea which sees an essential connection bewteen causation and (human) action.

A logical presupposition of manipulative causation is (familiarity with) recurrent situations of generically identical states, fragments of world states, with which we (know we) can interfere. Such (knowledge of) ability entails, i.e. presupposes also knowledge of how the world will develop if we do *not* interfere with it.

Another logical basis for this kind of causation is (the existence of some degree of) logical atomism, i.e. the conceptual and verificational separability of states of affairs between which a causal connection is either asserted or denied. In particular, it must be possible to come to know the occurrence of the alleged cause-factor independently of (coming to know) the occurrence of the alleged effect-factor, and conversely.

A third presupposition is (familiarity with) regularities, for example that *q* regularly follows upon *p* in our experience. This presupposition entails familiarity with recurrent situations but not necessarily situations with which we have learnt to interfere.

In a world where these suppositions are not fulfilled there is no room for manipulative causation either. If we were placed in such a world our notion of *action* (interference with nature) and this notion of causation would have no application.

The presuppositions, however, can be satisfied to a greater or lesser extent and the notion of manipulative causation can accordingly have a more or less restricted applicability. If we identify 'causation' with 'manipulative causation' these restrictions could be said to set limits to the reign of causation. If we refrain from this identification, we should have to reckon with different 'types' of causation.

It will be agreed offhand, I think, that manipulative causation is at home *primarily* in the natural sciences, including both the physical sciences and the life sciences. But is *all* causation in the natural sciences of the kind I here call manipulative? And is causation of this type applicable to the human sciences at all?

The answer to the first question will partly depend upon what one is willing to call 'causation' in the contexts of natural science—and also upon where we wish to draw the border between natural and 'not-natural' science. There is no need to insist upon any sharp border at all—and there is good reason not to be over-strict with the meaning of 'causation'. But this being granted, it seems to me that one can make a strong case for the thesis that causation in the natural sciences (better: causation in nature) is primarily and on the whole of the manipulative type. I shall advance a few arguments in support of this view.

When a regularity is recorded between phenomena which are not subject to direct interference by manipulation—for example because they take place in remote parts of the universe—we are, I think, on the whole hesitant to speak of them as 'causally related' or of the regularity as a 'causal law'. The regularity is rather what Mill[3] called an 'empirical law'. We may, e.g. doubt whether there is not a cause for the regularity itself so that when, say, r regularly follows upon q this is because of the previous occurrence of p. Now it often happens that observed regularities are raised to the rank of laws because of their being explained, i.e. deduced from laws. And thereby they in fact often assume a 'causal' appearance as well. Why is this?

The answer, I think, is that the laws themselves from which the observed uniformity has been deduced are established by laboratory procedures— and not just by passive observations. Our knowledge of causes and effects in remote regions in space, or, as in geological or palaeontological research, in time, is based on and 'mediated' by our knowledge of natural laws for which we have sufficient experimental evidence from our laboratories.

In speaking of 'laws of nature' I have here in the first place been thinking of such laws as those of falling bodies, or the Gas Law, or Ohm's Law, or Snell's Law. They are typically 'experimentalist laws'. But not all laws have this character, to be sure. Some laws of a very general nature are more like conceptual principles, constitutive of the frame of reference within which experiments are conducted and results interpreted. The discovery of the law of inertia, e.g. is a fascinating chapter of experimental science. But the law itself is not a causal law, nor was it discovered through experiments. It is rather a conceptual frame for distinguishing a 'causeless' state of affairs from states for the existence or origination of which we have to look for causes. And something similar is true of such laws as the principle of the conservation of energy or the law of entropy, etc. It is not very natural to think of them as *causal*.

10. It is a traditional matter of debate whether, or to what extent, causal categories are applicable to the human sciences. The question raised and the answers given in these debates are often all too sweeping and vague. A useful way of clarifying things is, I think, to try to relate ideas concerning manipulative causation to questions of explanation and prediction in the realm of human action.

[3] J. S. Mill, *A System of Logic* (1843), Book III, ch. 16.

Explanation of action is often and typically, even if not exclusively, given in terms of intentions, motives, and reasons. We also say that in acting an agent is aiming at something, an end of action, and we explain his conduct in terms of his aims and ends. Such explanations are called teleological.

It can hardly be called in question that teleological explanations are 'legitimate' within their appropriate orbit. But it is very much an open question what their logical status is, and in particular, how they are related to causal explanations.

Many recent authors have stressed what they take to be a basic difference between causal explanations on the one hand and intentionalist, motivational, or teleological explanations on the other hand. The supposed difference is this: In a causal relation cause and effect are logically independent. But the relation of actions to their motivating reasons, it is said, is not one between logically independent terms.

I think those philosophers are right, who point to this difference between the two types of explanation. But the way in which they have presented the Logical Connection Argument, as it is called, has often been faulty or else unconvincing. Let q be the result of a certain agent's action, i.e. the state of affairs which is there when this agent has done a certain thing. And let p be the reason which prompted his action, e.g. the fact that he wanted something for which this action was instrumental or intended to achieve something for which the action was necessary. I shall here lump all such action-prompting factors, be they intentions, motives, aims, or ends, under one label 'reasons'.

Now let p, the reason, be there on an occasion prior to the one when the action is supposed to follow. We must then think of p as remaining present until the action is effected. For, otherwise it would cease to be a reason for the agent to act upon. (We shall refer to a change in p as a 'change of mind'.) q, on the other hand, must be absent on the occasion when the action is initiated. For, otherwise, there would be no opportunity for performing the action. This occasion, moreover, must be such that not only the agent himself but also the person who describes the case or explains the action feels confident that q will not come about unless the agent acts. So we have to reckon with at least two causally possible world-segments here, one leading to q and another one leading to not-q. This alone excludes that q could, of causal necessity, follow upon p. If it did, the agent would not have acted.

We could, of course, have predicted the action, once p was known to be there. And we might have been very confident indeed of the truth of the prediction, thinking that once the agent has this reason, he will certainly act accordingly. This would be a comparable confidence to the one which we have in an action situation of our own, the confidence that the world will not change in a certain respect unless we interfere. This 'practical certainty', however, is not derived from belief in causal laws.

But here someone may say that we are begging the question. Once p is there and remains, q *must* follow and not-q is no longer a causal possibility in the action-situation—even though the agent may think it is. If reasons operate like causes, then, when the reasons are there, the agents are no longer free to *let* the world take the course which it would have taken independently of their action. To think otherwise is to be under an illusion. In this argument there is some truth and some error.

When viewing the action from before it has taken place, but when the reason for its performance is already there, there is no such 'must' at all. The reason may 'drop out' before the action has taken place, i.e. the agent may change his mind. Or the reason may continue to be there for him to act—and the agent may try but fail to accomplish the action. Or something may happen which prevents him.

Assume, however, that the agent has performed the action. This rules out the possibility that he tried but was not successful, or that he was prevented. Assume also that his reason for acting was continuously present. Then, to say that he acted *because* of that reason is indeed to make a statement of necessity. But not, I think, a causal one. For the omission of the action would now be a criterion or standard whereby we judge that the agent has changed his mind. When both the action and the reason *for it*, i.e., the reason why he acted, are there, then their connection is conceptual, logical, and not causal. This, on my understanding of this complex problem, is the gist of truth contained in the so-called Logical Connection Argument.

It is indeed a 'logical illusion' to think that an agent could, without changing his mind, act contrary to the reasons for his action—in our example, *let* the world stay at not-q instead of taking it to q. Having had a reason can, after the action, be said to have necessitated the action. Having a reason, however, can never be said to necessitate an agent not to change his mind before he acts. The existence of reasons therefore does not obliterate the bifurcation of possibilities which is characteristic of an action situation. This is why it is no 'causal illusion' to think of an agent as free even when his actions flow from so-called 'compelling reasons'.

Yet someone may still protest against this conceptual separation between causal explanations and explanations of action. Reasons too can be manipulated, first of all. There are numberless ways in which we can produce reasons for a man to act upon and then watch his behaviour—like any other event in nature. Starve a man and he will seize the first opportunity of getting food, threaten him at gun point and he will raise his arms, put requests or orders to him and under normal circumstances you can count upon his reaction. Why think that this is all that unique and different from causal relationships of stimuli and responses?

The answer is that we need not think of this as different from causation at all. We can ignore the bifurcations in the acting-situations as pictured in our topological tree; we can think that there is essentially only one continuation from p to q, and attribute a failure of the effect to materialize to the intervention of some unforeseen 'counteracting cause' which explains the failure. This is exactly analogous to procedures familiar from the methodology and practice of the natural sciences.

Such a view of human behaviour is indeed possible and may also be fruitful. It is a view largely accepted, I should think, in 'scientific' social and psychological studies. It can be called a *reified* view of man as an agent, using for it a term well known from Hegelian and Marxist philosophy.

To discuss the scope and limits of this reified view of man would be to enter a jungle of controversy in the philosophy of the social sciences. This we cannot do here. Let it only be said in conclusion that what I have done in this paper has been to argue for *one* essential limitation to the reification and thus also 'causalization' of action. This limitation is set by the implicit dependence of the very notion of cause on an (unreified) concept of agency and action. To regard things as being causally related is the intellectual privilege of agents who think they are free to interfere with the world. This thought is the basis of man's technology and mastery of nature. But only through a misunderstanding of its conceptual foundations can man snare himself in the deterministic connections which his scientific intelligence unravels in nature.

VIII

ON THE NATURE
AND THE OBSERVABILITY
OF THE CAUSAL RELATION

C. J. DUCASSE

THE aim of this paper is to set forth two related theses. The first is that the correct definition of the causal relation is to be framed in terms of one single case of sequence, and that constancy of conjunction is therefore no part of it, but merely, under certain conditions, a corollary of the presence of the causal relation. The second thesis is that the causal relation, when correctly defined, is as directly observable as many other facts, and that the alleged mysteriousness of the causal tie is therefore a myth due only to a mistaken notion of what a tie is.

1. MEANING OF 'A CORRECT DEFINITION'

The problem of giving a 'correct' definition of the causal relation is that of making analytically explicit the meaning which the term 'cause' has in actual concrete phrases that our language intuition acknowledges as proper and typical cases of its use. For obviously it is one thing to 'know what cause means' in the cheap sense of being able to understand intuitively such an assertion as that the Santa Barbara earthquake caused the collapse of numberless chimneys; and it is another and a much more difficult and rarer thing to 'know what cause means' in the sense of being able to give a correct definition of it. To say that a definition of it is correct means that that definition can be substituted for the word 'cause' in any such assertion as the above, in which the word occurs, *without in the least changing the meaning which the assertion is felt to have.* Any ventured definition of such a philosophical term as cause is thus capable of being correct or incorrect in strictly the same sense as that in which a scientific hypothesis is so, viz. either it fits the facts or it does not. The only difference is that in the case of scientific hypotheses the facts are perceptual objects and their relations, while in the case of philosophical hypotheses the facts are the intuited meanings of actual phrases in which the word to be defined occurs. The

From *Journal of Philosophy*, 23 (1926); reprinted in *Truth, Knowledge, and Causation* (London: Routledge and Kegan Paul, 1968), pp. 1–14. Reprinted by permission of the author and the editor of the journal.

great inductive method of hypothesis–deduction–verification is thus no less that of philosophy than that of science.

2. TWO PRELIMINARY REMARKS

Before attempting to formulate a definition of the term 'cause', attention must briefly be called to two essential preliminary points.[1]

1. The first is that nothing can, in strict propriety, ever be spoken of as a cause or an effect, except an *event*. And by an event is to be understood either a change or an absence o f change (whether qualitative or relational) of an object.[2] On the other hand, objects themselves (in the sense of substances, e.g. gold; or things, e.g. a tree) never can properly be spoken of as causes or effects,[3] but only as agents or patients, as components or compounds, as parts or wholes. These relations, although closely allied to the causal relation, are nevertheless distinct from it, and cannot be discussed here.

2. The second point to be borne in mind is that when the term 'causal connection' is used, any one of four distinct objective relations may actually be meant, namely, objectively sufficient to, necessary to, necessitated by, contingent upon. And to these four relations correspond respectively the four functional terms, cause, condition, effect, resultant. So that, more explicitly, if a given particular event is regarded as having been *sufficient to* the occurrence of another, it is said to have been its *cause*; if regarded as having been *necessary to* the occurrence of another, it is said to have been a *condition of* it; if regarded as having been *necessitated by* the occurrence of another, it is said to have been its *effect*; and if regarded as having been *contingent upon* the occurrence of another, it is said to have been a *resultant* of that other. Much confusion has resulted in discussions of causality from the failure to keep these four relations at all times clearly distinguished, Mill, indeed, pushing perversity to the point of convincing himself and some of his readers that there was no sound basis for a distinction between cause and condition. But it is, on the contrary, essential to remember that to be sufficient is one thing, to be necessary another thing, and to be *both* sufficient and necessary (which is what Mill's definition would make cause mean) yet a third thing.

[1] In a monograph on causation by the writer, these two points are argued at some length. See *Causation and the Types of Necessity* (Univ. of Washington Press, 1924), pp. 52 ff.

[2] More technically, an event can be defined as either a change or an absence of change in the relation of an object to either an intensive or an extensive standard of reference, during a specified time interval.

[3] Cf. Schopenhauer, *The Fourfold Root of the Principle of Sufficient Reason*, trans. Hillebrand, pp. 38 ff.; and Wundt, *Logik*, 3rd ed., i.586.

Of the four relations, cause, condition, effect, resultant, which a given particular event may have to another with which it is connected, we shall have space here to discuss only the first, namely, cause. And we shall, moreover, confine ourselves to cases—much the more frequent—where the events contemplated are changes, rather than absences of change.

3. DEFINITION OF CAUSE

Taking it as an admitted fact of the language that if the occurrence of a particular change sufficed to the occurrence of a given other it is then said to have caused that other, the all-important question now arises how such sufficing is to be defined. I suggest that the correct definition of it, framed in terms of a hypothetical situation, is as follows:

Considering two changes, C and K (which may be either of the same or of different objects), the change C is said to have been sufficient to, i.e. to have caused, the change K, if:

1. The change C occurred during a time and through a space terminating at the instant I at the surface S.[4]

2. The change K occurred during a time and through a space beginning at the instant I at the surface S.

3. No change other than C occurred during the time and through the space of C, and no change other than K during the time and through the space of K.

More roughly, but in briefer and more easily intuited terms, we may say that *the cause of the particular change K was such particular change C as alone occurred in the immediate environment of K immediately before.*

4. SOME BEARINGS OF THE DEFINITION

A number of important points may be noted in connection with the above definition of cause.

1. The first is that it presents the causal relation as involving not two terms only, but essentially three terms, namely, (a) the environment of an object, (b) some change in that environment, (c) the resulting change in the object. As soon as it is clearly realized that the expression 'the cause of an event' thus has any meaning at all only in terms of some definite environment, either concretely given or abstractly specified, Mill's contention that the distinction between cause and conditions is arbitrary and capricious is seen to be absurd. To take up the environment into the 'cause', as Mill's

---

[4] The limit of a change of a solid is obviously a surface, not a point.

definition of cause[5] tries to do, is impossible because the cause consists of a change in that environment. No event can be spoken of as the cause of anything, except relatively to certain conditions; and vice versa, as regards conditions.

2. The second remark for which the definition of cause above gives occasion concerns the immediate spatial and temporal contiguity of cause and effect. The alleged impossibility of such immediate contiguity is the chief ground upon which Russell has advocated the extrusion of the term 'cause' from the philosophical vocabulary.[6] The difficulties raised by him, however, are easily disposed of if two things are kept in mind. The first is that the terms 'a time' and 'a place' are ambiguous. It is essential to distinguish clearly 'a time' in the sense of an instant, i.e. a *cut* of the time series, from 'a time' in the sense of a *segment* of the time series, limited by two cuts. And similarly with regard to the space order, the cuts of it (viz. point, lines, or surfaces according as one-, two-, or three-dimensional space is considered) are to be carefully distinguished from the *parts* of space, which have such cuts as limits. The second thing to bear in mind is that an event (whether a change or an 'un-change')[7] cannot be said to occur *at* a time (cut), but only *during* a time (segment); nor *at* a point (or other cut of space), but only *through* a space (between cuts). Thus, a change is essentially a process which has extent both in time and in space, and is therefore divisible; any division yielding segments of the process that are themselves extended in time and space and therefore further divisible, *ad infinitum*.[8] The immediate contiguity of cause and effect in space and time, specified in our definition, then means only that one identical space–time *cut* marks both the end of the cause process and the beginning of the effect process; the one extending up to, and the other from, that cut; the cut itself, however (by the very nature of a cut as distinguished from a segment), having no space–time

[5] 'The cause . . . is the sum total of the conditions, positive and negative taken together . . . which being realized, the consequent invariably follows' (*Syst. of Logic*, bk. III, ch. v, No. 3). This definition is obviously in flagrant contradiction with Mill's characterization of the cause as the single difference in the circumstances, in the canon of the 'Method of Difference'.

[6] 'On the Notion of Cause', *Proceedings of the Aristotelian Society*, 13 (1912–13).

[7] The apt term 'unchange' is borrowed from Dr. Charles Mercier's book, *Causation and Belief*.

[8] A stage might, however, conceivably be reached, at which the parts obtained by the division of a change, would, *in terms of the particular test of changing used at the previous stages of division*, be themselves not changes, but unchanges (though, of course, none the less extended in time and space and therefore divisible). That is, the assertion that something changes, or, equally, does not change, remains ambiguous so long as some definite test of such change has not been specified as standard. Thus the assertion might be true in terms of one test and false in terms of another. Cf. 'A Liberalistic View of Truth', by the writer, in the *Philosophical Review* for November 1925.

dimension at all.[9] With cause and effect and their space–time relation[10] so conceived, there is no possibility that, as Russell contended, some other event should creep in between the cause and the effect and thwart the production of the effect. Nor are we compelled, as he also contended, to trim down indefinitely the beginning part of the cause (and, *mutatis mutandis*, the end part of the effect) on the ground that the early part of the cause is not necessary to the effect so long as the end part of the cause occurs. For, once more, the cause means something which was sufficient, and not as the objection assumes, something which was both sufficient and necessary, to the effect. Thus the space–time limit of the cause process at the outer end is as elastic as we please, and varies with the space–time scope of the particular description of the cause that we give in each concrete case. And the same is true of the outer end of the effect process.[11]

3. The third observation to be made on the definition of cause proposed is that it defines the cause of a particular event in terms of but a single occurrence of it, and thus in no way involves the supposition that it, or one like it, ever has occurred before or ever will again. The supposition of recurrence is thus wholly irrelevant to the meaning of cause; that supposition is relevant only to the meaning of law. And recurrence becomes related at all to causation only when a law is considered which happens to be a generalization of facts themselves individually causal to begin with. A general proposition concerning such facts is, indeed, a causal law, but it is not causal because general. It is general, i.e. a law, only because it is about a class of resembling facts; and it is causal only because each of them already happens to be a causal fact individually and in its own right (instead of, as Hume would have it, by right of its co-membership with others in a class of pairs of successive events). The causal relation is essentially a relation between concrete individual events; and it is only so far as these events exhibit likeness to others, and can therefore be grouped with them into kinds, that it is possible to pass from individual causal facts to

---

[9] In practice, no space–time dimension of a relevant order of magnitude. Clock ticks and graduation lines as used are never perfectly dimensionless.

[10] This view of the space–time relation of cause and effect, I was gratified to find, is also that set forth by Mr. Johnson in vol. III of his *Logic* (p. 74), which appeared at virtually the same time as the monograph on causation referred to above.

[11] It is interesting to note that the analysis of the space–time relation of cause and effect given above reveals an essential connection between the two notions of Change and of Causation. For, taking any given change process, by specifying a space–time cut of it, one splits it into a cause and an effect; and, on the other hand, taking any given cause and its effect, by abstracting from the particular space–time cut in terms of which as common limit the cause process is distinguished from the effect process, one obtains a process describable as one change. This calls to mind Kant's very inadequately argued contention in the Second Analogy, that (objective) change involves the category of causation.

causal laws. On the other hand, in the case of laws obtained, not by experimentation and generalization of the result of it by abstraction, but in a purely statistical manner (the only manner directly relevant to Hume's notion of cause), it is only quite accidentally that the terms of such 'constant conjunctions' as these laws describe stand one to the other as cause and effect. Much more frequently they are not such and are not regarded as such; and uniformity of succession thus constitutes not at all the meaning of the cause–effect relation, but at the most only evidence of the existence of some causal connection, perhaps very remote and indirect, *and yet to be discovered*, between the terms of the succession. A causal connection explains the regularity of the succession, but is not constituted by such regularity, which is but a corollary of the causal connection whenever the cause or the chain of causes happens to occur again. Hume himself, indeed, on the very page of the *Enquiry* where he gives his definition of cause (in terms of regularity of succession), says that that definition is 'drawn from circumstances foreign to the cause'; 'from something extraneous and foreign to it'. And it was to avoid having to say, as Hume's definition would require, that day was the cause of night and night the cause of day, that Mill added, in his own definition, the requirement of 'unconditionality' to that of invariability of sequence—without perceiving, however, that as soon as 'unconditionality' was introduced, invariability became superfluous. For if the effect 'unconditionally' follows from the cause, i.e. is *necessitated by* the cause, then, obviously, as often as the cause recurs the effect *must* recur also. But this so-called unconditionality of an effect upon a cause, i.e. the necessitation of the effect by the cause, was the very thing which Mill had declared was not revealed by mere observed regularity of sequence. It must then be ascertained by the experimental 'method of difference', i.e. by the analytical observation of an individual case. But Mill never sees that this amounts to *defining* cause in terms of single difference in one experiment. Hume refers to single difference as a 'Rule' by which to judge of causes and effects,[12] and Mill, borrowing the blunder, throughout persists in regarding single difference as a 'method' for the roundabout ascertainment of something other than itself, viz. of invariable sequence; instead of, and properly, regarding it as the very definition of cause. This is perhaps in part explicable by the fact that Mill never clearly perceived the difference between experimentation and generalization[13] by abstraction; he never was adequately conscious that it is one thing to introduce a single difference, i.e. make a single change, in a given concrete set of circumstances, and note what happens; and a very different thing to compare two such experiments,

[12] *Treatise*, bk. I, part III, No. 15.
[13] This has been noted by Jevons, *Pure Logic and Other Minor Works*, p. 251.

one of which yielded a certain effect and the other failed to, and note what single difference there was between the single antecedent changes introduced in the two cases into the (same) set of circumstances.

4. As a last remark upon the definition of cause in terms of a single case given above, it may be noted that it is the only one which is faithful to the manner in which the word 'cause' is actually used by every person whose English has not been contaminated by Hume. As Russell himself notes, we cannot without 'intolerable circumlocution'[14] avoid speaking of one particular event as causing another particular event. And, I ask, why seek to avoid it, when just that is so plainly what we do mean? When any philosophically pure-minded person sees a brick strike a window and the window break, he judges that the impact of the brick was the cause of the breaking, *because* he believes that impact to have been the only change which took place then in the immediate environment of the window. He may, indeed, have been mistaken, and acknowledge that he was mistaken, in believing that impact to have been the only change in the environment. But if so he will nevertheless maintain that *if* it had been the only change, it would have been the cause. That is, he will stand by the definition of cause, and admit merely that what he perceived was not a true case of what he meant and still means by cause.

5. THE OBSERVABILITY OF THE CAUSAL RELATION

This now brings us to the second of the two theses mentioned at the beginning of this paper, namely, that concerning the observability of the causal relation. Hume's view that no connection between a cause and its effect is objectively observable would be correct only under the assumption that a 'connection' is an entity of the same sort as the terms themselves between which it holds, that is, for Hume and his followers, a sense impression. For it is true that neither a colour, nor an odour, nor a sound, nor a taste, nor any other sense impression, 'connecting' the cause and the effect, is observable between them. Indeed, we must even add that if a sense impression were present between those said to constitute the cause and the effect, it would, from its very nature as a sense impression, be quite incapable of doing any connecting and would itself but constitute one more of the entities to be connected. This is true in particular of the feeling of expectation which Hume would have us believe is what the words 'necessary connection' ultimately denote.

But there is fortunately no need for us to attempt to persuade ourselves that whenever people during the past centuries have talked of objective

[14] *Scientific Method in Philosophy*, p. 220.

connection they thus have not really meant it at all. For the fact is that causal connection is not a sensation at all, but a relation. The nature of that relation has already been minutely described above. It is, as we have seen, a relation which has individual concrete events for its terms; and, as analysed by us, its presence among such events is to be observed every day. We observe it whenever we perceive that a certain change is the *only* one to have taken place immediately before, in the immediate environment of another.

But at this point it becomes necessary for us to consider two apparently weighty objections, which can be urged against the observability of what we have defined as constituting the causal relation. One of them is that we are never theoretically certain that we have observed as much as the definition demands; and the other is that, on the other hand, we are often certain that the cause is less than the definition would permit us so to call. Each of these difficulties in turn must be carefully examined.

1. The first of them, more explicitly stated, is this: We never can be certain that the change which we have observed in any given case was, as the definition requires, the *only* change that occurred then and there, and therefore it is always possible that a part of the cause has escaped us. In considering this objection, it is, of course, well to bear in mind that our definition specifies contiguity in space as well as in time of the cause to the effect, and in addition permits us to set the *outer* space–time limit of the environment to be observed as near to the effect as we find convenient; so that the definition relieves us of the sometimes alleged obligation to observe the antecedent change of the entire universe. But even confining our observation to as externally limited a region of the contiguous space–time as we please, the possibility still always remains that we have not in a given case observed the whole of the change in that environment.

This predicament, it must frankly be admitted, is inescapable. But we must state also, and with all possible emphasis, that it is not peculiar to the definition of causation proposed.[15] Nor, indeed, is it, in its essence, peculiar even to definitions of cause. Rather it is a predicament involved *in every attempt to observe a universal negative*. Thus, even such an assertion as that 'this man is Mr. So-and-so' is theoretically always precarious in exactly the same manner, for there is no theoretically absolute guarantee that the man before us is not someone else, who merely happens to be exactly like Mr. So-and-so in the particular respects to which our observation has

---

[15] The corresponding difficulty with the Humean definition of cause as regular sequence is that experience never can guarantee that exceptions to the regularity of the sequence have not escaped our observation; or, more generally, that the sample of the character of the sequence, which we have observed, is a 'fair sample'.

turned.[16] The predicament mentioned, thus, does not constitute the least evidence against the correctness of our definition of cause, for the very same difficulty would arise no matter what other definition were proposed.

All that we are then called upon to do in connection with that predicament is, first, to call attention to its existence and nature, and sagely class it as a fact illustrating the platitude that life is a precarious business in many ways; and, second, to state explicitly the proviso subject to which cases of causation as defined are observable. This proviso is obviously that *the change which we observed in the antecedently contiguous space–time was really the only change which occurred in it.* That is not something which we know to be true, but only something which we hope is true, and which for *practical* purposes we must suppose true; i.e. it is a *postulate*—the first of those underlying the present theory of causation. There is, however, no doubt that when, as in the laboratory, we have a high degree of control over the environment, and good opportunity to observe what occurs in it at a given moment, we do make the assumption just stated.

2. The second of the difficulties which we have to examine is of a logical rather than of a practical nature. It arises from the fact that in the face of the definition of cause given, we cannot without a contradiction refuse to take into the cause *any part* of the total change observed in the contiguous space–time environment of the effect; while, on the contrary, we very frequently in fact seem so to use the word 'cause' as to do just that. Thus, at the instant a brick strikes a window pane, the pane is struck, perhaps by the air waves due to the song of a canary near by. Yet we usually would say that the cause of the breakage was the impact of the brick, and that the impact of the air waves, although it was part of the prior total change in the contiguous space–time, was no part of the cause. This being the way in which the word 'cause' actually is used, how, then, can a definition which forbids us to call the cause anything less than *the whole* of the prior change in the contiguous space–time be regarded as a correct analysis of the meaning which the term 'cause' actually possesses?

The contradiction, however, is only apparent, and depends upon a confusion between two different questions, due in turn to a certain ambiguity in the expression 'the cause of an event'. The first of the two questions is, *what did cause,* i.e. *what did then and there suffice to, the occurrence of that concrete individual event?* The second question, on the other hand, is really a double question, for it assumes the answer to the first as already possessed, and goes on to ask, *which part of what did suffice would be left if*

---

[16] This difficulty becomes particularly acute when the opportunity for observation is limited, as, e.g. in establishing one's identity over the telephone; or, again, in the endeavour of psychical researchers to check up the alleged identity of the 'controls' of their mediums.

*we subtracted from what did suffice such portions of it as were unnecessary
to such an effect?* This is a perfectly significant question, for to say 'sufficient to' is one thing; and to say 'no more than sufficient to' is another thing:
a hundred-pound rock may well have been that which sufficed to the
crushing of a worm, but it cannot be said to have been no more than what
would have sufficed, since the tenth part of it would also have been enough.
The second and double question, moreover, is usually that which we mean
to ask when we inquire concerning the cause of an event; but, as will appear
directly, it is not, like the first, really an inquiry after the cause of one
individual concrete event strictly as such. It is, on the contrary, an inquiry
concerning *what is common to it and to the causes of certain other events
of the same kind.* This much of a generalization, indeed, is indissolubly
involved in the mere assigning of *a name* to the cause and to the effect
perceived; although *it is not involved in the merely perceiving them.* This is
an extremely important point, which constitutes the very key to the whole
matter. That this is so will become fully evident if the significance of the
second of the two questions above is more explicitly analysed.

If we inquire what exactly is required to define the meaning of that
(double) question, we find that at least *two* hypothetical cases are needed.
For to say that in a given case a certain change *sufficed* to the occurrence
of a given event, means, as we have seen, that no other change than it did
occur in the prior contiguous space–time; and to say that a certain portion
of that change was *unnecessary* means that in a case where that portion of
the change did *not* occur—*which case therefore cannot be the very identical
case, but only a case that is otherwise similar*—an(other) event of the same
sort as the effect considered nevertheless did result. But now the fact that
at least two hypothetical cases are thus necessary to define the meaning of
our second question above implies that that question is wholly meaningless
with regard to one single concrete event. It is a question not, like the first,
concerning the cause of one single concrete event, but concerning what was,
or would be, *common to the causes* of at least two such.

The apparent contradiction which we faced is therefore now disposed of,
for if, by 'the cause of an event', we really mean the cause of one individual
concrete event, and not merely of some case of a sort of event, then we must
include in our answer *the whole* of the antecedent change in the contiguous
space–time. And if, on the other hand, our answer leaves out any part of
that change (as it often does), then the only question to which it can be a
correct answer is one as to *what was common to the individual causes* of two
or more individual events of a given sort. Thus, if we say that the impact
of a brick was the cause of the breaking of the window, and that the song
of the canary had no part in it, then the words 'the breaking of the window'

do not refer to an individual event considered in its full concreteness, but only to a *case-of-a-kind*, uniquely placed and dated indeed, but not qualitatively specified otherwise than by the characters that define its kind, viz. 'breaking of window'. And it is solely owing to this that we can truly say that the song of the canary had nothing to do with it, for that means, then, nothing to do with what occurred *in so far as what occurred is viewed merely as a case of breakage of a window*. As already explained, to say that the song of the canary was unnecessary is not to say that it was not part of what did then and there suffice; it *is* to say only that in *another* case, otherwise similar, where the song did not occur, an effect of the *same sort*, viz. breaking, nevertheless did occur.

The whole of our answer to the objection we have been discussing may, after all this detail, be summarized by saying that the expression 'the cause of the breaking of this window' has two senses, one strict, and the other elliptical. In the strict sense, it means 'the fully concrete individual event which caused all the concrete detail of this breaking of this window'. In the elliptical (and indeed more practically interesting) sense, it means 'that which the cause of this breaking of this window has in common with the individual causes of certain other individual events of the same sort'.

6. THE GENERALIZATION OF OBSERVED CAUSAL FACTS

It is, of course, to be acknowledged that, as the parenthesis in the last sentence suggests, we are interested in causes and effects primarily for practical purposes, and that for such purposes causal knowledge is of direct value only so far as it has been generalized. This means that the interest of strictly concrete individual facts of causation to us is chiefly the indirect one of constituting raw material for generalization. And this explains why we so naturally and so persistently confuse the question, what did cause one given concrete event, with the very different question, in what respects does that cause resemble the causes of certain other events of the same sort previously observed in similar environments. For it is from the answer to this second question that we learn what in such environments is the most we must do to cause the occurrence of another event of the given sort. And evidently just that is the very practically valuable information that we desire ultimately to obtain. But although it is true that, as practical beings, we are not directly interested in concrete individual facts of causation, it is not true that there are no such facts; nor, as we have seen, is it true that generality or recurrence is any part of the meaning of cause.

To round out the outline of the theory of the causal relation which this paper sets forth, there remains only to state the two postulates which condition, respectively, the validity of the descriptions by names which we formulate to fit sets of individual causal facts, and the validity of the applications we make of such generalizing descriptions to new cases.

The postulate which conditions the correctness of any answer we venture to give to the problem of description, viz. the problem in what respects the cause of a given concrete event resembles the causes of certain others of the same sort previously observed in similar environments, [17] is that *the respects of resemblance which we include in our answer* (through the name by which we describe the cause) *are really the only ones that there were*. This postulate, which may be called that of the *descriptibility* of our causal observations, is then the second postulate of our theory. The first, which it will be recalled was that no change that was not observed occurred in the prior contiguous space–time environment, may be called that of the *observability* of causal facts. And the third postulate, which we may term that of the *applicability* of our descriptions of our observations of causal facts to new cases, is that *the new case (or cases) differs from those on the basis of which the description was formulated not otherwise nor more widely than they differed among themselves*.

---

[17] Mill correctly states that 'It is inherent in a description to be the statement of a resemblance, or resemblances,' *Logic*, p. 452.

IX

COUNTERFACTUALS

W. S. SELLARS

1. In his important paper on counterfactual conditionals,[1] Nelson Goodman interprets his problem as that of 'defining the circumstances under which a given counterfactual holds while the opposing counterfactual with the contradictory consequent fails to hold'.[2] As examples of such opposing counterfactuals, he gives 'If that piece of butter had been heated to 150° F, it would have melted,' and 'If that piece of butter had been heated to 150° F, it would not have melted.'

2. After a quick survey of some varieties of counterfactual and related statements, he finds that 'a counterfactual is true if a certain connection obtains between the antecedent and the consequent',[3] and turns to the task of explaining this connection. He points out, to begin with, that 'the consequent [of a counterfactual] seldom follows from the antecedent by logic alone'.[4] and never in the case of the empirical counterfactuals with which he is primarily concerned. Nor, in the case of the latter, does the consequent follow from the antecedent alone by virtue of a law of nature. For 'the assertion that a connection holds is made on the presumption that certain circumstances not stated in the antecedent obtain'.

When we say

If that match had been scratched, it would have lighted, we mean that the conditions are such—i.e. the match is well made, is dry enough, oxygen enough is present, etc.—that 'That match lights' can be inferred from 'That match is scratched.' Thus the connection we affirm may be regarded as joining the consequent with the conjunction of the antecedent and other statements that truly describe the relevant conditions. Notice especially that our assertion of the

From 'Counterfactuals, Dispositions and the Causal Modalities', *Minnesota Studies in the Philosophy of Science*, ed. Feigl, Scriven, and Maxwell (Minneapolis: University of Minnesota Press, 1958), vol. 2, pp. 227–48. © 1958 University of Minnesota. Reprinted by permission of the publishers.

[1] Nelson Goodman, 'The Problem of Counterfactual Conditionals', *Journal of Philosophy*, 44 (1947), 113–28; reprinted in his book, *Fact, Fiction and Forecast* (Cambridge, Mass., 1955), pp. 13–34. Page references in the following are to *Fact, Fiction and Forecast*.

[2] p. 14.   [3] p. 16.   [4] p. 16.

counterfactual is *not* conditioned upon these circumstances obtaining. We do not assert that the counterfactual is true if the circumstances obtain; rather, in asserting the counterfactual we commit ourselves to the actual truth of the statements describing the requisite relevant conditions (p. 17).

'There are', he concludes, 'two major problems, though they are not independent and may even be regarded as aspects of a single problem ... The first ... is to define relevant conditions: to specify what sentences are meant to be taken in conjunction with the antecedent as a basis for inferring the consequent.'[5] The second is to define what is meant by a law of nature.

For

even after the particular relevant conditions are specified, the connection obtaining will not ordinarily be a logical one. The principle that permits inference of
> That match lights

from
> That match is scratched. That match is dry enough.
> Enough oxygen is present. Etc.

is not a law of logic but what we call a natural or physical or causal law (p. 17).

3. Goodman first takes up the problem of relevant conditions. He has implied, in the passages just quoted, that whenever we assert a counterfactual, we have in mind a *specific* set of relevant conditions, those conditions, indeed, which the relevant law of nature requires to obtain in order that we may infer 'That match lights' from 'That match is scratched.' Instead, however, of focusing attention on these *specific* conditions, and exploring their bearing on the truth or falsity of the counterfactual, Goodman begins from scratch. Thus he writes,

It might seem natural to propose that the consequent follows by law from the antecedent and a description of the actual state-of-affairs of the world, that we need hardly define relevant conditions because it will do no harm to include irrelevant ones (pp. 17–18),

points out that

if we say that the statement follows by law from the antecedent and *all* true statements, we encounter an immediate difficulty: among true sentences is the negate of the antecedent, so that from the antecedent and all true sentences everything follows. Certainly this gives us no way of distinguishing true from false counterfactuals (p. 18),

and embarks on the task of so narrowing the class of true auxiliary sentences that we can account for this difference. A compact but lucid argument, in which he introduces a series of restrictions on the membership of this class, leads him to the following tentative rule:

[5] Ibid., pp. 16–17.

... a counterfactual is true if and only if there is some set S of true sentences such that S is compatible with C [the consequent of the counterfactual in question] and with $\sim C$ [the contradictory consequent], and such that $A \cdot S$ is self-compatible [A being the antecedent] and leads by law to C; while there is no set S' compatible with C and with $\sim C$, and such that $A \cdot S'$ is self-compatible and leads by law to $\sim C$ (p. 21).

4. It is at this point that Goodman explodes his bomb.

The requirement that $A \cdot S$ be self-compatible is not strong enough; for S might comprise true sentences that although *compatible with A*, were such that *they would not be true if A were true*. For this reason, many statements that we would regard as definitely false would be true according to the stated criterion. As an example, consider the familiar case where for a given match M, we would affirm

(i) If match M had been scratched, it would have lighted,

but deny

(ii) If match M had been scratched, it would not have been dry. According to our tentative criterion, statement (ii) would be quite as true as statement (i). For in the case of (ii), we may take as an element in our S the true sentence

Match M did not light,

which is presumably compatible with A (otherwise nothing could be required along with A to reach the opposite as the consequent of the true counterfactual statement (i)). As our total $A \cdot S$ we may have

Match M is scratched. It does not light. It is well made.

Oxygen enough is present . . . etc.;

and from this, by means of a legitimate general law, we can infer

It was not dry.

And there would seem to be no suitable set of sentences S' such that $A \cdot S'$ leads by law to the negate of this consequent. Hence the unwanted counterfactual is established in accord with our rule.

'The trouble,' Goodman continues, without pausing for breath, 'is caused by including in our S a true statement which although compatible with A would not be true if A were. Accordingly we must exclude such statements from the set of relevant conditions; S, in addition to satisfying the other requirements already laid down, must be not merely compatible with A but 'jointly tenable' or *cotenable* with A. A is cotenable with S, and the conjunction $A \cdot S$ self-cotenable, if it is not the case that S would not be true if A were' (pp. 21–2).

5. This new requirement, however, instead of saving the rule leads it to immediate shipwreck.

... in order to determine whether or not a given S is cotenable with A, we have to determine whether or not the counterfactual 'If A were true, then S would not be true' is itself true. But this means determining whether or not there is a suitable S_1, cotenable with A, that leads to $\sim S$ and so on. Thus we find ourselves involved in an infinite regressus or a circle; for cotenability is defined in terms of counterfactuals, yet the meaning of counterfactuals is defined in terms of cotenability.

In other words, to establish any counterfactual, it seems that we first have to determine the truth of another. If so, we can never explain a counterfactual except in terms of others, so that the problem of counterfactuals must remain unsolved (p. 23).

As of 1947, Goodman, 'though unwilling to accept this conclusion, [did] not . . . see any way of meeting the difficulty.'[6] That he still regards this difficulty as genuine, and the line of thought of which it is the culmination philosophically sound, is indicated by the fact that he has made 'The Problem of Counterfactual Conditionals' the starting point of his recent re-examination[7] of the same nexus of problems. Indeed, Goodman explicitly tells us that the four chapters of which this new study consists, and of which the first is a reprinting of the 1947 paper, 'represents a consecutive effort of thought on a closely integrated group of problems',[8] and that this first chapter contains 'an essentially unaltered description of the state of affairs from which the London lectures took their departure'.[9]

6. It is my purpose in the opening sections of this essay, devoted as it is to fundamentally the same group of problems, to show that Goodman's puzzle about cotenability arises from a failure to appreciate the force of the verbal form of counterfactuals in actual discourse, and of the general statements by which we support them; and that this failure stems, as in so many other cases, from too hasty an assimilation of a problematic feature of ordinary discourse to formalism by reference to which we have succeeded in illuminating certain other features.

7. Let me begin by asking whether it is indeed true that in 'the familiar case where for a given match M, we would affirm

(i) If match M had been scratched, it would have lighted' we *would* 'deny

(ii) If match M had been scratched, it would not have been dry.'

Goodman himself points out in a note that 'Of course, some sentences similar to (ii), referring to other matches under special conditions may be true.'[10] Perhaps he has something like the following case in mind:

Tom: If M had been scratched, it would have been wet.
Dick: Why?
Tom: Well, Harry is over there, and he has a phobia about matches. If he sees anyone scratch a match, he puts it in water.

[6] Ibid., p. 23.
[7] *Fact, Fiction and Forecast.* This book, of which the first part is a reprinting of the 1947 paper, contains the University of London Special Lectures in Philosophy for 1953.
[8] Op. cit., p. 7.
[9] Ibid., p. 9.
[10] Ibid., p. 33 (note 7 to p. 21).

But just *how* is Goodman's 'familiar case' different from that of the above dialogue? Why are we so confident that (ii) is false whereas (i) is true? Part of the answer, at least, is that we are taking for granted in our reflections that the only features of the case which are relevant to the truth or falsity of (ii) are such things as that the match was dry, that it was not scratched, that it was well made, that sufficient oxygen was present, that it did not light, 'etc.'[11] and that the generalization to which appeal would properly be made in support of (ii) concerns only such things as being dry, being scratched, being well made, sufficient oxygen being present, lighting, etc. For as soon as we modify the case by supposing Tom to enter and tell us (a) that if *M* had been scratched, Harry would have found it out, and (b) that if Harry finds out that a match has been scratched, he puts it in water, the feeling that (ii) is obviously false disappears.

8. In asking us to consider this 'familiar case', then, Goodman, whether he realizes it or not, is asking us to imagine ourselves in a situation in which we are to choose between (i) and (ii) knowing (a) that only the above limited set of considerations are relevant; and (b) that scratching dry, well-made matches in the presence of oxygen, etc. causes them to light. It is, I take it, clear that if we did find ourselves in such a situation, we would indeed accept (i) and reject (ii).

To call attention to all this, however, is not yet to criticize Goodman's argument, though it does give us a better understanding of what is going on. Indeed, it might seem that since we have just admitted that once we are clear about the nature of the case on which we are being asked to reflect, we would, in the imagined circumstances, accept (i) but reject (ii), we are committed to agree with Goodman that the criterion under examination is at fault. For according to it would not (ii) be true?

9. It is not my purpose to defend Goodman's tentative criterion against his criticisms. There are a number of reasons why it won't do as it stands, as will become apparent as we explore the force of counterfactuals in their native habitat. I will, however, in a sense, be defending it against the specific objection raised by Goodman. For it is because he *misinterprets* the fact that we would accept (i) but reject (ii) that he is led to the idea that the criterion must be enriched with a disastrous requirement of cotenability. And once this fact is properly interpreted, it will become clear that while there is *something* to Goodman's idea that a sound criterion must

---

[11] Goodman's 'etc.' should not mislead us. Its scope, though vague, is limited by the context, and does not include, positively or negatively, every *possible* circumstance, e.g. the presence of a pyrophobe.

include a requirement of cotenability, this requirement turns out to be quite harmless, to be quite free of regress or paradox.

10. But is it, on second thought, so obvious that even if we *were* in the circumstances described above, we would reject (ii)? After all, knowing that M didn't light, but was well made, that sufficient oxygen was present, etc. and knowing that M wasn't scratched but was dry, would we not be entitled to say,

> (iii) If it had been true that M was scratched, it would also have been true that M was not dry?

The fact that this looks as though it *might* be a long-winded version of (ii) gives us pause.

If, however, we are willing to consider the possibility that (ii) is after all true, the reasoning by which Goodman seeks to establish that if the tentative criterion were sound, (ii) as used in our 'familiar case' would be true, becomes of greater interest. The core of this reasoning is the following sentence:

As our total $A \cdot S$ we may have
   Match M is scratched. It does not light. It is well made.
   Oxygen enough is present . . . etc.
and from this, by means of a legitimate general law, we can infer
   It was not dry (pp. 21–2).

But although Goodman assures us that there is a 'legitimate general law' which permits this inference, he does not take time to formulate it, and once we notice this, we also notice that he has nowhere taken time to formulate the 'legitimate general law' which authorizes (i). The closest he comes to doing this is in the introductory section of the paper, where he writes:

When we say
   If that match had been scratched, it would have lighted
we mean that the conditions are such—i.e., the match is well made, is dry enough, oxygen enough is present, etc.—that 'That match lights' can be inferred from 'That match is scratched.' (p. 17).

11. Now the idea behind the above sentence seems to be that the relevant law pertaining to matches has the form

$(x)(t)$ x is a match $\cdot x$ is dry at $t \cdot x$ is scratched at $t \cdot implies \cdot x$ lights at t

(where to simplify our formulations, the conditions under which matches light when scratched have been boiled down to being dry.) And it must indeed be admitted that if this were the 'legitimate general law' which authorizes

If M had been scratched, it would have lighted

given 'M was dry' and 'M was not scratched', there would be reason to expect the *equivalent* 'legitimate general law'

$(x)(t)$ x is a match $\cdot$ x does not light at t $\cdot$ x is scratched at t $\cdot$ *implies* $\cdot$ x is not dry at t

to authorize

If M had been scratched, it would not have been dry

given 'M did not light' and 'M was not scratched'.

Or, to make the same point from a slightly different direction, if we were to persuade ourselves that the laws which stand behind true counterfactuals of the form

If x had been . . . it would have . . .

are of the form

$$(x)(t)A(x,t) \cdot B(x,t) \supset C(x,t),$$

we would, in all consistency, expect the equivalent laws

$$(x)(t)A(x,t) \cdot {\sim}C(x,t) \supset {\sim}B(x,t)$$
$$(x)(t)B(x,t) \cdot {\sim}C(x,t) \supset {\sim}A(x,t)$$

to authorize counterfactuals of the same form. And if we were to persuade ourselves that

[Given that M was dry, then, although M was not scratched,] if M had been scratched, it would have lighted

has the form

[Given that x was A at t, then, although x was not B at t,] if x had been B at t, x would have been C at t

we would expect the equivalent general laws to authorize such counterfactuals as

[Given that M did not light, then, although M was not scratched,] if M had been scratched, it would not have been dry

and

[Given that M did not light, then, although M was not dry,] if M had been dry, it would not have been scratched.

12. But as soon as we take a good look at these counterfactuals, we see that something is wrong. For in spite of the fact that 'M was not dry' can be inferred from 'M was scratched' together with 'M did not light,' we most certainly would not agree that—given 'M did not light' and 'M was not scratched'—

If M had been scratched, it would not have been dry.

What is wrong? One line of thought, the line which leads to cotenability, takes Goodman's 'familiar case' as its paradigm and, after pointing out that we are clearly entitled to say

(1) [Since M was dry,] if M had been scratched, it would have lighted

but not

(2) [Since M did not light,] if M had been scratched, it would not be dry,

continues somewhat as follows:

(1) is true.
(2) is false.
According to (1) M would have lighted if it had been scratched.
But (2) presupposes that M did not light.
Thus (1) being true, a presupposition of (2) would not have been true if M had been scratched.
So, (1) being true, a presupposition of (2) would not have been true if its 'antecedent' had been true.
Consequently, (1) being true, the truth of (2) is incompatible with the truth of its 'antecedent'—surely a terrible thing to say about any conditional, even a counterfactual one . . .

and concludes, (A) that the falsity of (2) follows from the truth of (1); (B) in knowing that (1) itself is true we must be knowing that there is no true counterfactual according to which a presupposition of (1) would not have been true if *its* [the new counterfactual's] antecedent had been true; and, in general (C) that in order to know whether any counterfactual, Γ, is true we need to know that there is no true counterfactual Γ', which specifies that the S required by Γ' would not have been the case if Γ's antecedent had been true. In Goodman's words, '. . . in order to determine whether or not a given S is cotenable with A, we have to determine whether or not the counterfactual "If A were true, then S would not be true" is itself true.

But this means determining whether or not there is a suitable S_1, cotenable with A, that leads to $\sim S$ and so on. Thus we find ourselves involved in a regressus or a circle . . .'

13. Now there are, to say the least, some highly dubious steps in the reasoning delineated above. I do not, however, propose to examine it, but rather to undercut it by correctly locating the elements of truth it contains. That there is *something* to the above reasoning is clear. The truth of (1) *does* seem to be incompatible with the truth of (2); and the falsity of (2) *does* seem to rest on the fact that if M had been scratched, it would have lighted.

Perhaps the best way of separating out the sound core of the above reasoning is to note what happens if, instead of exploring the logical relationship between the two counterfactuals (1) and (2), we turn our attention instead to corresponding subjunctive conditionals not contrary to fact in a new 'familiar case' which differs from Goodman's in that these subjunctive conditionals rather than counterfactuals are appropriate. Specifically, I want to consider the 'mixed' subjunctive conditionals,

(1') *If M is dry*, then if M were scratched, it would light,

and

(2') *If M does not light*, then if M were scratched, it would not be dry.

Is it not clear as in Goodman's case that (1') is true but (2') false? Indeed, that the falsity of (2') is a consequence of the truth of (1')? Here, however, there is no temptation to say that (2') is false for the reason that in order for it to be true a state of affairs would have to obtain which would not obtain if M were scratched. For (2'), unlike (2) does not require as a necessary condition of its truth that M does not light.

14. How, then, is the incompatibility of (2') with (1') to be understood? The answer is really very simple, and to get it, it is only necessary to ask 'Why would we reject (2')?' For to this question the answer is simply that it is just not the case that by scratching dry matches we *cause* them, provided they do not light, to become wet. And how do we know this? Part of the answer, of course, is the absence of favourable evidence for this generalization; not to say the existence of substantial evidence against it. But more directly relevant to our *philosophical* puzzle is the fact that in our 'familiar case' we are granted to know that scratching dry matches causes them to light. And if this generalization is true—and it must be remembered that we are using 'x is dry' to stand for 'x is dry and x is well made, and sufficient oxygen is present, etc.'—then the other generalization *can't*

be true. The two generalizations are, in a very simple sense, incompatible. For if scratching dry matches causes them to light, then the expression 'scratching dry matches *which do not light*' describes a kind of situation which cannot (physically) obtain. And we begin to suspect that Goodman's requirement of cotenability mislocates the sound idea that (to use a notation which, whatever its shortcomings in other respects, is adequate for the purpose of making *this* point) if it is a law that

$$(x)Ax \cdot Sx \cdot \supset \cdot Cx$$

then it can't—*logically* can't—be a law that

$$(x)Ax \supset \sim Sx.$$

15. But we have not yet pinpointed Goodman's mistake. To do so we must take a closer look at our reasons for rejecting (2′). We said above that we would reject it simply because it is not the case that by scratching dry matches we cause them to become wet. Perhaps the best way of beginning our finer-grained analysis is by making a point about our two subjunctive conditions (1′) and (2′) which parallels a point which was made earlier about counterfactuals (1) and (2).

Suppose that the 'legitimate general law' which authorizes (1′) had the form

$$(x)(t)A(x,t) \cdot S(x,t) \cdot \supset \cdot C(x,t);$$

would not (2′) be authorized by

$$(x)(t)A(x,t) \cdot \sim C(x,t) \cdot \supset \cdot \sim S(x,t)?$$

and hence—in view of the logical equivalence of these two general implications—be true if (1′) is true? Clearly we must do some thinking about the form of the 'legitimate general laws' which authorize subjunctive conditionals of the form

if *x* were . . . it would . . .

and which stand behind contrary-to-fact conditionals of the form

if *x* had been . . . it would have . . .

This thinking will consist, essentially, in paying strict attention to the characteristics of subjunctive conditionals, counterfactuals, and lawlike statements in their native habitat, rather than to their supposed counterparts in *PM*ese.

16. We pointed out above that if we were asked why we would reject (2′) in the context in which it arose, we would say that it is not the case that scratching dry matches causes them to become wet, if they don't light. We now note that if (1′) were challenged we would support it by saying that scratching dry matches does cause them to light, or that matches light when scratched, provided they are dry, or, perhaps, that if a dry match is scratched it will light, or something of the sort. Is it proper to represent these statements by the form

$$(x)(t)F(x,t) \cdot G(x,t) \cdot \supset \cdot H(x,t)?$$

If we leave aside for the moment the fact that there is something odd about the expression 'x is a match at t,' and focus our attention on the other concepts involved, it does not take much logical imagination to see that while 'there is no law against' representing 'x is scratched at t' by '$Sc(x,t)$', 'x is dry at t' by '$D(x,t)$', and 'x lights at t' by '$L(x,t)$', to do so is to obscure rather than make manifest the logical form of 'If a dry match is scratched, it lights.' For it is by no means irrelevant to the logic of this generalization that matches *begin to burn* when they are scratched. And it is a familiar fact that

As B when Ded—provided the circumstances, C, are propitious,

concerns something *new* that A's *begin to do* when *changed* in a certain respect in certain *standing conditions*—which need not, of course, be 'standing still.'

17. I do not, by any means, wish to suggest that all empirical generalizations are of the above form. Clearly,

Eggs stay fresh longer if they are not washed,

which authorizes the counterfactual

If this egg had not been washed, it would have stayed fresh longer,

is not of this form. But our problem, after all, is that of understanding just why it is clear that—in Goodman's 'familiar case'—we would affirm

(i) If M had been scratched, it would have lighted

but reject

(ii) If M had been scratched, it would not have been dry,

and to do this we must get the hang of generalizations of the former kind.

18. Now, *being dry* is obviously not the same thing as *becoming dry*, nor *beginning to burn* as *burning*, and though we can imagine that someone might say 'matches *burn* when scratched,' this would, strictly speaking, be either incorrect or false—incorrect if it was intended to express the familiar truth about matches; false if it was intended to express the idea that matches *burn* when they are *being scratched* as iron rusts while exposed to moisture. (Having made this point, I can now rephrase it by saying that if it were correct to use 'matches burn when scratched' in the former sense, this would simply mean that 'burn' has an *idiomatic* use in which it is equivalent to 'begin to burn'.)

With this in mind, let us examine the apodosis of Goodman's (ii), namely, '. . . it (*M*) would not have been dry'. If we suppose that this is intended to have the force of 'would have *become* wet', we can, indeed, assimilate

If *M* had been scratched, it would not have been dry

to the form

If *x* had been *D*ed, it would have *B*ed

of which (i) is such a straightforward example. For *becoming wet* would seem to be a legitimate example of *B-ing*.

But while there are true generalizations to the effect that doing certain things to matches in certain favourable circumstances causes them to become wet, none of them seem to involve scratching. Again, a match which *becomes wet* must have *been dry*, and approaching Goodman's 'familiar case'—as we do—in the knowledge that scratching dry (etc.) matches cause them to light, we cannot consistently say both

[Since *M* was dry, etc.,] if *M* had been scratched, it would have lighted

and

[Since *M* was dry, etc.,] if *M* had been scratched, it would have become wet

unless we suppose that the circumstances in which scratching dry matches causes them to become wet (the 'etc.' of the second 'since-' clause) differs in at least one respect from the circumstances in which scratching dry matches causes them to light (the 'etc.' of the first 'since-' clause). And it is clearly no help—in the absence of this supposition—to add to the second counterfactual the proviso, 'provided *M* does not light'; for this proviso, given the truth of the first counterfactual, is physically inconsistent with the conjunction of the antecedent of the second counterfactual with the 'since-' clause on which it rests.

19. If, therefore, we interpret '. . . it (*M*) would not have been dry' as '. . . it (*M*) would have become wet,' we run up against the fact that a generalization is implied which is not only patently false, but *inconsistent*— given the stipulations of the case—with one which we know to be true. And this is, as we have already noted, the sound core of Goodman's cotenability requirement. Two counterfactuals cannot both be true if they imply logically inconsistent generalizations. If one counterfactual is true, no counterfactual which involves an antecedent-cum-circumstances which is specified to be physically self-incompatible by the generalization implied by the first counterfactual can *also* be true. On the other hand, cotenability *thus understood* leads to no 'infinite regressus or . . . circle', for while one has not confirmed a generalization *unless* one has *disconfirmed* logically incompatible generalizations, this does not mean that *before* establishing one thing one must *first* establish something else, *and so on*. For the process of confirming a generalization *is* the process of disconfirming logically incompatible generalizations.

20. Suppose, however—as is indeed obvious—that we are not to interpret '. . . would not have been dry' as '. . . would have become wet'; does another interpretation of (ii) lie within groping distance? The answer is Yes—but, as before, on condition that we are prepared to make certain changes in its wording. Let us begin this groping with an examination of— not (ii) but—the closely related counterfactual,

If *M* had been scratched without lighting, then it . . .

then it *what*? Should we say '. . . *would* not have been dry'? or '. . . *could* not have been dry'? Clearly the latter. The difference, in this context, between 'w' and 'c' is all important. It is the difference between

(A) Matches *will not* be (stay) dry, if they are scratched without lighting

and

(B) Matches *cannot* be dry, if they do not light when scratched.

(A) introduces, as we have seen, a new generalization into our 'familiar case'—one which is inconsistent with

(C) Matches *will* light when scratched, provided they are dry,

which is the generalization implied by (i). (B), on the other hand, far from being inconsistent with (C) would seem to be just another version of it.

And it is clear, on reflection, that (C) is the only 'will-' statement which expresses the fact that scratching dry matches causes them to light. Thus, we can say that

A dry match will light when scratched

but not

A match which does not light when scratched *will* not be dry.

To be sure, we *can* say—with a little license—

A match which does not light when scratched *will be found* not to be dry

so that the above claim is not *quite* true. But the point being made is clear enough, and, in any case, we shall be examining the 'exception' in a moment.

21. We begin, therefore, to suspect that corresponding to generalizations of the form

*B*ing *A*s causes them to *D*—provided *C*

there is only one correctly formed counterfactual of the form 'If *x* had been *Y*ed it would have . . .' namely

[Since *C*,] if *this* had been *B*ed, it would have *D*ed

which is not to say that each such generalization might not authorize a number of counterfactuals having a *different* form. Beating about the bushes for other asymmetries pertaining to our familiar generalization about matches, we notice that while it tells us that scratching matches causes them to light, *it doesn't tell us the cause of matches not being dry*; and that while it enables us to *explain* the fact that a match lighted on a certain occasion by pointing out that it was scratched and was dry, *it doesn't enable us to explain the fact that a match was not dry by pointing out that it was scratched without lighting*.

On the other hand, the generalization does enable us to explain *how we know* that a given match was not dry. 'I know that it wasn't dry, *because* it didn't light when scratched.' '*M can't* have been dry, because it was scratched, but did not light.' '*Since M* was scratched, but did not light, it can't have been dry.' '*M* was scratched without lighting, so it wasn't dry.' All these point to the hypothetical

(*M* was scratched without lighting) *implies* (*M* was not dry),

and, indeed, to the general hypothetical

The fact that a match is scratched without lighting *implies* that it was not dry.

22. I have already pointed out how misleading it is to characterize the 'legitimate general law' which authorizes the counterfactual

If M had been scratched, it would have lighted

as a 'principle which permits the inference of

That match lights

from

That match is scratched. That match is well made. Enough oxygen is present. Etc.'[12]

For the fact that if there is a principle which authorizes the inference of S_3 from $S_1 \cdot S_2$, there will also be a principle which authorizes the inference of $\sim S_2$ from $S_1 \cdot \sim S_3$ leads one to expect that the same general fact about matches which, in Goodman's 'familiar case', supports the above counterfactual, will also support

If M had been scratched, it would not have been dry,

an expectation which is the ultimate source of the puzzlement exploited by Goodman's paper.

23. This is not to say that it is *wrong* to interpret our generalization about matches as a 'season inference ticket'. It is rather that the connection between the generalization and the counterfactual, 'If M had been scratched, it would have lighted,' rests on features of the generalization which are not captured by the concept of a season inference ticket, and which, therefore, the logical form of a general hypothetical does not illuminate. Thus, while

$(m)(t)\ m$ is scratched at $t \cdot m$ is dry at $t \cdot implies \cdot m$ lights at t[13]

does, *in a sense*, have the force of 'dry matches light if scratched,' or 'scratching dry matches causes them to light,' this mode of representation must be supplemented by a commentary along the lines of the above analysis, if its relation to 'If M had been scratched, it would have lighted' is to be understood; while if our familiar fact about matches is assimilated without further ado to the form

$(x)(t)A(x,t) \cdot B(x,t) \cdot C(x,t) \ldots \cdot \supset \cdot L(x,t)$

all chance of clarity has been lost.

[12] *Fact, Fiction and Forecast*, p. 17.
[13] I have used the so-called 'tenseless present'—a typical philosophical invention—to simplify the formulation of this general hypothetical, without, in this context, doing it too much violence.

24. We have connected the fact that scratching a match *is doing* something to it, with the fact that we expect

... if *M* had been scratched ...

to be preceded, at least tacitly, by an expression referring to *standing conditions*, thus

[Since *M* was dry,] ...

and to be followed by an expression referring to a *result*, thus

... it would have lighted.

It is important to bear in mind that the distinction between the *standing conditions*, the *doing* and the *result* is an *objective* one. It is not relative to a particular way of formulating the general fact that dry matches light when scratched. The equivalent formulas

$$(x)(t) \; D(x,t) \supset \cdot Sc(x,t) \supset L(x,t)$$
$$(x)(t) \sim L(x,t) \supset \cdot Sc(x,t) \supset \sim D(x,t)$$
$$(x)(t) \sim L(x,t) \supset \cdot D(x,t) \supset \sim Sc(x,t)$$

do *not* give us three different ways of cutting up the above fact about matches into a standing condition, a doing and a result or *consequence*; although, *in a purely logical sense*, '$\sim L(x,t)$' may be said to formulate a 'condition' under which '$(x)(t) \; Sc(x,t) \supset \sim D(x,t)$' holds, and '$Sc(x,t)$' and '$\sim D(x,t)$' respectively to be the 'antecedent' and the 'consequent' of this implication.

The fact that '$D(x,t)$' formulates a 'condition' in a sense in which '$\sim L(x,t)$' does not, is, though obvious, the key to our problem. For it is just because 'If *M* were scratched ...' and 'If *M* had been scratched ...,' are expressions for something being done to something (in a certain kind of circumstance) that we expect them to be followed, not just by a 'consequent', but by (expressions for) a *consequence*, and also expect the context to make it clear just what conditions or circumstances are being implied to obtain. There is, however, a manner of formulating this same content which does not evoke these expectations, and which *does* focus attention on specifically logical relationships. Consider, for example, the following conditions,

If it were the case that *M* was scratched without lighting, it would be the case that *M* was not dry.
If it had been the case that *M* was scratched without lighting, it would have been the case that *M* was not dry.

Clearly, to wonder what else would have to be the case, if it were the case that M was scratched without lighting, is not the same thing as to wonder what the *consequence* of striking a match would be, given that it failed to light.

Does this mean that in our familiar case, we would accept

If it had been the case that M was scratched, it would have been the case that M was not dry (or would not have been the case that M was dry)

although we reject

If M had been scratched, it would not have been dry?

The answer is *almost* Yes. We are getting 'warmer', though there is still work to be done. I shall introduce the next step by discussing examples of quite another sort.

25. Consider the following (where n is a number, perhaps the number of planets):

(1) if n were divisible by 3 and 4, it would be divisible by 12;
(2) if n were divisible by 3, then if n were divisible by 4, it would be divisible by 12;
(3) since n is divisible by 3, if n were divisible by 4, it would be divisible by 12;
(4) since n is divisible by 3, if n had been divisible by 4, it would have been divisible by 12;

and then the following (where n is, say, the number of chess pieces on a side):

(5) if n were not divisible by 12, but divisible by 3, it would not be divisible by 4;
(6) if n were not divisible by 12, then if n were divisible by 3, it would not be divisible by 4;
(7) since n is not divisible by 12, if n were divisible by 3, it would not be divisible by 4;
(8) since n is not divisible by 12, if n had been divisible by 3, it would not have been divisible by 4.

The crucial step, in each series, is from the first to the second, i.e. from (1) to (2), and from (5) to (6). (1) and (5) are clearly true. What of the others? What, to begin with, shall we say about (2)? The point is a delicate one. At first glance, it looks quite acceptable, a sound inference ticket. But would we not, perhaps, be a bit happier if it read

(2') if n were divisible by 3, then if it were *also* divisible by 4, it would be divisible by 12?

What of (3)? It calls attention to the argument,

n is divisible by 3
So, if n were divisible by 4, it would be divisible by 12.
(Call the conclusion of this argument C_1.) The principle of the argument is the complex hypothetical (2). And the question arises, How does this argument differ from one that would be authorized by (1)? Consider the argument

n is divisible by 3
So, if it were *also* divisible by 4, it would be divisible by 12.

There is clearly a sense in which the conclusion of this argument (call it C_2) is more cautious than that of the preceding argument. For C_2 carries with it a reference to, and a commitment to the truth of, its premise, which is lacking in C_1. The difference can be put by noting that while C_1, as a conclusion, may imply that one has *come to know that* 'n is divisible by 12' can be inferred from 'n is divisible by 4' *by virtue of knowing that n is divisible by 3*; it does not imply that *what* one has come to know is {that 'n is divisible by 12' can be inferred from 'n is divisible by 4' *given that n is divisible by 3*}. And by not implying this, indeed by implying that what one has come to know is that 'n is divisible by 12' can *without qualification* be inferred from 'n is divisible by 4,' it is false. To infer from p the legitimacy of the inference *from q to r*, is not the same thing at all as to infer from p the legitimacy of the inference *from q to r, given p*.

26. In the symbolism of modal logic, there is all the difference in the world between '$p \cdot q \cdot < \cdot r$' and '$p < (q < r)$' even though the corresponding formulas in the system of material implication are equivalent. The former authorizes the argument.

I. p
    So, $q \supset r$

but not, as does the latter

II. p
    So, $q < r$.

And while argument II defends the subjunctive conditional

If q were the case, r would be the case,

argument I does not. The only resembling subjunctive conditional defended by the assertion *that p*, and an appeal to '$p \cdot q \cdot < \cdot r$' is

If *q* were the case *as well as p*, *r* would be the case,

and while this latter carries with it the assertion *that p*, it does not do so in the same way as does

[Since *p* is the case,] if *q* were the case, *r* would be the case.

For this points to argument II with its stronger conclusion.

27. Turning back to our two lists of conditional statements about numbers, we can now see that the counterfactual corresponding to (1) is not (4), but rather

(4') Since *n* is divisible by 3, if it had *also* been divisible by 4, it would have been divisible by 12

On the other hand, (4) does correspond to (2). Again, (6) has the same force as (5) only if it is interpreted as

(6') If *n* were not divisible by 12, then if it were *also* the case that it *was* divisible by 3, it would not be divisible by 4.

and (5) authorizes (8) only if it is interpreted as

(8') Since *n* is not divisible by 12, if it had *also* been the case that it *was* divisible by 3, it would not have been divisible by 4.

28. It is worth noting, in this connection, that it is not only in cases like our match example, where we are dealing with particular matters of fact, that a generalization may enable us to explain *how we know* a fact, without enabling us to explain the fact itself. Thus, while

If *n* is divisible by 3 and 4, it is divisible by 12

enables us to explain the fact that a certain number is divisible by 12 ('It is divisible by 12 *because* it is divisible by 3 and by 4.'), it does not enable us to explain the fact that a certain number is not divisible by 4, though it does enable us to explain how we happen to know that the number is not divisible by 4. ('I know that it is not divisible by 4, because though it is divisible by 3, it is not divisible by 12.' 'He knows that it is not divisible by 4, because he knows that though it is divisible by 3, it is not divisible by 12.' 'It can't be divisible by 4, because, though it is divisible by 3, it is not divisible by 12.') It would simply be a mistake to say, 'It is not divisible by 4, because, though divisible by 3, it is not divisible by 12.'

One is tempted to put this by saying that just as one explains a particular matter of empirical fact by 'showing how it comes about', and not simply by subsuming it under the 'consequent' of a general hypothetical, the 'antecendent' of which it is known to satisfy, so one explains such a fact as that a certain number is divisible by 12, or not divisible by 4, not simply by subsuming it under the 'consequent' of any old mathematical truth under the 'consequent' of which it can be subsumed, but only by applying a mathematical truth which, so to speak, takes us in the direction of the 'genesis' of the property in question in the mathematical order, i.e. which starts us down (or up?) the path of what, in a neatly formalized system, would be its 'definition chain'. Certainly 'n is divisible by 12, because it is divisible by 3 and by 4' has something of this flavour, while 'n is not divisible by 4, because, though divisible by 3, it is not divisible by 12' does not. But to say anything worthwhile on this topic, one would have to say a great deal more than there is space for on this occasion.

29. Now the moral of these mathematical examples is that the counterfactual most resembling Goodman's (ii) which *is* authorized by our (simplified) generalization about matches, is, explicitly formulated,

(ii′) *Since M did not light*, if it had *also* been the case that it was scratched it would have been the case that it was not dry,

and it would be correct to boil this counterfactual down to
If it had been the case that M was scratched, it would have been the case that M was not dry

only if the context makes it clear that there is a tacit *also* in the statement, and indicates in what direction the additional presupposition is to be found.

Why, then, it may be asked, should we not conclude that (i) itself is simply a shorter version, appropriately used in certain contexts, of

(i′) Since M was dry, if it had *also* been the case that M was scratched, it would have been the case that M lighted?

(Clearly it is not a shorter version of

Since M was dry, if it had *also* been scratched . . .

for *this* would imply that something else must be *done* to the match besides scratching it, to make it light.)

The answer should, by now, be obvious. It is part of the logic of generalizations of the form

Xing Y's causes them to Z, provided . . .

that when we say

> If *this* Y had been Xed, it would have Zed,

it is understood that it is because *this* Y was in certain (in principle) specifiable circumstances that it would have Zed if it had been Xed. In other words, the fact that it is proper to say, simply

> If M had been scratched, it would have lighted

rests on the relation of the statement to the *objective* distinction between *standing conditions*, what is *done* and its *result*.

X

LAW STATEMENTS AND COUNTERFACTUAL INFERENCE

RODERICK M. CHISHOLM

THE problems I have been invited to discuss arise from the fact that there are two types of true synthetic universal statement: statements of the one type, in the context of our general knowledge, seem to warrant counterfactual inference and statements of the other type do not. I shall call statements of the first type 'law statements' and statements of the second type 'non-law statements'. Both law and non-law statements may be expressed in the general form, 'For every x, if x is S, x is P.' Law statements, unlike non-law statements, seem to warrant inference to statements of the form, 'If a, which is not S, were S, a would be P' and 'For every x, if x were S, x would be P.' I shall discuss (I) this distinction between law and non-law statements and (II) the related problem of interpreting counterfactual statements.[1]

I

Let us consider the following as examples of law statements:

L1. Everyone who drinks from this bottle is poisoned.

L2. All gold is malleable.

And let us consider the following as examples of non-law statements:

N1. Everyone who drinks from——bottle wears a necktie.

N2. Every Canadian parent of quintuplets in the first half of the twentieth century is named 'Dionne'.

From *Analysis*, 15 (1955), 97–105, reprinted by permission of Basil Blackwell Publishers.

[1] Detailed formulations of this problem are to be found in the following works: W. E. Johnson, *Logic*, Vol. III, chapter I; C. H. Langford, review of W. B. Gallie's 'An Interpretation of Causal Laws', *Journal of Symbolic Logic*, vi (1941), 67; C. I. Lewis, *An Analysis of Knowledge and Valuation*, Part II; Roderick M. Chisholm, 'The Contrary-to-fact Conditional', *Mind*, 55 (1946), 289–307 (reprinted in H. Feigl and W. S. Sellars, *Readings in Philosophical Analysis*); Nelson Goodman, 'The Problem of Counterfactual Conditionals', *Journal of Philosophy*, 44 (1947), 113–28 (reprinted in L. Linsky, *Semantics and the Philosophy of Language*); F. L. Will, 'The Contrary-to-fact Conditional', *Mind*, 56 (1947), 236–49; and William Kneale, 'Natural Laws and Contrary to Fact Conditionals', *Analysis*, 10 (1950), 121–5. See further references below and in Erna Schneider, 'Recent Discussion of Subjunctive Conditionals', *Review of Metaphysics*, vi (1953), 623–47. My paper, referred to above, contains some serious errors.

Let us suppose that L1 and N1 are concerned with the same bottle (perhaps it is one of short duration and has contained only arsenic). Let us suppose, further, that the blank in N1 is replaced by property terms which happen to characterize the bottle uniquely (perhaps they describe patterns of finger-prints). I shall discuss certain philosophical questions which arise when we make the following 'pre-analytic' assumptions. From L1 we can infer.

L1.1 If Jones had drunk from this bottle, he would have been poisoned.

and from L2 we can infer

L2.1 If that metal were gold, it would be malleable.

But from N1 we cannot infer

N1.1 If Jones had drunk from——bottle, he would have worn a necktie.

and from N2 we cannot infer

    N2.1 If Jones, who is Canadian, had been parent of quintuplets during the first half of the twentieth century, he would have been named 'Dionne'.

I shall not defend these assumptions beyond noting that, in respects to be discussed, they correspond to assumptions which practically everyone does make.

There are two preliminary points to be made concerning the interpretation of counterfactual statements. (1) We are concerned with those counter-factuals whose antecedents, 'if a were S', may be interpreted as meaning the same as 'if a had property S'. There is, however, another possible interpretation: 'if a were S' could be interpreted as meaning the same as 'if a were identical with something which in fact does have property S'.[2] Given the above assumptions, N2.1 is false according to the first interpretation, which is the interpretation with which we are concerned, but it is true according to the second (for if Jones were identical with one of the Dionnes, he would be named 'Dionne'). On the other hand, the statement

    N2.2 If Jones, who is Canadian, had been parent of quintuplets during the first half of the twentieth century, there would have been at least two sets of Canadian quintuplets

is true according to the first interpretation and false according to the second. (2) It should be noted, secondly, that there is a respect—to be discussed at greater length below—in which our counterfactual statements may be thought of as being elliptical. If we assert L1.1, we might, nevertheless, accept the following qualification: 'Of course, if Jones had emptied the bottle, cleaned it out, filled it with water, and *then* drunk from it, he might not have been poisoned.' And, with respect to L2.1, we might accept this qualification: 'If that metal were gold it would be malleable—provided,

---

[2] Compare K. R. Popper, 'A Note on Natural Laws and so-called "Contrary-to-fact Conditionals" ', *Mind*, 58 (1949), 62–6.

of course, that what we are supposing to be contrary-to-fact is that statement "That metal is not gold" and *not* the statement "All gold is malleable." '

Can the relevant difference between law and non-law statements be
described in familiar terminology without reference to counterfactuals,
without use of modal terms such as 'causal necessity', 'necessary condition',
'physical possibility', and the like, and without use of metaphysical terms
such as 'real connections between matters of fact'? I believe no one has
shown that the relevant difference *can* be so described. I shall mention
three recent discussions.

(1) It has been suggested that the distinction between law statements and
non-law statements may be made with respect to the universality of the
non-logical terms which appear in the statements. A term may be thought
of as being universal, it has been suggested, if its meaning can be con-
veyed without explicit reference to any particular object; it is then said
that law statements, unlike non-law statements, contain no non-logical
terms which are not universal.[3] (These points can be formulated more
precisely.) This suggestion does not help, however, if applied to what we
have been calling 'law statements' and 'non-law statements', for L1 is a
law statement containing the *non*-universal non-logical term 'this bottle'
and N1 (we have supposed) is a non-law statement all of whose non-logical
terms *are* universal. It may be that, with respect to ordinary usage, it is
incorrect to call L1 a 'law statement'; this point does not affect our problem,
however, since we are assuming that L1, whether or not it would ordinarily
be called a 'law statement', does, in the context of our general knowledge,
warrant the inference to L1.1.

(2) It has been suggested that the two types of statement might be
distinguished epistemologically. P. F. Strawson, in his *Introduction to
Logical Theory*, suggests that in order to *know*, or to have good evidence or
good reason for believing, that a given non-law statement is true, it is
necessary to know that all of its instances have in fact been observed; but
in order to know, or to have good evidence or good reason for believing,
that a given law statement is true, it is *not* necessary to know that all of its

---

[3] Compare C. G. Hempel and Paul Oppenheim, 'Studies in the Logic of Explanation', *Philosophy of Science*, 15 (1948) 135–75 (reprinted in H. Feigl and M. Brodbeck,
Readings in the Philosophy of Science). It should be noted that these authors (i) attempt
to characterize laws with respect only to formalized languages, (ii) concede that 'the
problem of an adequate definition of purely qualitative (universal) predicates remains
open', and (iii) propose a distinction between 'derived' and 'fundamental' laws. The
latter distinction is similar to a distinction of Braithwaite, discussed below. See also
Elizabeth Lane Beardsley, 'Non-Accidental and Counterfactual Sentences', *Journal of
Philosophy*, 46 (1949), 573–91; review of the latter by Roderick M. Chisholm, *Journal
of Symbolic Logic*, 16 (1951), 63–4.

instances have been examined. (We need not consider the problem of defining 'instance' in this use.) 'An essential part of our grounds for accepting' a non-law statement must be 'evidence that there will be no more' instances and 'that there never were more than the limited number of which observations have been recorded' (p. 199). Possibly this suggestion is true, but it leaves us with our problem. For the suggestion itself requires use of a modal term; it refers to what a man *needs* to know, or what it is *essential* that he know, in order to know that a law statement is true. But if we thus allow ourselves the use of modal terms, we could have said at the outset merely that a law statement is true. But if we thus allow ourselves the use of modal terms, we could have said at the outset merely that a law statement describes what is 'physically necessary', etc., and that a non-law statement does not.

(3) R. B. Braithwaite, in *Scientific Explanation*, suggests that a law statement, as distinguished from a non-law statement, is one which 'appears as a deduction from higher-level hypotheses which have been established independently of the statement' (p. 303). 'To consider whether or not a scientific hypothesis would, if true, be a law of nature is to consider the way in which it could enter into an established scientific deductive system' (ibid.). In other words, the question whether a statement is law-like may be answered by considering certain logical, or epistemological, relations which the statement bears to certain *other* statements. Our non-law statement N2, however, is deducible from the following two statements: (i) 'Newspapers which are generally reliable report that all parents of quintuplets during the first half of the twentieth century are named "Dionne",' and (ii) 'If newspapers which are generally reliable report that all parents of quintuplets during the first half of the twentieth century are named "Dionne", then such parents are named "Dionne".' Statements (i) and (ii) may be considered as 'higher level' parts of a 'hypothetical-deductive system' from which the non-law statement N2 can be deduced; indeed (i) and (ii) undoubtedly express the grounds upon which most people accept N2. It is not enough, therefore, to describe a non-law statement as a statement which 'appears as a deduction from higher level hypotheses which have been established independently'. (I suggest, incidentally, that it is only at an advanced stage of inquiry that one regards a synthetic universal statement as being a non-law statement.)

II

Even if we allow ourselves the distinction between law statements and non-law statements and characterize the distinction philosophically, by reference, say, to physical possibility (e.g. 'All *S* is *P*' is a law statement provided it is not physically possible that anything be both S and not P, etc.), we find that contrary-to-fact conditionals still present certain difficulties of interpretation.[4] Assuming that the distinction between law statement and non-law statement is available to us, I shall now make some informal remarks which I hope will throw light upon the ordinary use of these conditionals.

Henry Hiz has suggested that a contrary-to-fact conditional might be interpreted as a metalinguistic statement, telling us something about what can be inferred in a given system of statements. 'It says that, if something is accepted in this system to be true, then something else can be accepted in this system to be true.'[5] This suggestion, I believe, can be applied to the ordinary use of contrary-to-fact conditionals, but it is necessary to make some qualifying remarks concerning the relevant 'systems of statements'.

Let us consider one way of justifying the assertion of a contrary-to-fact conditional, 'If a were S, a would be P.' The antecedent of the counterfactual is taken, its indicative form, as a *supposition* or *assumption*.[6] One says, in effect, 'Let us *suppose* that a is S,' even though one may believe that a is not S. The indicative form of the consequent of the counterfactual —viz. 'a is P'—is then shown to follow logically from the antecedent taken with certain other statements already accepted. This demonstration is then taken to justify the counterfactual. The point of asserting the counterfactual may be that of *calling attention to*, *emphasizing*, or *conveying*, one or more of the premises which, taken with the antecedent, logically imply the consequent.

In simple cases, where singular counterfactuals are asserted, we may thus think of the speaker: (i) as having deduced the consequences of a singular supposition, viz. the indicative form of the counterfactual antecedent, taken with a statement he interprets as a law statement; and (ii) as being concerned in part to call attention to, emphasize, or convey, the statement interpreted as a law statement. We can usually tell, from the context of a man's utterance, what the supposition is and what the other statements are with which he is concerned. He may say, 'If that were gold, it would be malleable'; it is likely, in this case, that the statement interpreted as a law statement is L2, 'All gold is malleable;' it is also likely that this is the statement he is concerned to emphasize.

F. H. Bradley suggested, in his *Principles of Logic*, that when a man

[4] Modal analyses of law statements are suggested by Hans Reichenbach, *Elements of Symbolic Logic*, Ch. VIII, and Arthur Burks, 'The Logic of Causal Propositions', *Mind*, 60 (1951), 363–82.

[5] Henry Hiz, 'On the Inferential Sense of Contrary-to-fact Conditionals', *Journal of Philosophy*, 48 (1949), 586–7.

[6] Compare S. Jaskowski, 'On the Rules of Suppositions in Formal Logic', *Studia Logica*, 1 (Warsaw, 1934), and A. Meinong, *Über Annahmen*, concerning this use of 'assumption'.

asserts a singular counterfactual 'the real judgement is concerned with the individual's *qualities*, and asserts no more than a connection of adjectives.'[7] Bradley's suggestion, as I interpret it, is that the *whole* point of asserting a singular counterfactual, normally, is to call attention to, emphasize, or convey the statement interpreted as a law statement. It might be misleading, however, to say that the man is *affirming* or *asserting* what he takes to be a law statement, or statement describing a 'connection of adjectives', for he has not formulated it explicitly. It would also be misleading to say, as Bradley did (p. 89), that the man is merely *supposing* the law statement to be true, for the law statement is something he *believes*, and not merely supposes, to be true. If he were merely supposing 'All gold is malleable,' along with 'That is gold.' then it is likely he would include this supposition in the antecedent of his counterfactual and say 'If that were gold and if all gold were malleable, then that would be malleable.' Let us say he is *presupposing* the law statement.

We are suggesting, then, that a man in asserting a counterfactual is telling us something about what can be deduced from some 'system of statements' when the indicative version of the antecedent is added to this system as a *supposition*. We are referring to the statements of this system (other than the indicative version of the antecedent) as the *presuppositions* of his assertion. And we are suggesting that, normally, at least part of the point of asserting a counterfactual is to *call attention to*, *emphasize*, or *convey*, one or more of these presuppositions.

The statements a man presupposes when he asserts a counterfactual will, presumably, be statements he accepts or believes. But they will not include the denial of the antecedent of his counterfactual (even if he believes this denial to be true) and they will not include any statements he would treat as non-law statements.[8] And normally there will be many other statements he believes to be true which he will deliberately exclude from his presuppositions. The peculiar problem of interpreting ordinary counterfactual statements is that of specifying which, among the statements the asserter believes, he intends to *exclude* from his presuppositions. What statements he will exclude will depend upon what it is he is concerned to call attention to, emphasize, or convey.

Let us suppose a man accepts the following statements, taking the uni-

[7] Op. cit., p. 90. Compare D. J. O'Connor, 'The Analysis of Conditional Sentences', *Mind*, 60 (1951), 360; Robert Brown and John Watling, 'Counterfactual Conditionals', *Mind*, 61 (1952), 226.

[8] Instead of saying his presuppositions include no statement he treats as a law statement, it might be more accurate to say this: if his presuppositions include any statement *N* he would interpret as a non-law statement, then *N* and the man's supposition cannot be so formulated that the supposition constitutes a substitution-instance of *N*'s antecedent.

versal statements to be law statements: (1) All gold is malleable; (2) No cast-iron is malleable; (3) Nothing is both gold and cast-iron; (4) Nothing is both malleable and not malleable; (5) That is cast-iron; (6) That is not gold; and (7) That is not malleable. We may contrast three different situations in which he asserts three different counterfactuals having the same antecedents.

First, he asserts, pointing to an object his hearers don't know to be gold and don't know not to be gold, 'If that *were* gold, it would be malleable.' In this case, he is supposing the denial of (6); he is excluding from his presuppositions (5), (6), and (7); and he is concerned to emphasize (1).

Secondly, he asserts, pointing to an object he and his hearers agree to be cast-iron, 'If *that* were gold, then some gold things would not be malleable.' He is again supposing the denial of (6); he is excluding (1) and (6), but he is no longer excluding (5) or (7); and he is concerned to emphasize either (5) or (2).

Thirdly, he asserts, 'If that were gold, the some things would be both malleable and not malleable.' He is again supposing the denial of (6); he is now excluding (3) and no longer excluding (1), (5), (6), or (7); and he is now concerned to emphasize (1), (2), or (5).

Still other possibilities readily suggest themselves.

If, then, we were to ask 'What if that were gold?' our question would have a number of possible answers—e.g. the subjunctive forms of the denial of (7), the denial of (1), and the denial of (4). Any one of these three answers might be appropriate, but they would not *all* be appropriate in conjunction. Which answer is the appropriate one will depend upon what we wish to know. If, in asking 'What if that were gold?', we wish to know of some law statement describing gold, the denial of (7) is appropriate; if we wish to know what are the properties of the thing in question, the denial of (1) is appropriate; and if we wish to know whether the thing has properties such that a statement saying nothing gold has those properties is a law statement, the denial of (4) is appropriate. The counterfactual question 'What if that were gold?' is, therefore, clearly ambiguous. But in each case, the question could be formulated clearly and unambiguously.

Counterfactuals are similar to *probability* statements in that each type of statement is, in a certain sense, elliptical. If we ask 'What is the probability that this man will survive?' our question is incompletely formulated; and a more explicit formulation would be, 'With respect to such-and-such evidence, what is the probability that this man will survive?' Similarly, if we ask 'What would American policy in Asia be if Stevenson were President?' our question is incompletely formulated; a more explicit formulation would be, 'Supposing that Stevenson were President, and presupposing so-and-so, but not so-and-so, what would be the consequences with respect to American policy in Asia?' But there is an important respect in which counterfactual statements *differ* from such probability statements. If a man wishes to know what is the probability of a certain statement, i.e. if he wishes to know the truth of a categorical probability statement, then, we may say, he should take into consideration *all* the relevant evidence available to him; the premises of his probability inference should omit no relevant statement which he is justified in believing.[9] But this 'requirement of total evidence' cannot be assumed to hold in the case of counterfactual inference. If a man asks 'What would American policy in Asia be, if Stevenson were President?' and if his question may be interpreted in the way in which it ordinarily would be interpreted, then there are many facts included in his store of knowledge which we would expect him to *overlook*, or *ignore* in answering his question; i.e. there are many facts which we would expect him deliberately to *exclude* from his presuppositions. Normally we would expect him to exclude the fact that Eisenhower's programme is the one which has been followed since 1953; another is the fact that Mr. Dulles is Secretary of State. But there are other facts, which may also be included in the man's store of knowledge, whose status is more questionable. Does he intend to exclude the fact that Congress was Republican; does he intend to exclude those Asiatic events which have occurred as a result of Eisenhower's policies; does he intend to exclude the fact that Stevenson went to Asia in 1953? There is no point in insisting either that he consider or that he exclude these facts. But, if he wishes to be understood, he should tell us which are the facts that he is considering, or presupposing, and which are the ones he is excluding.

Bradley suggested the ambiguity of some counterfactual statements may be attributed to the fact that 'the supposition is not made evident' (op. cit., p. 89). In our terminology, it would be more accurate to say that the *presupposition* is not made evident; for the supposition is usually formulated explicitly in the antecedent of the counterfactual statement. (But when a man says, 'If that thing, which is not *S*, were *S* . . .', the subordinate indicative clause expresses neither a supposition nor a presupposition.) Ideally it might be desirable to formulate our counterfactuals in somewhat the following way: 'Supposing that that is *S*, and presupposing so-and-so, then it follows that that is *P*.' In practice, however, it is often easy to tell, from the context in which a counterfactual is asserted, just what it is that is being presupposed and what it is that is being excluded.[10]

---

[9] Compare Rudolf Carnap, *Logical Foundations of Probability*, pp. 211 ff.

[10] 'The Contrary-to-fact Conditional' (pp. 303–4; Feigl–Sellars, p. 494). I discuss what I take to be certain conventions of ordinary language pertaining to this point.

Although I have been using the terms 'counterfactual' and 'contrary-to-fact' throughout this discussion, it is important to note that, when a man arrives at a conditional statement in the manner we have been discussing, his supposition—and thus also the antecedent of his conditional—need *not* be anything he believes to be false. For example, a man in deliberating will consider the consequences of a supposition, taken along with certain presuppositions, and he will also consider the consequences of its denial, taken along with the same presuppositions. It is misleading to say, therefore, that the conditionals he may then affirm are 'counterfactual', or 'contrary-to-fact', for he may have no beliefs about the truth or falsity of the respective antecedents and one of these antecedents will in fact be true.[11] A better term might be 'suppositional conditional' or, indeed, 'hypothetical statement'.

[11] Compare Alan Ross Anderson, 'A Note on Subjunctive and Counterfactual Conditionals', *Analysis*, 12 (1951), 35–8; Roderick M. Chisholm, review of David Pears's 'Hypotheticals', *Journal of Symbolic Logic*, 15 (1950), 215–16.

XI

BELIEF-CONTRAVENING SUPPOSITIONS AND THE PROBLEM OF CONTRARY-TO-FACT CONDITIONALS

NICHOLAS RESCHER

IV

. . .

Thesis 1: Every belief-contravening supposition is by nature ambiguous. Its specific content is unclear in that its conflicts with cognate beliefs always require further adjudication. Within the environment of other accepted beliefs, a belief-contravening supposition is necessarily contextually ambiguous.

. . .

IV

Thesis 2: The revision in a family of related beliefs that is necessitated by a belief-contravening supposition is not merely a matter of logic.

. . .

VII

. . .

Thesis 3: A belief-contravening thesis requires a revision of the family of related beliefs, but it does not entail any set of specific changes that go to make up a particular revision. This recasting is not only not a matter of logic (Thesis 2), but cannot even be achieved by any automatic or mechanical methods.

This discussion up to this point can be summarized briefly. Belief-contravening suppositions lead us into a mire of ambiguity from which no

From *Philosophical Review*, 60 (1961), 176–96 (with sections I to III, and parts of IV–VII, omitted). Reprinted by permission of the author and the editor of the journal.

road map of logical revision or mechanical manipulation can extricate us. If such suppositions are viewed as a sort of 'make-believe', then we must recognize that the problem of where to 'draw the line' between make-believe on the one hand and the 'real thing' upon the other is a subtle one that cannot be solved in any automatic way whatever.

VIII

At this juncture an exasperated objector might be tempted to protest as follows: 'The whole tenor of the discussion goes in the direction of arguing that belief-contravening suppositions lead to a logical dead-end from which no exit is possible. The conclusion thus seems to emerge that such suppositions cannot reasonably be made. But we all know that they can! And indeed this has already been conceded in the preliminary survey of actual situations in which they arise. The foregoing analysis must therefore be incorrect, or at least it must have overlooked some basic and essential factor.'

So protests our objector and he is quite right. His objection conveys a valid charge. Our discussion has thus far been primarily destructive because it has managed to be oblivious of an essential consideration. We have overlooked the fact that a supposition is something we are challenged or asked or requested to make (perhaps, to be sure, only by ourselves). This puts suppositions into a dialectic framework in which the opportunity to put questions and obtain answers is inevitably present. We can refuse to enter into a supposition, not of course on grounds of mere obstinacy, but for the perfectly valid reason that we find it ambiguous, that we are unclear as to its meaning, that we cannot say just what it is that we are requested to assume. The essential fact is that belief-contravening supposition is not a rational resource of theoretical inquiry but a dialectical device requiring an interlocutor (who may, of course, be simply ourselves). This interlocutor must, if he wants us to make a belief-contravening supposition, be willing and able to respond to questions intended to clarify ambiguities and remove perplexities present in the supposition that he is requesting us to make. Consequently he must be prepared to adjudicate questions as to how the supposition that he puts to us is to be construed in relation to our other, relevant beliefs.

The crucial point is this: Anyone (including ourselves) who invites us to make a belief-contravening supposition must be ready to adjudicate doubtful interpretations and to resolve uncertainties as to the bearing of the assumption upon other relevant beliefs. Since this cannot, as we have seen, be done on the basis of logical inference from the supposition itself, it requires an additional, extra-logical resource. Supplemental information must therefore be provided within the dialectical setting within which the supposition arises. And where this requirement for the availability of supplemental information is not satisfied, the assumption itself cannot properly be made—not because it is meaningless, but because it has too many alternative meanings, because of the contextual ambiguity which infects belief-contravening suppositions.

These considerations serve to substantiate our fourth thesis:

Thesis 4: Belief-contravening suppositions outrun the possibility of logical resolution because of their contextual ambiguity, which can only be removed by further information not available from the supposition itself. We must rely upon the dialectical setting of a belief-contravening supposition to resolve the logical impasse which would otherwise vitiate the assumption in question on grounds of ambiguity.

IX

This thesis brings me to the end of my analysis of belief-contravening suppositions. In the brief remainder of this paper, I should like to undertake an application of the foregoing results. I want to bring them to bear on clarifying an important topic that has received a great deal of attention in recent philosophical literature, namely, the problem of contrary-to-fact conditionals.

X

A preliminary distinction is needed. There are, as I see it, two major types of counterfactual conditionals. The first type consists of what may be termed nomological counterfactuals. Such contrary-to-fact conditionals are simply a counterfactual specification of a covering law. Consider, for example, the conditionals:

Example 7: If Julius Caesar had been a lion, he would have had a tail.

Example 8: If Smith had eaten an ounce of arsenic, he would have died.

We have said virtually all that needs to be said about these counterfactuals when we are able to refer them to the appropriate covering laws:

All lions have tails.
All people who eat an ounce of arsenic die.

To be sure, even with these conditionals the now accustomed element of radical ambiguity can be detected. For we could rebut the foregoing counterfactuals by:

Example 9: If Julius Caesar had been a lion, there would have been a tail-less lion (because Caesar had no tail).

Example 10: If Smith had eaten an ounce of arsenic, this dosage would not invariably have proved fatal (because Smith is still alive).

These rebutting counterfactuals, however, are effectively ruled out in the cases under consideration. For we may analyse the nomological counterfactuals in terms of belief-contravening suppositions as illustrated in the following example:

Example 11:
Beliefs: (1) Caesar was not a lion (known fact).
       (2) Caesar had no tail (known fact).
       (3) All lions have tails (accepted covering law).

Assume: Caesar was a lion.

Notice now that belief (1) must obviously be set aside, but that we have an option between rejecting (2) and (3). In Example 7 we reject (2), and in Example 9 we reject (3). However, Example 7 is 'natural' and Example 9 is 'artificial' because the nomological use of counterfactuals represents a determination to retain the appropriate covering generalization—that is, (3)—at the cost of adapting all else to it.

Let us consider yet another example:

Example 12.1: If Saladin had not died, he would be alive today.

This counterfactual seems perfectly 'natural' and can be viewed as essentially unambiguous and trouble-free only because we construe it in the light of the covering law:

All real persons (that is, persons who have been born) who have not died are alive today.

Once we reject this law—for instance, by envisaging some way of joining the non-living other than dying (for example, bodily assumption)—the contextual ambiguity typical of belief-contravening suppositions also infects this counterfactual, since we can now construct the rebutting counterfactual:

Example 12.2: If Saladin had not died, he would have 'gone yonder' by bodily assumption (since he is not alive today).

Thus in the case of nomological counterfactuals the situation is relatively simple in that we do here have the necessary guidance needed for the reconstitution of our residual beliefs in the face of the belief-contravening supposition represented by the antecedent of the counterfactual. We have this guidance because we treat the covering law as immune to rejection. This resolution suffices to inform us how to restructure our relevant beliefs.[1]

Thus the nomological type of counterfactual condition is not drastically troublesome. The problems that do remain here are not logical problems, but problems revolving about the concept of a law, that is, a generalization so secure that we are willing to retain it at practically all costs, and to let all else revolve about it when a belief-contravening supposition is made. But this is an extra-logical problem into which I shall not enter here.[2]

One possible complication should be noted briefly, namely that which arises when the applicability of the law in question is subject to fulfilment of certain 'boundary-value conditions' whose satisfaction must be stipulated by auxiliary hypotheses. Let me illustrate this complication by an example that has received much discussion in the literature, namely, the counterfactual 'If the match M had been struck, it would have lit.' Let us analyse this in terms of belief-contravening suppositions:

Example 13:

Beliefs: (1) All dry matches located in an oxygen-containing medium light when struck (covering law).
   (2) M is a dry match (auxiliary hypothesis 1).
   (3) M is located in an oxygen-containing medium (auxiliary hypothesis 2).
   (4) M has not been struck.
   (5) M has not lit.

Assumption: Assume M had been struck.

It is clear that this assumption directly requires that we reject (4), and that, since we are dealing with a nomological counterfactual, we are determined to retain (1). This appears to leave us with a choice among three alternatives if we wish to settle for the minimum of a single additional rejection:

---

[1] Goodman discusses the puzzle of the 'law': 'All coins in my pocket are made of silver.' But it is precisely because this is not a 'genuine law' (that is, one that we are determined to yield up only in the face of 'actual evidence' and not in the face of a 'mere assumption') that this does not validate the counterfactual: 'If this penny were in my pocket, then it would be made of silver.'

[2] It is clear that 'logical' is here used in its narrower sense, and not in the wider sense of inductive logic, which includes such matters as the theory of scientific method.

Alternative 1		Alternative 2		Alternative 3	
Retain	*Reject*	*Retain*	*Reject*	*Retain*	*Reject*
(1)	(4)	(1)	(4)	(1)	(4)
---	---	---	---	---	---
(3)	(2)	(2)	(3)	(2)	(5)
(5)		(5)		(3)	

If, however, we decide not only to regard our law (1) as sacred, but also the auxiliary assumptions which assure its applicability—(2) and (3)—it is clear that we are reduced to adopting Alternative 3. And in this way we can vindicate the 'plausible' counterfactual

If the match M had been struck, it would have lit.

over against its 'implausible' competitors.

If the match M had been struck, it would not have been dry.
If the match M had been struck, it would not have been located in an oxygen-containing medium.[3]

---

[3] In correspondence, Professor Nelson Goodman offers an interesting criticism of this analysis. Its substance is as follows: The covering law (1) has the form:
    (L) Whatever satisfies the condition s $C_1, C_2, \ldots, C_n$ must exhibit the characteristic C.
But any such law can be reformulated in n logically equivalent versions of the type:
    (L_i) Whatever satisfies the conditions $C_1, C_2, \ldots, C_{i-1}, C_{i+1}, \ldots, C_n, \sim C$ must exhibit the characteristic $\sim C_i$.
Now just as L justifies the 'correct' counterfactual on the present analysis, so L_i justifies its 'improper' alternatives.

To my mind, Goodman's remark does not establish the inadequacy of the present analysis of nomological counterfactuals, but rather illustrates the important fact that here, as in other branches of inductive logic, it is essential to take into account not only the *matter* (i.e. substantive content) of law statements, but their logical *form* as well. Despite their *deductive* equivalence (interdeducibility), L and the L_i are not automatically interchangeable in discussions within the domain of *inductive* logic. (The decisive illustration of this important fact is C. G. Hempel's well-known 'Swan Paradox' in confirmation-theory: despite their deductive equivalence, the generalizations 'All swans are white' and 'All non-white things are non-swans' call for very different verification procedures—for the former we must collect swans and examine their colour, while for the latter we must collect non-white objects and determine their kind.) Thus when a counterfactual based upon a law of form L is given, the move from L to its 'equivalent' L_i *en route* to the establishment of a rebutting counterfactual is *not* admissible.

I might add that if it were maintained that L and the L_i are fully equivalent, and that a choice among them is entirely arbitrary (even in inductive contexts), then all basis for exclusive justification of one among several mutually rebutting nomological counterfactuals is *ipso facto* abrogated. This would lead to the result that with nomological counterfactuals, as with the 'purely hypothetical' counterfactuals of section XVI below, the assertion of one among several mutually rebutting contenders is haphazard.

For my present purposes these brief considerations should suffice to exhibit the character of this class of nomological or law-governed counterfactuals. Let me conclude my examination of them by noting that, from the strictly logical point of view, such counterfactuals are relatively straightforward and trouble-free.

XI

The remaining type of counterfactual conditionals, that is to say those that are not nomological, I shall characterize as purely hypothetical counterfactuals. In addition to including the classic instance 'If wishes were horses, beggars would ride,' this class is typified by such well-known mutually rebutting trouble-makers as:

Example 14.1: If Bizet and Verdi were compatriots, Bizet would be an Italian.

Example 14.2: If Bizet and Verdi were compatriots, Verdi would be a Frenchman.

Example 15.1: If Georgia included New York City, this city would lie south of the Mason–Dixon line.

Example 15.2: If Georgia included New York City, this state would extend north of the Mason–Dixon line.

It is clear that, in the case of the purely hypothetical counterfactuals, these essentially opposed results cannot be avoided. The contextual ambiguity of the antecedent gives us no way of choosing among the various mutually rebutting counterfactuals. Perplexity is unavoidably upon us in these cases.

XII

The point that I wish to make is by now doubtless anticipated. Purely hypothetical counterfactuals are, I submit, in effect simply conditional statements based upon belief-contravening suppositions. So far as I have been able to determine, all of the really troublesome (that is, non-nomological) cases of contrary-to-fact conditionals are actually hypotheticals whose antecedents assert belief-contravening suppositions. (Indeed, those familiar with the literature on counterfactuals have doubtless noted that most of my examples of belief-contravening suppositions have been drawn from this source.) All of the standard examples of problematical contrary-to-fact conditionals to be found in the literature are conditional or hypothetical statements whose antecedent puts before us a palpably false (and thus belief-contravening) supposition and whose consequent asserts a purported consequence of this supposition. Our analysis of belief-contravening suppositions is thus immediately applicable. The difficulty arising from purely hypothetical counterfactuals is easily recognized as a difficulty about belief-contravening (or, in this case, 'knowledge-contravening') suppositions. And the difficulty vanishes as a logical problem once this fact is recognized. For as we have seen, the refractory nature of belief-contravening suppositions is inherent in their fundamentally ambiguous character. Belief-contravening suppositions are pitfalls of paradox because they covertly invite us to commit a fallacy of ambiguity. In making the corresponding counterfactually conditional statements we fall into the trap by accepting this invitation. A counterfactual condition leads to paradox not because it is meaningless, but because it is overly meaningful, being so ambiguous as to admit of contrary, or at least discordant, interpretations.

We find support for this position in the view of Quine, who summarizes his tantalizingly brief discussion of counterfactuals, or as he calls them 'contrafactual' conditionals, in *Methods of Logic* with the statement: 'The problem of contrafactual conditionals is in any case a perplexing one, and it belongs not to pure logic but to the theory of meaning or possibly the philosophy of science' (Section 3).

XIII

Let me thus conclude with a bold claim. I believe it warranted to maintain that the much-agitated puzzle of counterfactual conditionals can now be laid to rest as a *logical* problem. Counterfactuals fall into two classes. First we have the nomological counterfactuals. These do not pose any distinctively logical difficulties, although they may (and I think do) generate real problems for the proper understanding of the concept of a law. Secondly, we have the purely hypothetical counterfactuals. These, though unquestionably troublesome from the logical standpoint, raise only troubles and difficulties generally inherent in belief-contravening suppositions. And these difficulties are seen upon due analysis to come down to ambiguities which are of a material rather than formal kind, whose resolution calls for supplementary information rather than logical analysis, and whose removal is a practical problem in the use of these statements and not a theoretical problem in their logic.

Thus if my analysis is correct, the whole puzzling problem of counterfactual conditionals vanishes as a logical problem, because it is recognized that the only logical difficulties involved are all of them generated through the fallacy of ambiguity. And while the recognition of ambiguity does fall within the province of logic, its resolution is inevitably an extra-logical matter. I repeat therefore: the *logical* problem of contrary-to-fact conditionals can be laid to rest. *Requiescat in pace.*

XII

A THEORY OF
CONDITIONALS

ROBERT C. STALNAKER

I. INTRODUCTION

A CONDITIONAL sentence expresses a proposition which is a function of two other propositions, yet not one which is a *truth* function of those propositions. I may know the truth values of 'Willie Mays played in the American League' and 'Willie Mays hit four hundred' without knowing whether or not Mays would have hit four hundred if he had played in the American League. This fact has tended to puzzle, displease, or delight philosophers, and many have felt that it is a fact that calls for some comment or explanation. It has given rise to a number of philosophical problems; I shall discuss three of these.

My principal concern will be with what has been called the *logical problem of conditionals*, a problem that frequently is ignored or dismissed by writers on conditionals and counterfactuals. This is the task of describing the formal properties of the *conditional function*: a function, usually represented in English by the words 'if . . . then', taking ordered pairs of propositions into propositions. I shall explain informally and defend a solution, presented more rigorously elsewhere, to this problem.[1]

The second issue—the one that has dominated recent discussions of contrary-to-fact conditionals—is the *pragmatic problem of counterfactuals*. This problem derives from the belief, which I share with most philosophers writing about this topic, that the formal properties of the conditional function, together with all of the *facts*, may not be sufficient for determining the truth value of a counterfactual; that is, different truth valuations of conditional statements may be consistent with a single valuation of all

From *Studies in Logical Theory*, ed. N. Rescher (Oxford: Blackwell, APQ Monograph No. 2, 1968), reprinted by permission of the publishers.

I want to express appreciation to my colleague, Professor R. H. Thomason, for his collaboration in the formal development of the theory expounded in this paper, and for his helpful comments on its exposition and defence.

The preparation of this paper was supported in part by a National Science Foundation grant, GS–1567.

[1] R. C. Stalnaker and R. H. Thomason, 'A Semantic Analysis of Conditional Logic' [*Theoria*, 36 (1970), 23–42]. In this paper, the formal system, C2, is proved sound and semantically complete with respect to the interpretation sketched in the present paper. That is, it is shown that a formula is a consequence of a class of formulas if and only if it is derivable from the class in the formal system, C2.

non-conditional statements. The task set by the problem is to find and defend criteria for choosing among these different valuations.

This problem is different from the first issue because these criteria are pragmatic, and not semantic. The distinction between semantic and pragmatic criteria, however, depends on the construction of a semantic theory. The semantic theory that I shall defend will thus help to clarify the second problem by charting the boundary between the semantic and pragmatic components of the concept. The question of this boundary line is precisely what Rescher, for example, avoids by couching his whole discussion in terms of conditions for belief, or justified belief, rather than truth conditions. Conditions for justified belief are pragmatic for any concept.[2]

The third issue is an epistemological problem that has bothered empiricist philosophers. It is based on the fact that many counterfactuals seem to be synthetic, and contingent, statements about unrealized possibilities. But contingent statements must be capable of confirmation by empirical evidence, and the investigator can gather evidence only in the actual world. How are conditionals which are both empirical and contrary-to-fact possible at all? How do we learn about possible worlds, and where are the facts (or counterfacts) which make counterfactuals true? Such questions have led philosophers to try to analyse the conditional in non-conditional terms[3]—to show that conditionals merely appear to be about unrealized possibilities. My approach, however, will be to accept the appearance as reality, and to argue that one can sometimes have evidence about non-actual situations.

In Sections II and III of this paper, I shall present and defend a theory of conditionals which has two parts: a formal system with a primitive conditional connective, and a semantical apparatus which provides general truth conditions for statements involving that connective. In Sections IV, V, and VI, I shall discuss in a general way the relation of the theory to the three problems outlined above.

II. THE INTERPRETATION

Eventually, I want to defend a hypothesis about the truth conditions for statements having conditional form, but I shall begin by asking a more

---

[2] N. Rescher, *Hypothetical Reasoning* (Amsterdam, 1964).

[3] Cf. R. Chisholm, 'The Contrary-to-fact Conditional', *Mind*, 55 (1946), 289–307, reprinted in *Readings in Philosophical Analysis*, ed. by H. Feigl and W. Sellars (New York, 1949), pp. 482–97. The problem is sometimes posted (as it is here) as the task of analysing the *subjunctive* conditional into an indicative statement, but I think it is a mistake to base very much on the distinction of mood. As far as I can tell, the mood tends to indicate something about the attitude of the speaker, but in no way effects the propositional content of the statement.

practical question: how does one evaluate a conditional statement? How does one decide whether or not he believes it to be true? An answer to this question will not be a set of truth conditions, but it will serve as a heuristic aid in the search for such a set.

To make the question more concrete, consider the following situation: you are faced with a true–false political opinion survey. The statement is, 'If the Chinese enter the Vietnam conflict, the United States will use nuclear weapons.' How do you deliberate in choosing your response? What considerations of a logical sort are relevant? I shall first discuss two familiar answers to this question, and then defend a third answer which avoids some of the weaknesses of the first two.

The first answer is based on the simplest account of the conditional, the truth-functional analysis. According to this account, you should reason as follows in responding to the true–false quiz: you ask yourself, first, will the Chinese enter the conflict? and second, will the United States use nuclear weapons? If the answer to the first question is no, *or* if the answer to the second is yes, then you should place your X in the 'true' box. But this account is unacceptable since the following piece of reasoning is an obvious *non sequitur*: 'I firmly believe that the Chinese will stay out of the conflict; *therefore* I believe that the statement is true.' The falsity of the antecedent is never sufficient reason to affirm a conditional, even an indicative conditional.

A second answer is suggested by the shortcomings of the truth-functional account. The material implication analysis fails, critics have said, because it leaves out the idea of *connection* which is implicit in an if–then statement. According to this line of thought, a conditional is to be understood as a statement which affirms that some sort of logical or causal connection holds between the antecedent and the consequent. In responding to the true–false quiz, then, you should look, not at the truth values of the two clauses, but at the relation between the propositions expressed by them. If the 'connection' holds, you check the 'true' box. If not, you answer 'false'.

If the second hypothesis were accepted, then we would face the task of clarifying the idea of 'connection', but there are counter-examples even with this notion left as obscure as it is. Consider the following case: you firmly believe that the use of nuclear weapons by the United States in this war is inevitable because of the arrogance of power, the bellicosity of our president, raising pressure from congressional hawks, or other *domestic* causes. You have no opinion about future Chinese actions, but you do not think they will make much difference one way or another to nuclear escalation. Clearly, you believe the opinion survey statement to be true even though you believe the antecedent and consequent to be logically and causally independent of each other. It seems that the presence of a 'connection' is not a necessary condition for the truth of an if–then statement.

The third answer I shall consider is based on a suggestion made some time ago by F. P. Ramsey.[4] Consider first the case where you have no opinion about the statement, 'The Chinese will enter the Vietnam war.' According to your suggestion, your deliberation about the survey statement should consist of a simple thought experiment: add the antecedent (hypothetically) to your stock of knowledge (or beliefs), and then consider whether or not the consequent is true. Your belief about the conditional should be the same as your hypothetical belief, under this condition about the consequent.

What happens to the idea of connection on this hypothesis? It is sometimes relevant to the evaluation of a conditional, and sometimes not. If you believe that a causal or logical connection exists, then you will add the consequent to your stock of beliefs along with the antecedent, since the rational man accepts the consequences of his beliefs. On the other hand, if you already believe the consequent (and if you also believe it to be causally independent of the antecedent), then it will remain a part of your stock of beliefs when you add the antecedent, since the rational man does not change his beliefs without reason. In either case, you will affirm the conditional. Thus this answer accounts for the relevance of 'connection' when it is relevant without making it a necessary condition of the truth of a conditional.

Ramsey's suggestion covers only the situation in which you have no opinion about the truth value of the antecedent. Can it be generalized? We can of course extend it without problem to the case where you believe or know the antecedent to be true; in this case, no changes need be made in your stock of beliefs. If you already believe that the Chinese will enter the Vietnam conflict, then your belief about the conditional will be just the same as your belief about the statement that the United States will use the bomb.

What about the case in which you know or believe the antecedent to be false? In this situation, you cannot simply add it to your stock of beliefs without introducing a contradiction. You must make adjustments by deleting or changing those beliefs which conflict with the antecedent. Here, the familiar difficulties begin, of course, because there will be more than

---

[4] F. P. Ramsey, 'General Propositions and Causality' in Ramsey, *Foundations of Mathematics and other Logical Essays* (New York, 1950), pp. 237–57. The suggestion is made on p. 248. Chisholm, op. cit., p. 489, quotes the suggestion and discusses the limitations of the 'connection' thesis which it brings out, but he develops it somewhat differently.

one way to make the required adjustments.[5] These difficulties point to the pragmatic problem of counterfactuals, but if we set them aside for a moment, we shall see a rough but general answer to the question we are asking. This is how to evaluate a conditional:

First, add the antecedent (hypothetically) to your stock of beliefs; second, make whatever adjustments are required to maintain consistency (without modifying the hypothetical belief in the antecedent); finally, consider whether or not the consequent is then true.

It is not particularly important that our answer is approximate—that it skirts the problem of adjustments—since we are using it only as a way of finding truth conditions. It is crucial, however, that the answer should not be restricted to some particular context of belief if it is to be helpful in finding a definition of the conditional function. If the conditional is to be understood as a function of the propositions expressed by its component clauses, then its truth value should not in general be dependent on the attitudes which anyone has toward those propositions.

Now that we have found an answer to the question 'How do we decide whether or not we believe a conditional statement?' the problem is to make the transition from belief conditions to truth conditions; that is, to find a set of truth conditions for statements having conditional form which explains why we use the method we do use to evaluate them. The concept of a *possible world* is just what we need to make this transition, since a possible world is the ontological analogue of a stock of hypothetical beliefs. The following set of truth conditions, using this notion, is a first approximation to the account that I shall propose:

Consider a possible world in which A is true, and which otherwise differs minimally from the actual world. '*If A, then B*' is true (*false*) just in case B is true (*false*) in that possible world.

An analysis in terms of possible worlds also has the advantage of providing a ready-made apparatus on which to build a formal semantical theory. In making this account of the conditional precise, we use the semantical systems for modal logics developed by Saul Kripke.[6] Following Kripke, we first define a *model structure*. Let M be an ordered triple

[5] Rescher, op. cit., pp. 11–16, contains a very clear statement and discussion of this problem, which he calls the problem of the ambiguity of belief-contravening hypotheses. He argues that the resolution of this ambiguity depends on pragmatic considerations. Cf. also Goodman's problem of relevant conditions in N. Goodman, *Fact, Fiction, and Forecast* (Cambridge, Mass., 1955), pp. 17–24.

[6] S. Kripke, 'Semantical Analysis of Modal Logics, I', *Zeitschrift für mathematische Logik und Grundlagen der Mathematik*, 9 (1963), 67–96.

(K,R,λ). K is to be understood intuitively as the set of all possible worlds; R is the relation of relative possibility which defines the structure. If α and β are possible worlds (members of K), then $\alpha R\beta$ reads 'β is possible with respect to α'. This means that, where α is the actual world, β is a possible world. R is a reflexive relation; that is, every world is possible with respect to itself. If your modal intuitions so incline you, you may add that R must be transitive, or transitive and symmetrical.[7] The only element that is not a part of the standard modal semantics is λ, a member of K which is to be understood as the *absurd world*—the world in which contradictions and all their consequences are true. It is an isolated element under R; that is, no other world is possible with respect to it, and it is not possible with respect to any other world. The purpose of λ is to allow for an interpretation of 'If A, then B' in the case where A is impossible; for this situation one needs an impossible world.

In addition to a model structure, our semantical apparatus includes a *selection function*, f, which takes a proposition and a possible world as arguments and a possible world as its value. The s-function selects, for each antecedent A, a particular possible world in which A is true. The *assertion* which the conditional makes, then, is that the consequent is true in the world selected. A conditional is true in the actual world when its consequent is true in the selected world.

Now we can state the semantical rule for the conditional more formally (using the corner, $>$, as the conditional connective):

$A > B$ is true in α if B is true in $f(A,\alpha)$;
$A > B$ is false in α if B is false in $f(A,\alpha)$.

The interpretation shows conditional logic to be an extension of modal logic. Modal logic provides a way of talking about what is true in the actual world, in all possible worlds, or in at least one, unspecified world. The addition of the selection function to the semantics and the conditional connective to the object language of modal logic provides a way of talking also about what is true in *particular* non-actual possible situations. This is what counterfactuals are: statements about particular counterfactual worlds.

But the world selected cannot be just any world. The s-function must meet at least the following conditions. I shall use the following terminology for talking about the arguments and values of s-functions: where

[7] The different restrictions on the relation R provide interpretations for the different modal systems. The system we build on is von Wright's M. If we add the transitivity requirement, then the underlying modal logic of our system is Lewis's S4, and if we add both the transitivity and symmetry requirements, then the modal logic is S5. Cf. S. Kripke, op. cit.

$f(A,\alpha) = \beta$, A is the *antecedent*, α is the *base world*, and β is the *selected world*.

(1) For all antecedents A and base worlds α, A must be true in $f(A,\alpha)$.
(2) For all antecedents A and base worlds α, $f(A,\alpha) = \lambda$ only if there is no world possible with respect to α in which A is true.

The first condition requires that the antecedent be true in the selected world. This ensures that all statements like 'if snow is white, then snow is white' are true. The second condition requires that the absurd world be selected only when the antecedent is impossible. Since everything is true in the absurd world, including contradictions, if the selection function were to choose it for the antecedent A, then 'If A, then B and not B' would be true. But one cannot legitimately reach an impossible conclusion from a consistent assumption.

The informal truth conditions that were suggested above required that the world selected *differ minimally* from the actual world. This implies, first, that there are no differences between the actual world and the selected world except those that are required, implicitly or explicitly, by the antecedent. Further, it means that among the alternative ways of making the required changes, one must choose one that does the least violence to the correct description and explanation of the actual world. These are vague conditions which are largely dependent on pragmatic considerations for their application. They suggest, however, that the selection is based on an ordering of possible worlds with respect to their resemblance to the base world. If this is correct, then there are two further formal constraints which must be imposed on the s-function.

(3) For all base worlds α and all antecedents A, if A is true in α, then $f(A,\alpha) = \alpha$.
(4) For all base worlds α and all antecedents B and B', if B is true in $f(B',\alpha)$ and B' is true in $f(B,\alpha)$, then $f(B,\alpha) = f(B',\alpha)$.

The third condition requires that the base world be selected if it is among the worlds in which the antecedent is true. Whatever the criteria for evaluating resemblance among possible worlds, there is obviously no other possible world as much like the base world as the base world itself. The fourth condition ensures that the ordering among possible worlds is consistent in the following sense: if any selection established β as prior to β' in the ordering (with respect to a particular base world α), then no other selection (relative to that α) may establish β' as prior to β.[8] Conditions (3) and (4)

[8] If $f(A,\alpha) = \beta$, then β is established as prior to all worlds possible with respect to α in which A is true.

together ensure that the s-function establishes a total ordering of all selected worlds with respect to each possible world, with the base world preceding all others in the order.

These conditions on the selection function are necessary in order that this account be recognizable as an explication of the conditional, but they are of course far from sufficient to determine the function uniquely. There may be further formal constraints that can plausibly be imposed on the selection principle, but we should not expect to find semantic conditions sufficient to guarantee that there will be a unique s-function for each valuation of non-conditional formulas on a model structure. The questions, 'On what basis do we select a selection function from among the acceptable ones?' and 'What are the criteria for ordering possible worlds?' are reformulations of the pragmatic problem of counterfactuals, which is a problem in the application of conditional logic. The conditions that I have mentioned above are sufficient, however, to define the semantical notions of validity and consequence for conditional logic.

III. THE FORMAL SYSTEM

The class of valid formulas of conditional logic according to the definitions sketched in the preceding section, is coextensive with the class of theorems of a formal system, C2. The primitive connectives of C2 are the usual $\supset$ and $\sim$ (with v, &, and $\equiv$ defined as usual), as well as a conditional connective, $>$ (called the corner). Other modal and conditional concepts can be defined in terms of the corner as follows:

$$\Box A =_{DF} \sim A > A$$
$$\Diamond A =_{DF} \sim (A > \sim A)$$
$$A \gtrless B =_{DF} (A >)B \; \& \; (B > A)$$

The rules of inference of C2 are *modus ponens* (if A and $A \supset B$ are theorems, then B is a theorem) and the Gödel rule of necessitation (If A is a theorem, then $\Box A$ is a theorem). There are seven axiom schemata:

(a1) Any tautologous wff (well-formed formula) is an axiom;
(a2) $\Box (A \supset B) \supset (\Box A \supset \Box B)$;
(a3) $\Box (A \supset B) \supset (A > B)$;
(a4) $\Diamond A \supset .(A > B) \supset \sim (A > \sim B)$;
(a5) $A > (B \lor C) \supset .(A > B) \lor (A > C)$;
(a6) $(A > B) \supset (A \supset B)$;
(a7) $A \gtrless B \supset .(A > C) \supset (B > C)$.

The conditional connective, as characterized by this formal system, is intermediate between strict implication and the material conditional, in the sense that $\Box (A \supset B)$ entails $A > B$ by (a3) and $A > B$ entails $A \supset B$

by (a6). It cannot, however, be analysed as a modal operation performed on a material conditional (like Burks's causal implication, for example).[9] The corner lacks certain properties shared by the two traditional implication concepts, and in fact these differences help to explain some peculiarities of counterfactuals. I shall point out three unusual features of the conditional connective.

(1) Unlike both material and strict implication, the conditional corner is a non-transitive connective. That is, from $A > B$ and $B > C$, one cannot infer $A > C$. While this may at first seem surprising, consider the following example: *Premises.* 'If J. Edgar Hoover were today a Communist, then he would be a traitor.' 'If J. Edgar Hoover had been born a Russian, then he would today be a Communist.' *Conclusion.* 'If J. Edgar Hoover had been born a Russian, he would be a traitor.' It seems reasonable to affirm these premises and deny the conclusion.

If this example is not sufficiently compelling, note that the following rule follows from the transitivity rule: From $A > B$ to infer $(A \& C) > B$. But it is obvious that the former rule is invalid; we cannot always strengthen the antecedent of a true conditional and have it remain true. Consider 'If this match were struck, it would light,' and 'If this match had been soaked in water overnight *and* it were struck, it would light.'[10]

(2) According to the formal system, the denial of a conditional is equivalent to a conditional with the same antecedent and opposite consequent (provided that the antecedent is not impossible). That is, $\Diamond A \supset \sim(A > B) \equiv (A > \sim B)$. This explains the fact, noted by both Goodman and Chisholm in their early papers on counterfactuals, that the normal way to contradict a counterfactual is to contradict the consequent, keeping the same antecedent. To deny 'If Kennedy were alive today, we wouldn't be in this Vietnam mess,' we say, 'If Kennedy were alive today, we would so be in this Vietnam mess.'

(3) The inference of contraposition, valid for both the truth-functional horseshoe and the strict implication hook, is invalid for the conditional corner. $A > B$ may be true while $\sim B > \sim A$ is false. For an example in support of this conclusion, we take another item from the political opinion survey: 'If the U.S. halts the bombing, then North Vietnam will not agree

---

[9] A. W. Burks, 'The Logic of Causal Propositions', *Mind*, 60 (1951), 363–82. The causal implication connective characterized in this article has the same structure as strict implication. For an interesting philosophical defence of this modal interpretation of conditionals, see B. Mayo, 'Conditional Statements', *The Philosophical Review*, 66 (1957), 291–303.

[10] Although the transitivity inference fails, a related inference is of course valid. From $A > B$, $B > C$, and A, one can infer C. Also, note that the biconditional connective is transitive. From $A \geqq B$ and $B \geqq C$, one can infer $A \geqq C$. Thus the biconditional is an equivalence relation, since it is also symmetrical and reflexive.

to negotiate.' A person would believe that this statement is true if he thought that the North Vietnamese were determined to press for a complete withdrawal of U.S. troops. But he would surely deny the contrapositive, 'If North Vietnam agrees to negotiate, then the U.S. will not have halted the bombing.' He would believe that a halt in the bombing, and much more, is required to bring the North Vietnamese to the negotiating table.[11]

Examples of these anomalies have been noted by philosophers in the past. For instance, Goodman pointed out that two counterfactuals with the same antecedent and contradictory consequents are 'normally meant' as direct negations of each other. He also remarked that we may sometimes assert a conditional and yet reject its contrapositive. He accounted for these facts by arguing that semifactuals—conditionals with false antecedents and true consequents—are for the most part not to be taken literally. 'In practice,' he wrote, 'full counterfactuals affirm, while semifactuals deny, that a certain connection obtains between antecedent and consequent. . . . The practical import of a semifactual is thus different from its literal import.'[12] Chisholm also suggested paraphrasing semifactuals before analysing them. 'Even if you were to sleep all morning, you would be tired' is to be read 'It is false that if you were to sleep all morning, you would not be tired.'[13]

A separate and non-conditional analysis for semi-factuals is necessary to save the 'connection' theory of counterfactuals in the face of the anomalies we have discussed, but it is a baldly *ad hoc* manoeuvre. Any analysis can be saved by paraphrasing the counter-examples. The theory presented in Section II avoids this difficulty by denying that the conditional can be said, in general, to assert a connection of any particular kind between antecedent and consequent. It is, of course, the structure of inductive relations and causal connections which makes counterfactuals and semifactuals true or false, but it does this by determining the relationships among possible worlds, which in turn determine the truth values of conditionals. By treating the relation between connection and conditionals as an indirect relation in this way, the theory is able to give a unified account of conditionals which explains the variations in their behaviour in different contexts.

IV. THE LOGICAL PROBLEM: GENERAL CONSIDERATIONS

The traditional strategy for attacking a problem like the logical problem of conditionals was to find an *analysis*, to show that the unclear or object-

[11] Although contraposition fails, *modus tolens* is valid for the conditional: from $A > B$ and $\sim B$, one can infer $\sim A$.
[12] Goodman, op. cit., pp. 15, 32.
[13] Chisholm, op. cit., p. 492.

ionable phrase was dispensable, or replaceable by something clear and harmless. Analysis was viewed by some as an *unpacking*—a making manifest of what was latent in the concept; by others it was seen as the *replacement* of a vague idea by a precise one, adequate to the same purposes as the old expression, but free of its problems. The semantic theory of conditionals can also be viewed either as the construction of a concept to replace an unclear notion of ordinary language, or as an *explanation* of a commonly used concept. I see the theory in the latter way: no recommendation or stipulation is intended. This does not imply, however, that the theory is meant as a description of linguistic usage. What is being explained is not the rules governing the use of an English word, but the structure of a concept. Linguistic facts—what we would say in this or that context, and what sounds odd to the native speaker—are relevant as evidence, since one may presume that concepts are to some extent mirrored in language.

The 'facts', taken singly, need not be decisive. A recalcitrant counter-example may be judged a deviant use or a different sense of the word. We can claim that a paraphrase is necessary, or even that ordinary language is systematically mistaken about the concept we are explaining. There are, of course, different senses and times when 'ordinary language' goes astray, but such *ad hoc* hypotheses and qualifications diminish both the plausibility and the explanatory force of a theory. While we are not irrevocably bound to the linguistic facts, there are no 'don't cares'—contexts of use with which we are not concerned, since any context can be relevant as evidence for or against an analysis. A general interpretation which avoids dividing senses and accounts for the behaviour of a concept in many contexts fits the familiar pattern of scientific explanation in which diverse, seemingly unlike surface phenomena are seen as deriving from some common source. For these reasons, I take it as a strong point in favour of the semantic theory that it treats the conditional as a univocal concept.

V. PRAGMATIC AMBIGUITY

I have argued that the conditional connective is semantically unambiguous. It is obvious, however, that the context of utterance, the purpose of the assertion, and the beliefs of the speaker or his community may make a difference to the interpretation of a counterfactual. How do we reconcile the ambiguity of conditional sentences with the univocity of the conditional concept? Let us look more closely at the notion of ambiguity.

A sentence is ambiguous if there is more than one proposition which it may properly be interpreted to express. Ambiguity may be syntactic (if the sentence has more than one grammatical structure), semantic (if one of the words has more than one meaning), or pragmatic (if the interpretation depends directly on the context of use). The first two kinds of ambiguity are perhaps more familiar, but the third kind is probably the most common in natural languages. Any sentence involving pronouns, tensed verbs, articles, or quantifiers is pragmatically ambiguous. For example, the proposition expressed by 'L'état, c'est moi' depends on who says it; 'Do it now' may be good or bad advice depending on when it is said; 'Cherchez la femme' is ambiguous since it contains a definite description, and the truth conditions for 'All's well that ends well' depends on the domain of discourse. If the theory presented above is correct, then we may add conditional sentences to this list. The truth conditions for 'If wishes were horses, then beggers would ride' depend on the specification of an s-function.[14]

The grounds for treating the ambiguity of conditional sentences as pragmatic rather than semantic are the same as the grounds for treating the ambiguity of quantified sentences as pragmatic: simplicity and systematic coherence. The truth conditions for quantified statements vary with a change in the domain of discourse, but there is a single structure to these truth conditions which remains constant for every domain. The semantics for classical predicate logic brings out this common structure by giving the universal quantifier a single meaning and making the domain a parameter of the interpretation. In a similar fashion, the semantics for conditional logic brings out the common structure of the truth conditions for conditional statements by giving the connective a single meaning and making the selection function a parameter of the interpretation.

Just as we can communicate effectively using quantified sentences without explicitly specifying a domain, so we can communicate effectively using conditional sentences without explicitly specifying an s-function. This suggests that there are further rules beyond those set down in the semantics, governing the use of conditional sentences. Such rules are the subject-matter of a *pragmatics* of conditionals. Very little can be said, at this point, about pragmatic rules for the use of conditionals since the logic has not advanced beyond the propositional stage, but I shall make a few speculative remarks about the kinds of research which may provide a framework for treatment of this problem, and related pragmatic problems in the philosophy of science.

(1) If we had a functional logic with a conditional connective, it is

[14] I do not wish to pretend that the notions needed to define ambiguity and to make the distinction between pragmatic and semantic ambiguity (e.g. 'proposition' and 'meaning') are precise. They can be made precise only in the context of semantic and pragmatic theories. But even if it is unclear, in general, what pragmatic ambiguity is, it is clear, I hope, that my examples are cases of it.

likely that $(\forall x)(Fx > Gx)$ would be a plausible candidate for the form of a law of nature. A law of nature says, not just that every actual F is a G, but further that for every possible F, if it were an F, it would be a G. If this is correct, then Hempel's confirmation paradox does not arise, since 'All ravens are black' is not logically equivalent to 'All non-black things are non-ravens.' Also, the relation between counterfactuals and laws becomes clear: laws support counterfactuals because they entail them. 'If this dove were a raven, it would be black' is simply an instantiation of 'All ravens are black.'[15]

(2) Goodman has argued that the pragmatic problem of counter-factuals is one of a cluster of closely related problems concerning induction and confirmation. He locates the source of these difficulties in the general problem of projectability, which can be stated roughly as follows: when can a predicate be validly projected from one set of cases to others? or when is a hypothesis confirmed by its positive instances? Some way of distinguishing between natural predicates and those which are artificially constructed is needed. If a theory of projection such as Goodman envisions were developed, it might find a natural place in a pragmatics of condition-als. Pragmatic criteria for measuring the inductive properties of predicates might provide pragmatic criteria for ordering possible worlds.[16]

(3) There are some striking structural parallels between conditional logic and conditional probability functions, which suggests the possibility of a connection between inductive logic and conditional logic. A probability assignment and an s-function are two quite different ways of describing the inductive relations among propositions; a theory which draws a con-nection between them might be illuminating for both.[17]

VI. CONCLUSION: EMPIRICISM AND POSSIBLE WORLDS

Writers of fiction and fantasy sometimes suggest that imaginary worlds have a life of their own beyond the control of their creators. Pirandello's six characters, for example, rebelled against their author and took the story out of his hands. The sceptic may be inclined to suspect that this suggestion

---

[15] For a discussion of the relation of laws to counterfactuals, see E. Nagel, *Structure of Science* (New York, 1961), pp. 47–78. For a recent discussion of the paradoxes of confirmation by the man who discovered them, see C. G. Hempel, 'Recent Problems of Induction' in *Mind and Cosmos*, ed. by R. G. Colodny (Pittsburgh, 1966), pp. 112–34.

[16] Goodman, op. cit., especially Ch. IV.

[17] Several philosophers have discussed the relation of conditional propositions to conditional probabilities. See R. C. Jeffrey, 'If', *Journal of Philosophy*, 61 (1964), 702–3, and E. W. Adams, 'Probability and the Logic of Conditionals' in *Aspects of Inductive Logic*, ed. J. Hintikka and P. Suppes (Amsterdam, 1966), pp. 265–316. I hope to present elsewhere my method of drawing the connection between the two notions, which differs from both of these.

is itself fantasy. He believes that nothing goes into a fictional world, or a possible world, unless it is put there by decision or convention; it is a creature of invention and not discovery. Even the fabulist Tolkien admits that Faërie is a land 'full of wonder, but not of information'.[18]

For similar reasons, the empiricist may be uncomfortable about a theory which treats counterfactuals as literal statements about non-actual situations. Counterfactuals are often contingent, and contingent statements must be supported by evidence. But evidence can be gathered, by us at least, only in this universe. To satisfy the empiricist, I must show how possible worlds, even if the product of convention, can be subjects of empirical investigation.

There is no mystery to the fact that I can partially define a possible world in such a way that I am ignorant of some of the determinate truths in that world. One way I can do this is to attribute to it features of the actual world which are unknown to me. Thus I can say, 'I am thinking of a possible world in which the population of China is just the same, on each day, as it is in the actual world.' I am making up this world—it is a pure product of my intentions—but there are already things true in it which I shall never know.

Conditionals do implicitly, and by convention, what is done explicitly by stipulation in this example. It is because counterfactuals are generally about possible worlds which are very much like the actual one, and defined in terms of it, that evidence is so often relevant to their truth. When I wonder, for example, what would have happened if I had asked my boss for a raise yesterday, I am wondering about a possible world that I have already roughly picked out. It has the same history, up to yesterday, as the actual world, the same boss with the same dispositions and habits. The main difference is that in that world, yesterday I asked the boss for a raise. Since I do not know everything about the boss's habits and dispositions in the actual world, there is a lot that I do not know about how he acts in the possible world that I have chosen, although I might find out by watching him respond to a similar request from another, or by asking his secretary about his mood yesterday. These bits of information about the actual world would not be decisive, of course, but they would be relevant, since they tell me more about the non-actual situation that I have selected.

If I make a conditional statement—subjunctive or otherwise—and the antecedent turns out to be true, then whether I know it or not, I have said something about the actual world, namely that the consequent is true in it. If the antecedent is false, then I have said something about a particular

[18] J. R. Tolkien, 'On Fairy Stories' in *The Tolkien Reader* (New York, 1966), p. 3.

counterfactual world, even if I believe the antecedent to be true. The conditional provides a set of conventions for selecting possible situations which have a specified relation to what actually happens. This makes it possible for statements about unrealized possibilities to tell us, not just about the speaker's imagination, but about the world.

XIII

CAUSATION

DAVID LEWIS

HUME defined causation twice over. He wrote 'we may define a cause to be *an object followed by another, and where all the objects,'similar to the first, are followed by objects similar to the second.* Or, in other words *where, if the first object had not been, the second never had existed.*'[1]

Descendants of Hume's first definition still dominate the philosophy of causation: a causal succession is supposed to be a succession that instantiates a regularity. To be sure, there have been improvements. Nowadays we try to distinguish the regularities that count—the 'causal laws'—from mere accidental regularities of succession. We subsume causes and effects under regularities by means of descriptions they satisfy, not by over-all similarity. And we allow a cause to be only one indispensable part, not the whole, of the total situation that is followed by the effect in accordance with a law. In present-day regularity analyses, a cause is defined (roughly) as any member of any minimal set of actual conditions that are jointly sufficient, given the laws, for the existence of the effect.

More precisely, let C be the proposition that c exists (or occurs) and let E be the proposition that e exists. Then c causes e, according to a typical regularity analysis,[2] iff (1) C and E are true; and (2) for some non-empty set $\mathscr{L}$ of true law-propositions and some set $\mathscr{F}$ of true propositions of particular fact, $\mathscr{L}$ and $\mathscr{F}$ jointly imply $C \supset E$, although $\mathscr{L}$ and $\mathscr{F}$ jointly do not imply E and $\mathscr{F}$ alone does not imply $C \supset E$.[3]

From *Journal of Philosophy*, 70 (1973), 556–67. Reprinted by permission of the author and editor of the journal.

I thank the American Council of Learned Societies, Princeton University, and the National Science Foundation for research support.

[1] *An Enquiry concerning Human Understanding*, Section VII.

[2] Not one that has been proposed by any actual author in just this form, so far as I know.

[3] I identify a *proposition*, as is becoming usual, with the set of possible worlds where it is true. It is not a linguistic entity. Truth-functional operations on propositions are the appropriate Boolean operations on sets of worlds; logical relations among propositions are relations of inclusion, overlap, etc. among sets. A sentence of a language *expresses* a proposition iff the sentence and the proposition are true at exactly the same worlds. No ordinary language will provide sentences to express all propositions; there will not be enough sentences to go around.

Much needs doing, and much has been done, to turn definitions like this one into defensible analyses. Many problems have been overcome. Others remain: in particular, regularity analyses tend to confuse causation itself with various other causal relations. If c belongs to a minimal set of conditions jointly sufficient for e, given the laws, then c may well be a genuine cause of e. But c might rather be an effect of e: one which could not, given the laws and some of the actual circumstances, have occurred otherwise than by being caused by e. Or c might be an epiphenomenon of the causal history of e: a more or less inefficacious effect of some genuine cause of e. Or c might be a pre-empted potential cause of e: something that did not cause e, but that would have done so in the absence of whatever really did cause e.

It remains to be seen whether any regularity analysis can succeed in distinguishing genuine causes from effects, epiphenomena, and pre-empted potential causes—and whether it can succeed without falling victim to worse problems, without piling on the epicycles, and without departing from the fundamental idea that causation is instantiation of regularities. I have no proof that regularity analyses are beyond repair, nor any space to review the repairs that have been tried. Suffice it to say that the prospects look dark. I think it is time to give up and try something else.

A promising alternative is not far to seek. Hume's 'other words'—that if the cause had not been, the effect never had existed—are no mere restatement of his first definition. They propose something altogether different: a counterfactual analysis of causation.

The proposal has not been well received. True, we do know that causation has something or other to do with counterfactuals. We think of a cause as something that makes a difference, and the difference it makes must be a difference from what would have happened without it. Had it been absent, its effects—some of them, at least, and usually all—would have been absent as well. Yet it is one thing to mention these platitudes now and again, and another thing to rest an analysis on them. That has not seemed worth while.[4] We have learned all too well that counterfactuals are ill understood, wherefore it did not seem that much understanding could be gained by using them to analyse causation or anything else. Pending a better understanding of counterfactuals, moreover, we had no way to fight seeming counter-examples to a counterfactual analysis.

But counterfactuals need not remain ill understood, I claim, unless we cling to false preconceptions about what it would be like to understand them. Must an adequate understanding make no reference to unactualized

[4] One exception: Aardon Lyon, 'Causality', *British Journal for Philosophy of Science*, 18.1 (May 1967), 1–20.

possibilities? Must it assign sharply determinate truth conditions? Must it connect counterfactuals rigidly to covering laws? Then none will be forthcoming. So much the worse for those standards of adequacy. Why not take counterfactuals at face value: as statements about possible alternatives to the actual situation, somewhat vaguely specified, in which the actual laws may or may not remain intact? There are now several such treatments of counterfactuals, differing only in details.[5] If they are right, then sound foundations have been laid for analyses that use counterfactuals.

In this paper, I shall state a counterfactual analysis, not very different from Hume's second definition, of some sorts of causation. Then I shall try to show how this analysis works to distinguish genuine causes from effects, epiphenomena, and pre-empted potential causes.

My discussion will be incomplete in at least four ways. Explicit preliminary settings-aside may prevent confusion.

1. I shall confine myself to causation among *events*, in the everyday sense of the word: flashes, battles, conversations, impacts, strolls, deaths, touchdowns, falls, kisses, and the like. Not that events are the only things that can cause or be caused; but I have no full list of the others, and no good umbrella-term to cover them all.

2. My analysis is meant to apply to causation in particular cases. It is not an analysis of causal generalizations. Presumably those are quantified statements involving causation among particular events (or non-events), but it turns out not to be easy to match up the causal generalizations of natural language with the available quantified forms. A sentence of the form 'c-events cause E-events,' for instance, can mean any of

(a) For some c in C and some e in E, c causes e,

(b) For every e in E, there is some c in C such that c causes e,

(c) For every c in C, there is some e in E such that c causes e, not to mention further ambiguities. Worse still, 'Only c-events cause E-events' ought to mean

(d) For every c, if there is some e in E such that c causes e, then c is in C

if 'only' has its usual meaning. But no; it unambiguously means (b) instead! These problems are not about causation, but about our idioms of quantification.

3. We sometimes single out one among all the causes of some event and call it 'the' cause, as if there were no others. Or we single out a few as the 'causes,' calling the rest mere 'causal factors' or 'causal conditions'. Or we

---

[5] See, for instance, Robert Stalnaker, 'A Theory of Conditionals', in Nicholas Rescher, ed., *Studies in Logical Theory* (Oxford, 1968), [reprinted above, pp. 165–179]; and my *Counterfactuals* (Oxford, 1973).

speak of the 'decisive' or 'real' or 'principal' cause. We may select the abnormal or extraordinary causes, or those under human control, or those we deem good or bad, or just those we want to talk about. I have nothing to say about these principles of invidious discrimination.[6] I am concerned with the prior question of what it is to be one of the causes (unselectively speaking). My analysis is meant to capture a broad and non-discriminatory concept of casuation.

4. I shall be content, for now, if I can give an analysis of causation that works properly under determinism. By determinism I do not mean any thesis of universal causation, or universal predictability-in-principle, but rather this: the prevailing laws of nature are such that there do not exist any two possible worlds which are exactly alike up to some time, which differ thereafter, and in which those laws are never violated. Perhaps by ignoring indeterminism I squander the most striking advantage of a counterfactual analysis over a regularity analysis: that it allows undetermined events to be caused.[7] I fear, however, that my present analysis cannot yet cope with all varieties of causation under indeterminism. The needed repair would take us too far into disputed questions about the foundations of probability.

COMPARATIVE SIMILARITY

To begin, I take as primitive a relation of *comparative over-all* similarity among possible worlds. We may say that one world is *closer to actuality* than another if the first resembles our actual world more than the second does, taking account of all the respects of similarity and difference and balancing them off one against another.

(More generally, an arbitrary world w can play the role of our actual world. In speaking of our actual world without knowing just which world is ours, I am in effect generalizing over all worlds. We really need a three-place relation: world w_1 is closer to world w than world w_2 is. I shall henceforth leave this generality tacit.)

I have not said just how to balance the respects of comparison against each other, so I have not said just what our relation of comparative similarity is to be. Not for nothing did I call it primitive. But I have said what *sort* of relation it is, and we are familiar with relations of that sort. We do

---

[6] Except that Morton G. White's discussion of causal selection, in *Foundations of Historical Knowledge* (New York, 1965), pp. 105–81, would meet my needs, despite the fact that it is based on a regularity analysis.

[7] That this ought to be allowed is argued in G. E. M. Anscombe, *Causality and Determination: An Inaugural Lecture* (Cambridge, 1971) [reprinted above, pp. 63–81]; and in Fred Dretske and Aaron Snyder, 'Causal Irregularity', *Philosophy of Science*, 39.1 (March 1972), 69–71.

make judgements of comparative overall similarity—of people, for instance —by balancing off many respects of similarity and difference. Often our mutual expectations about the weighting factors are definite and accurate enough to permit communication. I shall have more to say later about the way the balance must go in particular cases to make my analysis work. But the vagueness of over-all similarity will not be entirely resolved. Nor should it be. The vagueness of similarity does infect causation; and no correct analysis can deny it.

The respects of similarity and difference that enter into the overall similarity of worlds are many and varied. In particular, similarities in matters of particular fact trade off against similarities of law. The prevailing laws of nature are important to the character of a world; so similarities of law are weighty. Weighty, but not sacred. We should not take it for granted that a world that conforms perfectly to our actual laws is *ipso facto* closer to actuality than any world where those laws are violated in any way at all. It depends on the nature and extent of the violation, on the place of the violated laws in the total system of laws of nature, and on the counter-vailing similarities and differences in other respects. Likewise, similarities or differences of particular fact may be more or less weighty, depending on their nature and extent. Comprehensive and exact similarities of particular fact throughout large spatio-temporal regions seem to have special weight. It may be worth a small miracle to prolong or expand a region of perfect match.

Our relation of comparative similarity should meet two formal constraints. (1) It should be a weak ordering of the worlds: an ordering in which ties are permitted, but any two worlds are comparable. (2) Our actual world should be closest to actuality, resembling itself more than any other world resembles it. We do *not* impose the further constraint that for any set A of worlds there is a unique closest A-world, or even a set of A-worlds tied for closest. Why not an infinite sequence of closer and closer A-worlds, but no closest?

COUNTERFACTUALS AND COUNTERFACTUAL DEPENDENCE

Given any two propositions A and C, we have their *counterfactual* $A \square \rightarrow C$: the proposition that if A were true, then C would also be true. The operation $\square \rightarrow$ is defined by a rule of truth, as follows. $A \square \rightarrow C$ is true (at a world w) iff either (1) there are no possible A-worlds (in which case $A \square \rightarrow C$ is *vacuous*), (2) some A-world where C holds is closer (to w) than is any A-world where C does not hold. In other words, a counterfactual is non-vacuously true iff it takes less of a departure from actuality to make the consequent true along with the antecedent than it does to make the antecedent true without the consequent.

We did not assume that there must always be one or more closest A-worlds. But if there are, we can simplify: $A \square \rightarrow C$ is non-vacuously true iff C holds at all the closest A-worlds.

We have not presupposed that A is false. If A is true, then our actual world is the closest A-world, so $A \square \rightarrow C$ is true iff C is. Hence $A \square \rightarrow C$ implies the material conditional $A \overset{\text{f}}{\supset} C$; and A and C jointly imply $A \square \rightarrow C$.

Let $A_1, A_2, \ldots$ be a family of possible propositions, no two of which are compossible; let $C_1, C_2, \ldots$ be another such family (of equal size). Then if all the counterfactuals $A_1 \square \rightarrow C_1, A_2 \square \rightarrow C_2, \ldots$ between corresponding propositions in the two families are true, we shall say that the C's *depend counterfactually* on the A's. We can say it like this in ordinary language: whether C_1 or C_2 or . . . depends (counterfactually) on whether A_1 or A_2 or . . . .

Counterfactual dependence between large families of alternatives is characteristic of processes of measurement, perception, or control. Let $R_1, R_2, \ldots$ be propositions specifying the alternative readings of a certain barometer at a certain time. Let $P_1, P_2, \ldots$ specify the corresponding pressures of the surrounding air. Then, if the barometer is working properly to measure the pressure, the R's must depend counterfactually on the P's. As we say it: the reading depends on the pressure. Likewise, if I am seeing at a certain time, then my visual impressions must depend counterfactually, over a wide range of alternative possibilities, on the scene before my eyes. And if I am in control over what happens in some respect, then there must be a double counterfactual dependence, again over some fairly wide range of alternatives. The outcome depends on what I do, and that in turn depends on which outcome I want.[8]

CAUSAL DEPENDENCE AMONG EVENTS

If a family $C_1, C_2, \ldots$ depends counterfactually on a family $A_1, A_2, \ldots$ in the sense just explained, we will ordinarily be willing to speak also of causal dependence. We say, for instance, that the barometer reading depends causally on the pressure, that my visual impressions depend causally on the scene before my eyes, or that the outcome of something under my control depends causally on what I do. But there are exceptions. Let

[8] Analyses in terms of counterfactual dependence are found in two papers of Alvin I. Goldman: 'Toward a Theory of Social Power', *Philosophical Studies*, 23 (1972), 221–68; and 'Discrimination and Perceptual Knowledge', presented at the 1972 Chapel Hill Colloquium.

G_1, G_2, ... be alternative possible laws of gravitation, differing in the value of some numerical constant. Let M_1, M_2, ... be suitable alternative laws of planetary motion. Then the M's may depend counterfactually on the G's, but we would not call this dependence causal. Such exceptions as this, however, do not involve any sort of dependence among distinct particular events. The hope remains that causal dependence among events, at least, may be analysed simply as counterfactual dependence.

We have spoken thus far of counterfactual dependence among propositions, not among events. Whatever particular events may be, presumably they are not propositions. But that is no problem, since they can at least be paired with propositions. To any possible event e, there corresponds the proposition $O(e)$ that holds at all and only those worlds where e occurs. This $O(e)$ is the proposition that e occurs.[9] (If no two events occur at exactly the same worlds—if, that is, there are no absolutely necessary connections between distinct events—we may add that this correspondence of events and propositions is one to one.) Counterfactual dependence among events is simply counterfactual dependence among the corresponding propositions.

Let c_1, c_2, ... and e_1, e_2, ... be distinct possible events such that no two of the c's and no two of the e's are compossible. Then I say that the family e_1, e_2, ... of events *depends causally* on the family c_1, c_2, ... iff the family $O(e_1)$, $O(e_2)$, ... of propositions depends counterfactually on the family $O(c_1)$, $O(c_2)$, ... As we say it: whether e_1 or e_2 or ... occurs depends on whether c_1 or c_2 or ... occurs.

We can also define a relation of dependence among single events rather than families. Let c and e be two distinct possible particular events. Then *e depends causally* on c iff the family $O(e)$, $\sim O(e)$ depends counterfactually

---

[9] Beware: if we refer to a particular event e by means of some description that satisfies, then we must take care not to confuse $O(e)$, the proposition that e itself occurs, with the different proposition that some event or other occurs which satisfies the description. It is a contingent matter, in general, what events satisfy what descriptions. Let e be the death of Socrates—the death he actually died, to be distinguished from all the different deaths he might have died instead. Suppose that Socrates had fled, only to be eaten by a lion. Then e would not have occurred, and $O(e)$ would have been false; but a different event would have satisfied the description 'the death of Socrates' that I used to refer to e. Or suppose that Socrates had lived and died just as he actually did, and afterwards was resurrected and killed again and resurrected again, and finally became immortal. Then no event would have satisfied the description. (Even if the temporary deaths are real deaths, neither of the two can be *the* death.) But e would have occurred, and $O(e)$ would have been true. Call a description of an event e *rigid* iff (1) nothing but e could possibly satisfy it, and (2) e could not possibly occur without satisfying it. I have claimed that even such commonplace descriptions as 'the death of Socrates' are non-rigid, and in fact I think that rigid descriptions of events are hard to find. That would be a problem for anyone who needed to associate with every possible event e a sentence $\phi(e)$ true at all and only those worlds where e occurs. But we need no such sentences—only propositions, which may or may not have expressions in our language.

on the family $O(c)$, $\sim O(c)$. As we say it: whether e occurs or not depends on whether c occurs or not. The dependence consists in the truth of two counterfactuals: $O(c) \ \square \rightarrow O(e)$ and $\sim O(c) \ \square \rightarrow \sim O(e)$. There are two cases. If c and e do not actually occur, then the second counterfactual is automatically true because its antecedent and consequent are true: so e depends causally on c iff the first counterfactual holds. That is, if e would have occurred if c had occurred. But if c and e are actual events, then it is the first counterfactual that is automatically true. Then e depends causally on c iff, if c had not been, e never had existed. I take Hume's second definition as my definition not of causation itself, but of causal dependence among actual events.

CAUSATION

Causal dependence among actual events implies causation. If c and e are two actual events such that e would not have occurred without c, then c is a cause of e. But I reject the converse. Causation must always be transitive; causal dependence may not be; so there can be causation without causal dependence. Let c, d, and e be three actual events such that d would not have occurred without c and e would not have occurred without d. Then c is a cause of e even if e would still have occurred (otherwise caused) without c.

We extend causal dependence to a transitive relation in the usual way. Let c, d, e, ... be a finite sequence of actual particular events such that d depends causally on c, e on d, and so on throughout. Then this sequence is a *causal chain*. Finally, one event is a *cause* of another iff there exists a causal chain leading from the first to the second. This completes my counterfactual analysis of causation.

COUNTERFACTUAL VERSUS NOMIC DEPENDENCE

It is essential to distinguish counterfactual and causal dependence from what I shall call *nomic dependence*. The family C_1, C_2, ... of propositions depends nomically on the family A_1, A_2, ... iff there are a non-empty set $\mathscr{L}$ of true law-propositions and a set $\mathscr{F}$ of true propositions of particular fact such that $\mathscr{L}$ and $\mathscr{F}$ jointly imply (but $\mathscr{F}$ alone does not imply) all the material conditionals $A_1 \supset C_1$, $A_2 \supset C_2$, ... between the corresponding propositions in the two families. (Recall that these same material conditionals are implied by the counterfactuals that would comprise a counterfactual dependence.) We shall say also that the nomic dependence holds *in virtue of* the premise sets $\mathscr{L}$ and $\mathscr{F}$.

Nomic and counter factual dependence are related as follows. Say that a proposition B is *counterfactually independent* of the family $A_1, A_2, \ldots$ of alternatives iff B would hold no matter which of the A's were true—that is, iff the counterfactuals $A_1 \,\square\!\!\rightarrow B, A_2 \,\square\!\!\rightarrow B \ldots$ all hold. If the C's depend nomically on the A's in virtue of the premise sets $\mathscr{L}$ and $\mathscr{F}$, and if in addition (all members of) $\mathscr{L}$ and $\mathscr{F}$ are counterfactually independent of the A's, then it follows that the C's depend counterfactually on the A's. In that case, we may regard the nomic dependence in virtue of $\mathscr{L}$ and $\mathscr{F}$ as explaining the counterfactual dependence. Often, perhaps always, counterfactual dependences may be thus explained. But the requirement of counterfactual independence is indispensable. Unless $\mathscr{L}$ and $\mathscr{F}$ meet that requirement, nomic dependence in virtue of $\mathscr{L}$ and $\mathscr{F}$ does not imply counterfactual dependence, and, if there is counterfactual dependence anyway, does not explain it.

Nomic dependence is reversible, in the following sense. If the family $C_1, C_2, \ldots$ depends nomically on the family $A_1, A_2, \ldots$ in virtue of $\mathscr{L}$ and $\mathscr{F}$, then also $A_1, A_2, \ldots$ depends nomically on family $AC_1, AC_2, \ldots$, in virtue of $\mathscr{L}$ and $\mathscr{F}$, where A is the disjunction $A_1 \vee A_2 \vee \ldots$. Is counterfactual dependence likewise reversible? That does not follow. For, even if $\mathscr{L}$ and $\mathscr{F}$ are independent of $A_1, A_2, \ldots$ and hence establish the counterfactual dependence of the C's on the A's, still they may fail to be independent of $AC_1, AC_2, \ldots$, and hence may fail to establish the reverse counterfactual dependence of the A's on the AC's. Irreversible counterfactual dependence is shown below: @ is our actual world, the dots are the other worlds, and distance on the page represents similarity 'distance'.

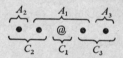

The counterfactuals $A_1 \,\square\!\!\rightarrow C_1, A_2 \,\square\!\!\rightarrow C_2$, and $A_3 \,\square\!\!\rightarrow C_3$ hold at the actual world; wherefore the C's depend on the A's. But we do not have the reverse dependence of the A's on the AC's, since instead of the needed $AC_2 \,\square\!\!\rightarrow A_2$ and $AC_3 \,\square\!\!\rightarrow A_3$ we have $AC_2 \,\square\!\!\rightarrow A_1$ and $AC_3 \,\square\!\!\rightarrow A_1$.

Just such irreversibility is commonplace. The barometer reading depends counterfactually on the pressure—that is as clear-cut as counterfactuals ever get—but does the pressure depend counterfactually on the reading? If the reading had been higher, would the pressure have been higher? Or would the barometer have been malfunctioning? The second sounds better: a higher reading would have been an incorrect reading. To be sure, there are actual laws and circumstances that imply and explain the actual accuracy of the barometer, but these are no more sacred than the actual laws and circumstances that imply and explain the actual pressure. Less sacred, in fact. When something must give way to permit a higher reading, we find it less of a departure from actuality to hold the pressure fixed and sacrifice the accuracy, rather than vice versa. It is not hard to see why. The barometer, being more localized and more delicate than the weather, is more vulnerable to slight departures from actuality.[10]

We can now explain why regularity analyses of causation (among events, under determinism) work as well as they do. Suppose that event c causes event e according to the sample regularity analysis that I gave at the beginning of this paper, in virtue of premise sets $\mathscr{L}$ and $\mathscr{F}$. It follows that $\mathscr{L}$, $\mathscr{F}$, and $\sim O(c)$ jointly do not imply $O(e)$. Strengthen this: suppose further that they do imply $\sim O(e)$. If so, the family $O(e)$, $\sim O(e)$, depends nomically on the family $O(c)$, $\sim O(c)$ in virtue of $\mathscr{L}$ and $\mathscr{F}$. Add one more supposition: that $\mathscr{L}$ and $\mathscr{F}$ are counterfactually independent of $O(c)$, $\sim O(c)$. Then it follows according to my counterfactual analysis that e depends counterfactually and causally on c, and hence that c causes e. If I am right, the regularity analysis gives conditions that are almost but not quite sufficient for explicable causal dependence. That is not quite the same thing as causation; but causation without causal dependence is scarce, and if there is inexplicable causal dependence we are (understandably!) unaware of it.[11]

EFFECTS AND EPIPHENOMENA

I return now to the problems I raised against regularity analyses, hoping to show that my counterfactual analysis can overcome them.

The *problem of effects*, as it confronts a counterfactual analysis, is as follows. Suppose that c causes a subsequent event e, and that e does not also cause c. (I do not rule out closed causal loops *a priori*, but this case is not to be one.) Suppose further that, given the laws and some of the actual circumstances, c could not have failed to cause e. It seems to follow that if the effect e had not occurred, then its cause c would not have occurred. We

[10] Granted, there are contexts or changes of wording that would incline us the other way. For some reason, 'If the reading had been higher, that would have been because the pressure was higher' invites my assent more than 'If the reading had been higher, the pressure would have been higher.' The counterfactuals from readings to pressures are much less clear-cut than those from pressures to readings. But it is enough that some legitimate resolutions of vagueness give an irreversible dependence of readings on pressures. Those are the resolutions we want at present, even if they are not favoured in all contexts.

[11] I am not here proposing a repaired regularity analysis. The repaired analysis would gratuitously rule out inexplicable causal dependence, which seems bad. Nor would it be squarely in the tradition of regularity analyses any more. Too much else would have been added.

have a spurious reverse causal dependence of c on e, contradicting our supposition that e did not cause c.

The *problem of epiphenomena*, for a counter actual analysis, is similar. Suppose that e is an epiphenomenal effect of a genuine cause c of an effect f. That is, c causes first e and then f, but e does not cause f. Suppose further that, given the laws and some of the actual circumstances, c could not have failed to cause e; and that, given the laws and others of the circumstances, f could not have been caused otherwise than by c. It seems to follow that if the epiphenomenon e had not occurred, then its cause c would not have occurred and the further effect f of that same cause would not have occurred either. We have a spurious causal dependence of f on e, contradicting our supposition that e did not cause f.

One might be tempted to solve the problem of effects by brute force: insert into the analysis a stipulation that a cause must always precede its effect (and perhaps a parallel stipulation for causal dependence). I reject this solution. (1) It is worthless against the closely related problem of epiphenomena, since the epiphenomenon e does precede its spurious effect f. (2) It rejects *a priori* certain legitimate physical hypotheses that posit backward or simultaneous causation. (3) It trivializes any theory that seeks to define the forward direction of time as the predominant direction of causation.

The proper solution to both problems, I think, is flatly to deny the counterfactuals that cause the trouble. If e had been absent, it is not that c would have been absent (and with it f, in the second case). Rather, c would have occurred just as it did but would have failed to cause e. It is less of a departure from actuality to get rid of e by holding c fixed and giving up some or other of the laws and circumstances in virtue of which c could not have failed to cause e, rather than to hold those laws and circumstances fixed and get rid of e by going back and abolishing its cause c. (In the second case, it would of course be pointless not to hold f fixed along with c.) The causal dependence of e on c is the same sort of irreversible counterfactual dependence that we have considered already.

To get rid of an actual event e with the least over-all departure from actuality, it will normally be best not to diverge at all from the actual course of events until just before the time of e. The longer we wait, the more we prolong the spatio-temporal region of perfect match between our actual world and the selected alternative. Why diverge sooner rather than later? Not to avoid violations of laws of nature. Under determinism *any* divergence, soon or late, requires some violation of the actual laws. If the laws were held sacred, there would be no way to get rid of e without changing all of the past; and nothing guarantees that the change could be kept negligible except in the recent past. That would mean that if the present were ever so slightly different, then all of the past would have been different—which is absurd. So the laws are not sacred. Violation of laws is a matter of degree. Until we get up to the time immediately before e is to occur, there is no general reason why a later divergence to avert e should need a more severe violation than an earlier one. Perhaps there are special reasons in special cases—but then these may be cases of backward causal dependence.

PRE-EMPTION

Suppose that c_1 occurs and causes e; and that c_2 also occurs and does not cause e, but would have caused e if c_1 had been absent. Thus c_2 is a potential alternate cause of e, but is pre-empted by the actual cause c_1. We may say that c_1 and c_2 overdetermine e, but they do so asymmetrically.[12] In virtue of what difference does c_1 but not c_2 cause e?

As far as causal dependence goes, there is no difference: e depends neither on c_1 nor on c_2. If either one had not occurred, the other would have sufficed to cause e. So the difference must be that, thanks to c_1, there is no causal chain from c_2 to e; whereas there is a causal chain of two or more steps from c_1 to e. Assume for simplicity that two steps are enough. Then e depends causally on some intermediate event d, and d in turn depends on c_1. Causal dependence is here intransitive: c_1 causes e via d even though e would still have occurred without c_1.

So far, so good. It remains only to deal with the objection that e does *not* depend causally on d, because if d had been absent then c_1 would have been absent and c_2, no longer pre-empted, would have caused e. We may reply by denying the claim that if d had been absent then c_1 would have been absent. That is the very same sort of spurious reverse dependence of cause on effect that we have just rejected in simpler cases. I rather claim that if d had been absent, c_1 would somehow have failed to cause d. But c_1 would still have been there to interfere with c_2, so e would not have occurred.

---

[12] I shall not discuss symmetrical cases of overdetermination, in which two over-determining factors have equal claim to count as causes. For me these are useless as test cases because I lack firm naïve opinions about them.

XIV

CAUSES AND COUNTERFACTUALS

JAEGWON KIM

A CONDITIONAL of the form 'If it were the case that A, it would be the case that B' points to some sort of dependency relationship between the propositions A and B—and, by extension, between the facts, events, states, etc. expressed by A and B. An analysis of counterfactuals would tell us exactly what this dependency relationship comes to. The causal relation, too, appears to be such a relationship: if an event c is a cause of an event e, then the occurrence of e depends in some sense on the occurrence of c. We say: but for the cause the effect would not have occurred. It is thus that Lewis wants to explain causal dependency in terms of counterfactual dependency.

Speaking only of actual events and skirting issues concerning the analysis of counterfactuals, we can summarize Lewis's account in the following two statements:

(1) An event e causally depends on an event c just in case if c had not occurred e would not have occurred.

(2) An event c is a cause of an event e just in case there is a chain of events from c to e, each event in this chain being causally dependent on its predecessor.

It follows that the counterfactual conditional 'If c had not occurred, e would not have occurred' entails, under Lewis's analysis, the causal statement 'c caused e.'

It seems, however, that the sort of dependency expressed by counterfactuals is considerably broader than strictly causal dependency and that causal dependency is only one among the heterogeneous group of dependency relationships that can be expressed by counterfactuals. Let us look at a few cases:

1. First, there are cases that exemplify some sort of 'logical' or 'analytical' dependency. Consider:

From *Journal of Philosophy*, 70 (1973), 570–2. Reprinted by permission of the author and editor of the journal.

If yesterday had not been Monday, today would not be Tuesday.

Should we say on the strength of this counterfactual that today's being Tuesday was caused by yesterday's being Monday? But perhaps these aren't *events*; but then consider:

If George had not been born in 1950, he would not have reached the age of 21 in 1971.

2. Second, there are cases in which one event is a constituent part of another, the two events satisfying the required counterfactual. For example, my writing the letter 'r' twice in succession is a constituent event in the event of my writing 'Larry'; and it is presumably true to say:

If I had not written 'r' twice in succession, I would not have written 'Larry'.

But I do not see a causal relation between these events.

3. Consider cases in which an agent does an action by doing another. Thus, by turning the knob, I open the window. The following counterfactual is true:

If I had not turned the knob, I would not have opened the window.

However, my turning the knob does not cause my opening the window (although it does cause the window's being open).

4. The kind of case that I find interesting is one in which one event 'determines' another without *causally* determining it. The second event depends asymmetrically on the first for its occurrence, but is not a *causal* consequence of it. When my sister gave birth to her first child, I became an uncle. My becoming an uncle was determined by, was dependent on, the birth of the child, but was not a causal effect of it. And the two events sustain the required counterfactual:

If my sister had not given birth at t, I would not have become an uncle at t.

If these examples are plausible, counterfactual dependency is too broad to pin down causal dependency. And as Lewis himself points out, cases of overdetermination raise special difficulties for his analysis; they constitute *prima facie* evidence that counterfactual dependency is also too narrow to capture causal dependency.

Lewis says that his account explains why the regularity analysis of causal relations work as well as it does. Lewis is surely right in attending to this problem: obviously, considerations involving law-like regularities are important in ascertaining causal relations, and any adequate theory of causation should explain that epistemological aspect of causal relations. I am not certain, however, that Lewis in fact provides an explanation here. His argument depends crucially on a lemma established earlier in his paper to the effect that if the family of propositions $C_1, \ldots, C_n$ depends nomically on $A_1, \ldots, A_n$ in virtue of $\mathscr{L}$ and $\mathscr{F}$, then $C_1, \ldots, C_n$ counterfactually depends on $A_1, \ldots, A_n$ provided that $\mathscr{L}$ and $\mathscr{F}$ are counterfactually independent of $A_1, \ldots, A_n$. However, the proof of this lemma nowhere makes use of the fact that $\mathscr{L}$ is a set of *laws*. (One conjectures, though, that the nomological nature of $\mathscr{L}$ may have something to do with $\mathscr{L}$'s counterfactual independence of $A_1, \ldots, A_n$.) It would seem that Lewis must show in greater detail how considerations of laws enter into our judgements of similarity between possible worlds, and hence how laws relate to counterfactuals, before we can properly understand how his counterfactual account relates to the classical regularity theory.

What is the function of causal statements? Why do we make causal judgements? The following are some of the more common contexts in which we engage in causal talk: (1) we make causal judgements to *explain* the occurrence of particular events; (2) we seek causal knowledge because of its *predictive* usefulness; (3) knowledge of causal connections often gives us power to *control* events; (4) causal attributions involving agents are important in the attribution of *moral responsibility*, *legal liability*, and so on; (5) causal concepts are often used in special technical senses in physical theory. In assessing the comparative merits of rival accounts of causation, we should consider not only the alleged counter-examples (e.g. over-determination, pre-emption, etc.) but also, and more importantly, how well the proposed analyses account for those aspects of causal judgements just mentioned, among others. If we compare the classical regularity theory with Lewis's account with this in mind, it is by no means clear that the latter fares significantly better than the former. But a final judgement would be premature; more would have to be known, for example, about the role of laws in Lewis's account of counterfactuals.

NOTES ON THE CONTRIBUTORS

J. L. MACKIE is a Fellow of University College, Oxford. His book *The Cement of the Universe: A Study of Causation* appeared in 1974.

R. TAYLOR is a member of the Philosophy Department at the University of Rochester. Among his publications is *Action and Purpose* (1966).

M. SCRIVEN is a member of the Philosophy Department at Berkeley, California. His book *Primary Philosophy* was published in 1966.

J. KIM, formerly at Cornell, is now at the University of Michigan. He has contributed many papers to the Journal of Philosophy and other periodicals.

G. E. M. ANSCOMBE has been Professor of Philosophy at Cambridge since 1970. She has been translator and co-editor of the posthumous works of Wittgenstein, and author of *An Introduction to Wittgenstein's Tractatus* (1959).

D. DAVIDSON, now at Princeton, was John Locke Lecturer in Oxford in 1969–70. He was the editor (with J. Hintikka) of *Words and Objections* (1969).

G. H. VON WRIGHT, formerly Professor of Philosophy at Cambridge, is now Research Professor in the Academy of Finland, and Professor at Large of Cornell University.

C. J. DUCASSE was formerly head of the Philosophy Department at Brown University. Among his many publications is *Truth, Knowledge, and Causation* (1968).

W. S. SELLARS is Professor of Philosophy at the University of Pittsburgh. He was John Locke Lecturer at Oxford in 1965–6, and his book *Science and Metaphysics* appeared in 1968.

R. M. CHISHOLM is Professor of Philosophy at Brown University. Among his many publications is *Perceiving* (1957).

N. RESCHER has been Professor of Philosophy at Pittsburgh since 1961. He has written widely on logic and the philosophy of science.

R. STALNAKER is a Professor at Cornell University.

D. K. LEWIS, now a member of the Philosophy Department at Princeton, is the author of *Convention* (1969).

BIBLIOGRAPHY

I. BOOKS

BEROFSKY, B., *Determinism* (Princeton, 1971).

BUNGE, M., *Causality* (Cambridge, Mass., 1959).

DUCASSE, C. J., *Causation and the Types of Necessity* (Seattle, 1924; Dover paperbacks, 1969).

GOODMAN, N., *Fact, Fiction and Forecast* (2nd ed., Indianapolis, 1965).

HART, H. L., and HONORÉ, A. M., *Causation and the Law* (Oxford, 1959).

MICHOTTE, A., *The Perception of Causality* (New York, 1963).

RESCHER, N., *Hypothetical Reasoning* (Amsterdam, 1964).

SUPPES, P., *A Probabilistic Theory of Causality* (Amsterdam, 1970).

VON WRIGHT, G. H., *Explanation and Understanding* (Ithaca, N.Y., 1971), pp. 34–82.

II. ARTICLES

ANDERSON, J., 'The Problem of Causality', *Australasian Journal of Philosophy*, 2 (1938), 127–42.

ANSCOMBE, G. E. M., 'Causality and Extensionality', *Journal of Philosophy*, 66 (1969), 152–9.

AYER, A. J., 'Why Cannot Cause Succeed Effect?', in *The Problem of Knowledge* (Harmondsworth (Penguin Books), 1956).

BLACK, M., 'Why Cannot an Effect Precede Its Cause?', *Analysis*, 16 (1955), 49–58.

BRAND, M., and SWAIN, M., 'On the Analysis of Causation', *Synthèse*, 21 (1970), 222–227.

BROMBERGER, S., 'What are Effects?', in R. J. Butler (ed.), *Analytical Philosophy*, 1st series (Oxford, 1966).

BURKS, A. W., 'The Logic of Causal Propositions', *Mind*, 60 (1951), 363–82.

CHISHOLM, R. M., and TAYLOR, R. T., 'Making Things to Have Happened', *Analysis*, 20 (1960), 73–82.

CHISHOLM, R. M., 'The Contrary-to-Fact Conditional', *Mind*, 55 (1946), 289–307.

COLLINWOOD, R. G., 'On the So Called Idea of Causation', *Proceedings of the Aristotelian Society*, 38 (1938), 85.

COLLINS, A., 'Explanation and Causality', *Mind*, 75 (1966), 482–500.

DRAY, W. H., 'Must Effects Have Causes?', in R. J. Butler (ed.), *Analytical Philosophy*, 1st series (Oxford, 1966).

DUMMETT, M., 'Bringing About the Past', *Philosophical Review*, 73 (1964), 338-59.

EWING, A. C., 'A Defence of Causality', in W. E. Kennick and M. Lazerowitz (eds.), *Metaphysics* (New Jersey, 1966), pp. 258–75.

FØLLESDAL, D., 'Quantification into causal contexts', in R. S. Cohen and M. W. Wartofsky (eds.), *Boston Studies in the Philosophy of Science*. vol. 2 (New York, 1965), pp. 263–74. Reprinted in L. Linsky (ed.), *Reference and Modality* (Oxford, 1971).

FØLLESDAL, D., 'A Model Theoretic Approach to Causal Logic', in *Det Kgl Norske Videnskabers Selskabs Skrifter*, 2 (1966).

GALE, R., 'Why a Cause Cannot Be Later Than Its Effect', *Review of Metaphysics*, 19 (1965–6), 209–34.

GASKING, D., 'Causation and Recipes', *Mind*, 6 (1955), 479–87.

GOROVITZ, S., 'Leaving the Past Alone', *Philosophical Review*, 73 (1964), 360–71.

GOROVITZ, S., 'Causal Judgments and Causal Explanations', *Journal of Philosophy*, 62 (1965), 695–711.

HAMPSHIRE, S., 'Subjunctive Conditionals', *Analysis*, 9 (1948), 9–14. Reprinted in M. Macdonald, *Philosophy and Analysis* (Oxford, 1954), 204–210.

HANSON, N. R., 'Causal Chains', *Mind*, 64 (1955), 289–311.

HIZ, H., 'On the Inferential Sense of Contrary-to-Fact Conditionals', *Journal of Philosophy*, 48 (1951), 586–7.

KIM, J., 'Causation, Nomic Subsumption, and The Concept of Event', *Journal of Philosophy*, 70 (1973), 217–36.

KNEALE, W., 'Natural Laws and Contrary-to-Fact Conditionals', *Analysis*, 10 (1950), 121–5. Reprinted in M. Macdonald, *Philosophy and Analysis* (Oxford, 1954).

LUCAS, J. R., 'Causation', in R. J. Butler (ed.), *Analytical Philosophy*, 1st series (Oxford, 1966).

MACKIE, J. L., 'Counterfactuals and Causal Laws', in R. J. Butler (ed.), *Analytical Philosophy*, 1st series (Oxford, 1966).

MADDEN, E. H., 'A Third View of Causality', *Review of Metaphysics*, 23 (1969), 67–84.

MANDELBAUM, M., 'Causal Analysis in History', *Journal of the History of Ideas*, 3 (1942),

MARC-WOGAU, K., 'On Historical Explanation', *Theoria*, 28 (1962), 213–3.

MARTIN, R., 'The Sufficiency Thesis', *Philosophical Studies*, 23 (1972), 205–11.

MONTAGUE, R., 'Logical Necessity, Physical Necessity, Ethics Quantifiers', *Inquiry*, 4 (1960), 259–69.

PAP, A., 'Philosophical Analysis, Translation Schemas, and the Regularity Theory of Causation', *Journal of Philosophy*, 49 (1952), 657–66.

PARRY, W. T., 'Re-examination of the Problem of Counterfactual Conditionals', *Journal of Philosophy*, 54 (1957), 85–94.

RUDDICK, W., 'Causal Connection', *Synthèse*, 18 (1968), 46–67.

RUSSELL, B., 'On the Notion of Cause', *Proceedings of the Aristotelian Society*, 13 (1912–13), 1–26. Reprinted in *Mysticism and Logic*. (Harmondsworth (Penguin Books), 1953).

SCHLICK, M., 'Causality in Contemporary Physics, I and II', *Philosophical Studies*, 12 (1962), 177–93, 281–98.

SHOPE, R. K., 'Explanations in terms of "The Cause"', *Journal of Philosophy*, 64 (1967), 312–20.

SHORTER, J. M., 'Causality and a Method of Analysis', in R. J. Butler (ed.), *Analytical Philosophy*, 2nd series (Oxford, 1968).

SIMON, H., and RESCHER, N., 'Cause and Counterfactual', *Philosophical Studies*, 33 (1966).

Sosa, E., 'Hypothetical Reasoning', *Journal of Philosophy*, 64 (1967), 293–305.

Stalnaker, R. C., and Thomason, R. H., 'A Semantic Analysis of Conditional Logic', *Theoria*, 36 (1970), 23–42.

Stevenson, C. L., 'If-Iculties', *Philosophical Studies*, 37 (1970), 27–49.

Taylor, R., 'Causation', *The Monist*, 47 (1962–3), 287–313.

Vendler, Z., 'Effects, Results and Consequences', in Butler, R. J. (ed.), *Analytical Philosophy*, 1st series (Oxford, 1966).

Vendler, Z., 'Causal Relations', *Journal of Philosophy*, 60 (1963).

Walters, R. S., 'The Problem of Counterfactual Conditionals', *Australasian Journal of Philosophy*, 39 (1961), 30–46.

Warnock, G. J., 'Every Event Has a Cause', in A. Flew (ed.), *Logic and Language*, (Oxford, 1951), 107–9.

Watling, J., 'The Problem of Contrary-to-Fact Conditionals', *Analysis*, 17 (1957), 73–80.

Von Wright, G. H., 'On Conditionals', in *Logical Studies* (London, 1957), pp. 127–65.

I have found helpful the longer bibliographies compiled by J. J. Cobarrubias, of Columbia University, and Gary Rosenkrantz, of Brown University.

INDEX OF NAMES

(not including authors mentioned only in the Bibliography)